EDUCATION AND THE HANDICAPPED
1760–1960

INTERNATIONAL LIBRARY OF SOCIOLOGY
AND SOCIAL RECONSTRUCTION

Founded by Karl Mannheim

Editor: W. J. H. Sprott

*A catalogue of books available in the INTERNATIONAL LIBRARY OF SOCIOLOGY AND
SOCIAL RECONSTRUCTION, and new books in preparation for the Library,
will be found at the end of this volume*

EDUCATION
AND THE HANDICAPPED
1760–1960

by

D. G. PRITCHARD

LONDON
ROUTLEDGE & KEGAN PAUL
NEW YORK: HUMANITIES PRESS

First published 1963
by Routledge & Kegan Paul Limited
Broadway House, 68–74 Carter Lane
London, E.C.4

Printed in Great Britain
by Compton Printing Ltd.
London and Aylesbury

Second impression 1966
Third impression 1970

SBN 7100 3420 2

CONTENTS

v

Contents

PREFACE

'THE Author will not be so uncandid as to offer any Apology for the appearance of the following pages.' Thus in 1834 did James Gall open his Preface to *A Historical Sketch of the Origin and Progress of Literature for the Blind*. His sentiments are echoed here. But even if no apology is offered thanks are.

It is with pleasure that I record my gratitude to those who have assisted me in many ways. Mr. E. Keates of the School for the Blind, Liverpool, and Mr. J. R. Waddington of the Victoria Settlement, Liverpool, both made unpublished papers available for my inspection. Miss P. Smith gave me information concerning the Invalid Children's Aid Association, and Mr. W. King, Principal of St. Loyes College, Exeter, supplied me with notes on which my reference to Dame Georgiana Buller is based. The staffs of the Picton Library, Liverpool, the Library of the Department of Education of the Deaf, Manchester, and the Public Record Office, London, have been most helpful. Miss P. M. Downie, Chief Librarian of the Ministry of Education, Mrs. S. L. Coghill, Librarian of the Royal National Institute for the Blind, and Dr. P. P. Gorman, Librarian of the Royal National Institute for the Deaf, drew to my attention various sources of information. Mr. H. A. Hewitt, Departmental Records Officer of the Ministry of Education, helped me to trace files relating to early special schools, and my colleague, Mr. O. M. V. Argles, Tutor-Librarian of the Institute of Education, performed a similar service in relation to books. Mr. Argles, Dr. J. Murphy, of the University of Liverpool, and my wife read the manuscript in whole or in part and made valuable suggestions. My wife also undertook the unenviable task of translating my handwriting into typescript. To all of these I express my thanks.

During the nineteenth century and part of the twentieth the children now known as physically handicapped and educationally sub-normal were termed physically defective and mentally defective; the schools that they and the blind and the deaf attended were frequently called institutions; the education they received bore the name of instruction. In the interest of historical accuracy the nineteenth-century terms have therefore been used when dealing with that period, and reference is made to the change of nomenclature when it occurs. Indeed it is the story of the advance in opinion and outlook from 1760 to 1960, which brought about the change from instruction to education, from institution to school, and from mentally defective to educationally sub-normal, that the book sets out to tell.

Frequent reference is made to the *Report of the Royal Commission on the Blind and the Deaf and Dumb* 1889 and the *Report of the Departmental Committee on Defective and Epileptic Children* 1898. In order to avoid cumbersome footnotes the *Reports* have been respectively abbreviated to *R.C.B.D.* and *C.D.E.C.*

References also occur in the footnotes to documents in the Ministry of Education Archives. All these documents have now been transferred to the Public Record Office, but as they were seen and examined at the Ministry of Education they are referred to as Ministry of Education Archives, Education Class......, Piece...... Documents which had earlier been transferred to the Public Record Office, and were examined there, are shown as Public Record Office, Education Class ......, Piece.......

D. G. P.

The University of Liverpool
December 1961

1

EARLIEST PROVISION FOR THE HANDICAPPED

ANY consideration of the history of the education of the handicapped must take into account the development of educational provision for ordinary children. When it is realized that less than one hundred years ago fewer than two-fifths of our children attended school, it is hardly surprising that the growth of special education is a recent manifestation. Schools had, of course, existed since the coming of Augustine in 597, though they were predominantly for clever boys of good family. Occasional parochial and chantry schools were to be found, but until the foundation of the Society for Promoting Christian Knowledge in 1698, no large-scale effort to give elementary education to the poorer classes had been made. During the eighteenth century the charity schools of the S.P.C.K. were augmented by dame schools, Sunday Schools and schools of industry. The quality of the education they provided was poor; its extent limited.

Schools for the handicapped did not appear until the second half of the eighteenth century. That they should lag behind was understandable, for educational and social trends are followed, not created, by provision for the handicapped. Furthermore, certain specialist techniques are necessary, and some of these are allied to and dependent upon advances in science, medicine and mental measurement, which themselves are recent. However, certain discoveries were ignored or forgotten. For fifty years the genius of Louis Braille was ignored in England; the fact that the deaf could speak, for a longer period.

Even if there were no schools, there were individual and isolated attempts to improve the lot of the handicapped. These followed an

1

earlier period, in which the handicapped had been sacrificed to the welfare of society, be that society the roving tribe or the Greek city state. The former found them a burden in their effort to survive, the latter in their effort to purify the race; a concept not entirely outmoded in the twentieth century. In Sparta the laws of Lycurgus approved the abandonment of idiots, and the exposure of handicapped infants. The Athenians, even under Solon and in the time of Plato, practised exposure, and killed outright their deaf children. The Spartans, with a finer sense of cruelty, merely put them in the great pit in Taygetus.

In the Christian era, as the teaching of Christ, and the Hebraic Law which exhorted that the handicapped should be aided, became known, the attitude towards them softened. Hospices for the blind were established; in Caesarea in the fourth century by St. Basil, and in the fifth by St. Lymnaeus in Syria. Of these little is known, nor of the first English hospice, Elsing Spittle, opened by a London merchant for one hundred blind men in 1329, and confiscated at the Reformation. Better known is the Hospice Nationale des Quinze-Vingts, Paris. Its foundation is generally attributed to Louis IX, St. Louis, about 1260, as an asylum for three hundred of his soldiers blinded in the Crusades. Its origins, in fact, are obscure, and it is probable that it was only rebuilt by Louis. Its successor still stands today, and for its purpose of providing asylum it has proved eminently successful. Unfortunately, it also provided a tradition of charity and begging, which both inhibited independence and became inseparably associated with the blind, for its inmates were for long encouraged to augment its funds by soliciting alms.

Other hospital brotherhoods were patterned on the Quinze-Vingts, but, as none of them attempted any training or instruction, of more import to the education of the blind were the block letters devised by Didymus. Blinded in early childhood, he became, under the late Roman Empire, Professor of philosophy and theology at the University of Alexandria. Sporadic and mainly unsuccessful attempts to teach the blind to read by touch continued until the seventeenth century. Even if they could be successfully taught, there would be nothing for them to read. Block letters could obviously not be made into a book. When, in 1651, Harsdorffer in Germany produced wax tablets by which the blind could write, there was far more purpose in learning to read. This was emphasized when the Swiss, Jacob Bernouilli, invented a frame which guided a pencil on paper. But still the difficulty of the block letters remained; and it was left to Valentin Haüy to adopt embossed print, invented some time earlier, to the use of the blind. Haüy's claim to fame rests on firmer foundations than this. He was the first to claim that the blind could and should be educated. At the Institution Nationale des Jeunes Aveugles in Paris, he substantiated his claim.

His attention was first drawn to the condition of the blind when he saw, outside a café in a fashionable boulevard, a group of blind men, grotesquely attired and wearing pasteboard spectacles, executing a discordant symphony to the delight of the passers-by. Determining to alleviate their lot, he sought out Maria von Paradis, the famous blind harpsichordist. She acquainted him with earlier work on behalf of the blind, and the methods of teaching then in existence. He modified and added to these, and tried out his ideas on François Leseuer, a blind waif he had found begging at the door of the church of Saint-Germain des Prés. Leseuer made a good pupil, and soon could read Roman letters if printed heavily enough to show in low relief on the reverse side. After witnessing a demonstration of Leseuer's ability, the Société Philanthropique decided to support Haüy's idea of founding a school. He relinquished his lucrative post at the Foreign Office, and with twelve blind children from an almshouse and funds from the Société he opened the Institution Nationale in 1784.

Two years later the school had thirty pupils, who were commanded to give an exhibition of their attainments before Louis XVI at Versailles, and by the year of the Revolution, the number had increased to fifty. Within the walls of the Institution, the blind, like the sighted without, responded to the call of liberty, and Haüy was faced with a popular rising, with which he dealt more tactfully and successfully than Louis was able to outside. This was the least of his troubles. The Revolution threatened to overthrow all charitable institutions. The members of the Société Philosophique went into hiding. Subscriptions ceased. In 1791 conditions improved materially when the National Assembly endowed the school with the house and funds of a suppressed convent. Educationally, however, they declined as the new rulers of France sought to dictate policy. Ten years later they decreed that the school should be closed and the children removed to the Quinze-Vingts. Haüy was thanked for his services and dismissed, and instruction of the children ceased. But he had not laboured in vain. His efforts had already gained the tribute of imitation, and his *Essai sur l'Education des Aveugles* enshrined his methods. In any case, in the year of Waterloo, the Institution Nationale became once again a separate entity, soon to receive its most famous pupil, and later teacher, Louis Braille; soon, too, to give further inspiration by the excellence of its music teaching.

The first efforts on behalf of the deaf are also ascribed to a saint.

It was for long believed that Bede's account of how, about 685, the Bishop of Hagulstad, St. John of Beverly, taught a dumb youth to speak, was an early example of the oral instruction of a deaf-mute. As, however, Bede makes no mention of deafness, it is at least possible that this was a case of recovery from aphasia.[1] Eight centuries pass before another record, which could refer to the instruction of the deaf, appears. Rodolphus Agricola, a native of Gröningen, mentions as within his knowledge that a deaf and dumb person had been taught to write and note down his thoughts.[2] This statement, when published, was received with considerable scepticism, mainly because of Aristotle's thesis that living persons deprived of hearing are not capable of education. It was left to Geronimo Cardano, mathematician, naturalist, physician and philosopher, to convince the sceptics. This sixteenth-century Italian, of great but ill-regulated talents, propounded the theoretical principle on which the education of the deaf became based. He realized that it was possible to substitute one sense for another. Thus, by using their sight the deaf could read, and so compensate for their deafness. Equally, by writing they could make up for their lack of speech. Through reading they could 'hear', through writing 'speak'. As for the world of ideas the deaf could enter this, too. For though writing be associated with speech, and speech with thought, written characters and ideas could be connected together without the intervention of sounds.

Such was Cardano's prestige, such the excellence of his argument, that it became accepted that the education of the deaf, albeit difficult, was not impossible. The way now lay open for efforts on behalf of the deaf. The first to tread it effectively was the Spanish philanthropist Pedro Ponce de Leon. Of noble birth, he entered the Benedictine monastery of San Salvador at Oña, Old Castile. There, tradition has it, he was inspired by Bede's account of St. John of Beverly to attempt lip-reading with the deaf. Contemporary evidence shows that, whatever his inspiration, he was successful. He had a series of pupils to whom he taught speech, reading, writing and arithmetic. They learnt to pray, to assist at Mass and to confess themselves in speech. Among them were the two brothers of the Constable of Castile; because of their ability to speak they became persons at law possessing the right to inherit titles and property. This economic and legal motive accounts in part for the early interest taken in Spain in the education of the deaf.

Ponce died in 1584, and the Spanish interest was continued by another Benedictine, Juan Paulo Bonet. Whereas Ponce had

---

[1] Bede, *Ecclesiastical History of England.* Edited J. A. Giles (1849), pp. 237–8.
[2] Agricola, *De Inventione Dialectica.*

concentrated on speech, Bonet turned his attention to signs. In 1620 he published a record of his experiences as a teacher of the deaf and the manual one-handed alphabet he had used.[1] As Ponce had given the deaf their first effective instruction, so Bonet gave to their teachers their first effective text-book. His alphabet, but very slightly modified, was still in use in France and the United States two hundred years later.

One of Bonet's pupils was seen by Charles I, when as Prince of Wales he made his unsuccessful matrimonial journey to Spain, and described by one of the Prince's suite.[2] His description helped to inspire the succession of seventeenth-century Britons who worked for the deaf. The physician, John Bulwer, published the first book in English on the education of the deaf.[3] In it he emphasized, what was still imperfectly realized in England, that lack of speech need not necessarily accompany deafness. George Dalgarno, a Scot who became an Oxford schoolmaster, produced a sound and practical manual alphabet, which became the basis of the two-handed alphabet of the English schools in the early nineteenth century.[4] John Wallis and William Holder were not only born in the same year, 1616, but each made the same claim of being the first English teacher to describe a successful method of teaching the deaf.[5] 'Whalley and Popham were the first two children in England to be taught, Wallis and Holder the first two teachers, as far as we know, and theirs the first quarrel.'[6] Their unedifying dispute conducted through the publications of the Royal Society, of which both were members, was unfortunately but the precursor of many which were to rift and delay the education of the deaf. But the very prominence of their quarrel served to highlight the problem of educating the deaf. The claims of Wallis, the mathematician, and Holder, the theologian, to have taught the deaf to speak were analysed and discussed by philosophers and men of letters. The question received attention, though it was attention of an academic not a practical nature.

Consequently, it was left once again to the Continent to take the lead. Towards the close of the seventeenth century, Johann Amman, a Swiss doctor practising in Amsterdam, successfully taught private pupils, and, more importantly, published his *Surdus Loquens*—the Speaking Deaf—which, like Bonet's work, was to have considerable

[1] Bonet, *Simplification of the Letters of the Alphabet and Method of Teaching Deaf-mutes to Speak*. Translated by H. N. Dixon (1890).
[2] Digby, *The Private Memoirs of Sir Kenelme Digby* (1827).
[3] Bulwer, *Philocophus, or the Deafe and Dumbe Man's Friend* (1648).
[4] Dalgarno, *Didascalocophus or the Deaf and Dumb Mans [sic] Tutor* (1680).
[5] Holder, *Elements of Speech* (1669).
[6] Hodgson, *The Deaf and their Problems* (1953), p. 101.

influence.[1] While Amman's writings had been important, it was the teaching ability of Jacob Rodriguez Pereira which earned him the gratitude of the deaf. Employing Bonet's alphabet, lip-reading and the subsequent acquisition of speech, his method differed little from his predecessors. Rather his genius lay in his ability to achieve outstanding results.

A Jew of Portuguese birth and Spanish ancestry, he was compelled by persecution to move to France. There, after successfully teaching his deaf sister to speak, he undertook the education of a sixteen-year-old deaf boy of noble family. Within two years, he was able to report extremely favourable results, which eventually came to the knowledge of the Academy of Sciences. That august body investigated and highly commended Pereira's teaching. He and his pupil were presented to Louis XV, and as a result he was given as his next pupil the godson of the Duc de Chaulnes. Again he achieved almost immediate and extraordinary success, and his pupil in later years even acquired a second language. Pereira demonstrated that the deaf could reach the heights. Rightly he was given a number of honours, among them election in 1760 to the Royal Society.

In the same year the first public school in the world for handicapped children opened its doors. Hitherto the education of the deaf had been confined to children of the wealthy. The motives of their teachers had varied. Some, like Ponce, were impelled by religion. Others, like Wallis and Holder, by prestige, while Pereira represented a new class, the professional tutor of the deaf. Disinterested humanitarianism had played but a small part. But for Charles Michel, Abbé de l'Epée, it was the primary consideration. Born at Versailles, where his father was architect to Louis XIV, he studied for the Church and became a deacon. A man of great piety and evangelistic views, given to introspection, he was unable to accept all the doctrines of the Church. His acceptance of Jansenism impelled Rome to advise the Bishop to refuse his ordination to the priesthood. He therefore turned to the law, and was admitted to the Bar. Advocacy, however, though well within his ability was insufficient for his reforming nature. He left it to work among the poor of Paris. To help him in this work, he decided to re-seek ordination. His humility was such that he was able to condemn as pride any feeling that he was right and the Church wrong. With this confession of faith and the aid of his uncle, the Bishop of Troyes, he was ordained. For long he laboured among the poor, and it was during his work

[1] He subsequently summarized his views in *Dissertatio de Loquela*, which much later was translated and published in England: Amman, *A Dissertation on Speech*. Translated by C. Baker (1873).

with them that he first met deaf children. Moved to compassion, he determined that the improvement of their lot should be his vocation. In 1760 he founded the Institution Nationale des Sourds-Muets in Paris.

The school was designed for poor children, and, moreover, un-selected poor children. Previous teachers had been able to select their pupils, who, in any case, with their good backgrounds could have been expected to be reasonably intelligent. But the Abbé's task was formidable. Not only was he attempting the education of those who had had no advantages, and many disadvantages, but he was also attempting their instruction in the mass, as opposed to the individual tuition of the earlier teachers. At first he knew little of the education of the deaf, but he soon acquainted himself with the writings of Bonet and Amman. He was ready to attempt their oral methods, but as the numbers in his school grew, he realized that it would be far easier to instruct large groups by manual methods. He adopted Bonet's alphabet and added to it an extremely effective system of arbitrary signs which he devised. These he published, to-gether with an account of his method of teaching, in 1784, by which time he was convinced, as against earlier opinion, that speech was not necessary in the education of the deaf, nor was it the best way of educating them.[1]

The entirely opposite, but traditional, view was expressed by Samuel Heinicke. In temperament and background, too, he was unlike the meek and well-connected De l'Epée. He was strong-willed, tenacious and resolute, and coming from German peasant stock he determined to escape his background. His ambition was to become a teacher or a preacher, and, as the first step in his circuitous journey, he enlisted in the Dresden Royal Life Guards, part of the forces of the Elector of Saxony. He devoted his free time to study, and became proficient in Latin, French and mathematics. His free time must have been considerable, for he also taught private students while in the army. One of these was a deaf and dumb boy, who so aroused his interest that he was about to leave the forces to specialize in the teaching of the deaf when the Seven Years War broke out. He was taken prisoner, but prison camps were not made for such men and he soon escaped to Hamburg, where he became organist and teacher at the nearby hamlet of Eppendorf. There he found another deaf and dumb child, and despite opposition he accepted him into his school. Using Amman's methods, he soon taught the child to speak. Other children were brought to him, and with each success his fame spread. His school received many visitors including the Elector of Saxony

[1] De l'Epée, *La Véritable Maniere d'Instruire les Sourds et Muets* (1784).

himself, who invited him to return to Saxony to open a school for the deaf. At Leipzig, in the spring of 1778, with a grant from the Elector and nine pupils from his school at Eppendorf, he established the first state school for handicapped children.

Heinicke's leading principle was that precision of thought is only possible where there is speech,[1] and therefore the deaf must acquire language. Meanwhile De l'Epée was showing the world that whether or not precision of thought required speech, education was certainly possible without it. This annoyed the quick-tempered Heinicke, who sent a letter to a German studying at the Paris school advising him to leave as De l'Epée's methods were harmful to educational progress. The Abbé thereupon wrote politely in French explaining his own methods and asking specific questions. Heinicke replied brusquely in German, which the priest could not read, and did not answer the questions. The Frenchman thus assumed that Heinicke could not understand French, and therefore wrote in Latin; and so in Latin the correspondence continued, each man laboriously propounding his own view but not answering the other's. At length De l'Epée passed the correspondence to the Zurich Academy with a request that the Academicians should rule on the best method. Heinicke haughtily refused to furnish them with any additional information regarding his methods, but there was no such difficulty as far as De l'Epée was concerned.

It was not therefore surprising that the Academy's report in 1783 should recommend the manual method, for while not necessarily better than the oral, they had at least seen it and knew that it worked, whereas they had doubts regarding Heinicke's method. This verdict, allied to the prejudice which Heinicke's temper, forceful nature and vigorous defence of his system created, gave a big boost to the manual method. Moreover, De l'Epée publicized his method, while Heinicke was loth to reveal the details of his. Consequently, a system, which would later have to be discarded, came to be widely used. It soon became known as the French method, while the oral system, which was adopted by the schools of Germany, was called the German. The respective systems came to be associated with national and religious differences, and their reconciliation became even more difficult. England followed first one, then the other, but for close on a hundred years used neither proficiently.

Before the close of the eighteenth century the first schools for the blind and deaf had therefore appeared. Nothing, however, had been done for children who were physically or mentally handicapped. Even in the Age of Enlightenment there were obvious reasons why

---

[1] Klares Denken ist dur in der Lautsprache möglich.

this was so. Public sympathy was more easily aroused by blindness and deafness than by physical handicap or mental sub-normality. The former was often repulsive to look at, the latter occasioned derision. In any case, both were frequently taken to be an indication of Divine displeasure, a chastisement from above upon the parents whose child was so afflicted. Hence, the unfortunate child became an object of dislike from the outset by parents and neighbours alike, and was consigned to an obscure corner. Moreover, many of those whom we would now consider to be educationally sub-normal would not in the eighteenth century be noticeably backward. When the ability to read and write is possessed by few, those who cannot read and write do not stand out. The child who would later be termed feeble-minded could successfully labour with his equally illiterate fellows. It was only when education became general that the problem of backwardness was discovered. In fact, as society becomes more complex and technological so will the dividing line between normality and sub-normality be drawn higher and higher.

As for the physically handicapped, it was hardly to be expected that much would be done for them, for it was only in the Augustan Age that science finally replaced superstition in medicine. Indeed the advancement of science was one of the outstanding features of the eighteenth century. But while medical and hospital services were still in their infancy, many of the handicapped, who would survive today, died. Of those who were born handicapped some were immediately deserted as foundlings. The Foundling Hospital, one of 154 new hospitals to be established between 1700 and 1825, was opened in London in 1745 as a first step in reducing the high mortality rate among deserted bastard children and the foundlings of the poor.

But even in the eighteenth century the way for the education of the mentally handicapped was being prepared. Already their custodial care had been attempted. St. Vincent de Paul and his Sisters of Charity had in the early seventeenth century included feeble-minded adults among the handicapped for whom they provided at the château which was eventually to become the Bicêtre, the Parisian asylum. Educationally, however, it was Francis Bacon and the seventeenth-century realists who first threw light on how those of low intelligence might be assisted.

Realism, with its emphasis on the use of the senses and the inductive method in education, was a reaction both to Scholasticism, with its preoccupation with Aristotelian logic and its fetish of theory unrelated to reality, and to the later humanistic education, with its emptiness of mere words and style. Here was the beginning of the replacement of literary and linguistic studies by material from nature and life; here the beginning of the scientific approach to education and the study of the child as an individual. Locke and Rousseau underlined these views. All knowledge, asserted Locke, came through the senses, and the natural curiosity of the child should be utilized. Books would therefore not be the most important source of learning; rather learning should be accompanied by pleasurable sensations. This sensationalism of Locke became the philosophical foundation of Rousseau's naturalism. Education, he maintained, should be based on the nature of the child, not on the requirements of an artificial society. The original capacities of each child should be allowed unrestricted expression. Such views led naturally to the concept of child study and the development of psychology, for if education was to be based on a child's capacities, then it was essential that these be studied.

Pereira and Itard were both influenced by these principles. The former urged that the deaf should be taught to see, by lip-reading, and to feel, by tactile vibration, the speech they could not hear. The latter drew upon this extension of sensationalism in his investigation as to whether ideation is innate or produced by sensory stimuli. His work belongs to the nineteenth century, but his inspiration came from an earlier period.

2

EIGHTEENTH CENTURY: THE FIRST ENGLISH SCHOOLS

TWO years before Rousseau wrote *Émile*, and in the same year as the first Parisian deaf entered De l'Epée's school, nine-year-old Charles Shirreff became a pupil of Thomas Braidwood. So began the long, and not always successful, association of the Braidwood family with the education of the deaf. So, too, began the first school for the deaf in Britain.

A Scot, Thomas Braidwood was educated at the University of Edinburgh, and after graduating established in the city a private school for the teaching of mathematics. It is doubtful whether it would have brought him fame. However, in 1760 at the age of forty-five, greatness was thrust upon him. He was approached by a wealthy Leith merchant, Alexander Shirreff, with a request that he should teach his son, deaf from the age of three. Braidwood saw the task as a challenge and accepted it. Here was no altruism of a De l'Epée, no religious fervour of a Ponce. Nevertheless, he possessed the teaching ability of a Pereira, and drawing upon his previous experience, he taught the boy by, what was to him, the natural method. He taught him to speak. Any words that Shirreff acquired were memorized by lip-reading and writing. He soon acquired many words, and Braidwood another pupil. Again he was successful, and again the success brought him further pupils. Gradually the mathematics school closed, and in its place appeared Mr. Braidwood's Academy for the Deaf and Dumb.

By 1766 Braidwood was advertising in the *Scots Magazine*,[1] in the manner of those days, by which an unidentified friend described his success in letter form. A similar advertisement the following year

---

[1] *Scots Magazine*, Vol. XXXI, January 1766.

showed that there were then six pupils at the school, and that Braidwood considered that he could 'undertake to teach anyone of a tolerable genius in the space of about three years to speak and to read distinctly'.[1] The letter-advertisements appear to have fulfilled their purpose, for by 1769 a further letter claimed that thirty pupils had been refused by the Academy. This was because the education was such that only a few pupils could be taken at a time. Consequently, the letter continued, the education of the pupils was expensive, and therefore two things were needed. First a fund should be established to help parents who could not afford to pay the fees, and secondly 'that he [Braidwood] shall communicate his skill to three or four ingenious young men'.[2] Apparently neither of these was forthcoming, and so he communicated his skill only to members of his own family, who swore not to reveal his methods. The first to be so honoured was his nephew, John Braidwood, who became his assistant in 1775.[3]

The Academy was by now well known, so much so that by 1780 it had admitted four pupils from the United States. The sloping street, in which it was situated, was known locally as Dumbiedykes, a name which it still bears, and which suggested to Walter Scott the name for one of his most popular characters in *The Heart of Midlothian*. Part of the fame of the school, however, was due to a visit paid to it in 1773 by Johnson and Boswell, and subsequently described by the former in his *Journey to the Western Islands of Scotland*. 'There is one subject of philosophical curiosity to be found in Edinburgh, which no other city has to shew; a college of the deaf and dumb, who are taught to speak, to read, to write, and to practice arithmetick, by a gentleman, whose name is Braidwood. The number which attends him is, I think, about twelve, which he brings together in a little school, and instructs according to their several degrees of proficiency.'[4]

Johnson realized that the instruction of the deaf was not new, and makes mention of Wallis and Holder. 'How far,' he continues, 'any former teachers have succeeded, it is not easy to know; the improvement of Mr. Braidwood's pupils is wonderful. They not only speak, write, and understand what is written, but if he that speaks looks

[1] *Scots Magazine*, Vol. XXXI, August 1767.

[2] *Ibid.*, July 1769, p. 342.

[3] John was later to marry Thomas's daughter. The sons of this marriage were grandsons of Thomas, and, as they bore the name of Braidwood, this misled a number of writers into thinking that John was the son of Thomas, e.g. Arnold, *Education of Deaf-Mutes* (1888), Vol. 1, p. 97, Frampton and Rowell, *Education of the Handicapped* (1939), Vol. 1, p. 66, Fay, 'The Braidwood Family', *American Annals of the Deaf and Dumb*, Vol. XXIII, No. 1, January 1878, p. 64.

[4] Johnson, *op. cit.* (1775), p. 380.

towards them, and modifies his organs by distinct and full utterance, they know so well what is spoken, that it is an expression scarcely figurative to say, they hear with the eye.'[1] The usually critical lexicographer was much impressed by what he saw, and full of praise for the work Braidwood was doing. Part of his description is so typical of the man that it is worth reproducing at length. 'This school I visited, and found some of the scholars waiting for their master, whom they are said to receive at his entrance with smiling countenance and sparkling eyes, delighted with the hope of new ideas. One of the young Ladies had her slate before her, on which I wrote a question consisting of three figures, to be multiplied by two figures. She looked upon it, and quivering her fingers in a manner which I thought very pretty, but of which I know not whether it was art or play, multiplied the sum regularly in two lines, observing the decimal place; but did not add the two lines together, probably disdaining so easy an operation. I pointed at the place where the sum total should stand, and she noted it with such expedition as seemed to shew that she had it only to write. It was pleasing to see one of the most desperate of human calamities capable of so much help: whatever enlarges hope, will exalt courage; after having seen the deaf taught arithmetick, who would be afraid to cultivate the Hebrides?'[2]

Johnson was not alone in singing the school's praises. Francis Green has left a glowing and comprehensive account of Braidwood's activities in his *Vox Oculis Subjecta*.[3] Green was an American, a man of learning, and a distinct Tory. He held no brief for the views of Adams, Lee and Patrick Henry; nor they for his. When, in 1775, the War of Independence started, Green left his Boston home for the England of George the Third. Hearing of Braidwood's school in Edinburgh, he journeyed thither, and his eight-year-old son, Charles, was the fourth American child to be admitted. The father remained in Britain for some time, during which he saw a great deal of the Academy. He speaks highly of the tone of the establishment. There was no harsh or repressive discipline 'as is sometimes practised upon persons unfortunately deprived of reason'.[4] He substantiates Samuel Johnson's impression when he states that the children loved both the school and their lessons. All the children were taught in the same room. The methods used were completely individual, as the teachers did not sit in one place, as was the custom in other schools, but moved about among the children giving help where necessary. Braidwood himself carried a small, spatula-like instrument, which he

---

[1] *Ibid.*, p. 381. [2] *Ibid.*, pp. 382–3.
[3] Green, *op. cit.* (1783), pp. 145–50. [4] *Ibid.*, p. 145.

used for placing the tongue in the correct position for the various sounds. Green places the ages of the pupils as between five and twenty, although Braidwood in one of his advertisements mentions one aged twenty-five. Be that as it may, such a wide range demanded the best of individual teaching; which apparently was what the children were given. After five years' instruction they could read, write and speak with ease.

In 1783 Braidwood decided that he should be nearer the centre of things, and moved his Academy to Hackney, which was then but a village outside London. There, in the following year, he took a second nephew, the nineteen-year-old Joseph Watson, as an assistant.[1] Watson was destined to become the first superintendent of the first public school for the deaf in this country. Even before Braidwood moved from Edinburgh he had conceived the idea of a public school, 'and some few inefficient steps were taken towards its accomplishment'. [2] Among the inefficient steps was an approach to the King who promised £100 towards the venture. However, when the London Asylum for the Deaf was eventually opened in 1792, Braidwood, who was by then seventy-seven, had no hand in the actual movement which brought it about. But nevertheless he played his part. His was the inspiration that such an institution should be founded. His was the Academy that trained its first headmaster. His was the teaching ability that showed that the deaf were worthy of schooling. His was the school where they first received such schooling. Of his uncle, Watson wrote: 'His indefatigable industry and great success would claim from me respectful notice, even if I could forget the ties of blood.'[3]

Despite his apparent contribution to the education of the deaf, Braidwood has not always been well-remembered. American writers in particular have been critical of him. Frampton and Rowell have stated that his school 'would be considered today an unethical monopoly and possibly a racket'.[4] The criticism stems from two sources, both intimately connected with the history of the education of the deaf in the United States. When Francis Green eventually returned to his own country he continued to write about the deaf, and urged that a school should be established for them. Such a school, of course, would be conducted on the oral lines of the Edinburgh Academy, for Green had also visited De l'Epée's school and had not been impressed. Green died in 1809; no school had been founded; but the seed had been sown. The other three Americans to

---

[1] Watson, *Instruction of the Deaf and Dumb* (1809), Introduction, p. xxiii.
[2] *Ibid.*, p. xxvi.   [3] *Ibid.*, pp. xxiii–xxiv.
[4] Frampton and Rowell, *Education of the Handicapped*, Vol. 1, p. 66.

be educated by Braidwood were all children of Major Thomas Bolling of Cobbs, Virginia. Colonel William Bolling, the hearing brother of the Bolling children, was so impressed by Green's advocacy and Braidwood's efforts on behalf of his kin that he persuaded John Braidwood, grandson of Thomas Braidwood, to open the first American school for the deaf at Baltimore. This was during the Anglo American War of 1812, the war in which the British burnt Washington. British stock was at its lowest, and it was necessary to obtain special permission to allow John Braidwood to stay in the United States. His stay was not a success. He was a difficult man with whom to work, and he was soon involved in acrimonious disputes. He left the school for the North, but returned a little later to start a new school, the first having failed, with the Rev. John Kirkpatrick, whom he agreed to instruct in the oral method. Again there were clashes of personality, and Kirkpatrick broke off relations with Braidwood. Shortly afterwards the school closed. Braidwood's sojourn in the United States had not endeared him, or his family, to the Americans.

The second point of criticism deals with Thomas Braidwood's secretiveness. At the same time as John was quarrelling in Maryland, twenty-eight-year-old Thomas Hopkins Gallaudet was attempting to teach the young deaf daughter of a neighbour, Dr. Mason Cogswell. Gallaudet had studied the works of Abbé Sicard, De l'Epée's successor, who had perfected the latter's sign and manual system. But Cogswell's friends raised money to send Gallaudet to Britain to learn the oral method. He arrived in 1815 to find that the teachers at the deaf institutions in Britain, at London, Birmingham and Edinburgh, were all pledged to maintain secrecy regarding their work. Three of the four institutions were, and the fourth had been until recently, under the superintendence of members of the Braidwood family. Thomas Braidwood's widowed daughter controlled the Hackney school; his grandson was Superintendent of the Birmingham Institution; Watson was still in command at the London Asylum; and John Braidwood had, but a few years earlier, left the Edinburgh Institution for America. Gallaudet was told that if he wished to learn the oral method he must bind himself for three years at a very low salary, after which he would be free to return to teach the deaf in the United States. Naturally, he refused the offer, and journeyed to Paris. There, Sicard gave him every opportunity to learn. After three months he returned to his homeland, taking with him a deaf teacher from the Paris school, Laurent Clerc. With the aid of Clerc and a grant from Congress, Gallaudet in 1817 opened the first public school for the deaf in the United States, at Hartford, Connecticut. The system employed was the French sign and manual.

Later schools copied Hartford, and fifty years were to pass before oral instruction was introduced to America.[1]

Hence the gravamen of the charge against Braidwood is that because of his insistence upon keeping his methods secret, schools in the United States were condemned to use a poorer system. A lesser and subsidiary charge that the grandson was a failure both as a man and a teacher obviously cannot be brought against the grandfather. But it can cloud the issue. What should be remembered is that Braidwood was living in an age of inventors, who if they did not cling to their inventions were liable to lose any financial gain that might be forthcoming. In any case, the Scot did offer to communicate his skill, and may well have been embittered by the lack of response. Even so, there was nothing particularly original about his methods. He taught, in fact, on the same principles as Wallis had described in *The Philosophical Transactions* of 1680.[2] But even if Braidwood was monopolistic, he would best be remembered for the happy boarding school which he created in an era which was marked by rebellions at Winchester, Eton, Harrow and Rugby. The revolt at Rugby in 1797 was so extensive that troops were called in, and the Riot Act read.

Revolution was not confined to the field of education. In 1791 appeared Thomas Paine's *Rights of Man*, which was to become the text-book of Radical England. Fanned by Paine, the flame which had engulfed France appeared to be spreading across the Channel. But the very excesses of the Revolution were producing a reaction. Taking their lead from Burke's *Reflections on the Revolution*, erstwhile supporters were outraged by the news which seeped through from France. Riots broke out in various parts of the Kingdom. Strangely, however, the riots were on behalf of the forces of conservatism, and in Birmingham, in 1791, Dissenting chapels were pillaged by the mob. Yet during the same year, and the year that followed, the first public institutions for blind and deaf children respectively were founded.

The genesis of the idea of an organization for the benefit of the blind in Liverpool came from the blind poet, Edward Rushton. Strong willed and quick tempered, he championed causes as ardently and wholeheartedly as he fought abuses. As a youth he had served aboard a slave ship, and had endeavoured, despite the protestations of the crew, to alleviate the lot of the captives below decks. When an epidemic of malignant ophthalmia broke out among the slaves, Rushton toiled selflessly among them. The relief that he brought to them was at the expense of his own sight. Although he was later to

---

[1] Fay, *Histories of American Schools for the Deaf* (1893), Vol. 1.
[2] Watson, *Instruction of the Deaf and Dumb*, pp. xii–xiii.

regain his sight partially, the experience drove him to assist others. His original conception was of a benefit club, but his friend, the blind musician, John Christie, persuaded him that the blind would benefit more from instruction in a trade, especially in music.

At this juncture, the scheme was mentioned to Henry Dannett, incumbent of St. John's Church, Liverpool. A man of Rushton's temperament but with greater tenacity, he took over the project, while Rushton applied his reforming zeal to another cause. By 1790 Dannett had collected £600, which was 'placed in the bank of Messrs. Caldwell and Smyth who are generous enough to allow the charity five per cent'.[1] In December he published a broadsheet[2] in which he announced his intention of opening 'The School of Instruction for the Indigent Blind', in two houses in Commutation Row, during the following month. There the blind would be instructed in 'Music or the Mechanical Arts, and so be rendered comfortable in themselves, and useful to their country'.

The original mechanical arts were to be numerous and varied,[3] and after a period of experiment the most lucrative and pleasant would be selected. While canvassing his plan and collecting money for it, Dannett had encountered some opposition. This took two forms. Objection was made to the teaching of music on the grounds that 'we shall have our streets full of Blind Fiddlers'. Dannett's reply was that violins were excluded. The intention was to instruct in organ playing, and this would be achieved through practice upon the harpsichord. In the second place, the critics considered that the blind would be unequal to any of the arts selected. Time alone, said Dannett, would show this.

Time, in fact, showed that they were equal to the tasks given. In January 1793, two years after the venture started, Dannett gave an account of his stewardship.[4] Eighty-one persons had sought admission at the outset, and although only twenty-five could be admitted immediately, the majority had subsequently attended, and the number present at any one time had on occasions risen as high as forty-five. Some of them had learnt trades and returned home; others had remained under instruction. Yet others had been dismissed for misconduct, or being blind minstrels, 'long inured to habits of idleness and dissipation, had soon become disgusted with useful industry', and had returned to their former lives.[5]

The oldest under instruction was sixty-eight, the youngest nine.

[1] Asylum for Indigent Blind, Minute Book, 1791–1803.
[2] A copy exists in the Minute Book.
[3] They included making nets and whip-lashes, lining hats, picking oakum, winding cotton and spinning worsted.
[4] Manuscript report 1791–3, in Minute Book.   [5] *Ibid.*

Despite this disparity in ages the scheme was a success, albeit a costly one. While they were still being taught their trades, the blind were incapable of earning anything. Yet their instructors had to be paid,[1] and they themselves had to be fed and, if married, given wages to support a family. Equally, the children who were taught music by John Christie were unproductive, and Christie, too, was being paid —at 6*d.* a lesson.

Consequently more funds were needed, and Dannett, who had for two years borne alone the burden of management and fund raising, handed over the establishment to a Committee of Management. The last entry in the Minute Book, in his firm, copper-plate hand, throws light upon the character of this devoted, gentle, man. He had recently discovered 'that Monsieur Huay [*sic*] had established a school on a somewhat similar plan in Paris . . . under the auspices of the late unfortunate Louis, who took great delight in visiting it. . . . This amiable Monarch had a heart to feel, and a hand always stretched out to relieve, the distress of his subjects. . . . One would have imagined that the humanity of his character, and the remembrance of his former beneficient deeds, would have softened the savage breasts, and preserved him from the brutal violence of his lawless murderers, who, by his death, have cast an indelible infamy upon a Nation, heretofore deemed civilized!'[2]

Under the Committee of Management the name was changed to the Asylum for the Indigent Blind. But this was as much a misnomer as the title of school had been, since none of those under instruction was resident. Regulations were formulated, a superintendent and matron were appointed, and the object of the Asylum was stated to be the instruction of the blind 'in some useful art or trade, to which their genius appears to be best adapted, and by which they will be enabled to earn something at their own homes'.[3] Admission was limited to those aged between fourteen and forty-five in the case of men, and twelve to forty-five in the case of women. They stayed at the Asylum for a maximum of four years. However, in the case of those being taught music, admission was confined to children aged between eight and sixteen, 'appearing to be of a promising genius'.[4] Their instruction lasted between four and eight years, and on leaving each was given five guineas with which to buy an instrument.

Christie had taught music from the beginning; and he had taught it solely to children. If there was an element of school at all at the

---

[1] The instructor in the making of whip-lashes was the most highly paid—at a guinea per week.

[2] Minute Book, 1791–1803.

[3] *Ibid.*, Committee Meeting, January 1794.   [4] *Ibid.*

Asylum, it was in this aspect—the musical education of blind children. But it was intended to be vocational, not scholastic. Even this was limited, for with only one blind teacher no more than six children could be accepted for music at any one time. Admittedly, children of twelve and over were eligible for the trade training, but until 1794 most of those receiving training were adults. After this date there was more concentration on children. Out of seventeen admitted during that year, ten were under the age of fifteen. The Superintendent may have regretted the change, for he received from the Asylum free coal and candles according to the number of blind that he shaved.

Henry Dannett had never intended that the Asylum should remain permanently in the two houses in which it opened. Before relinquishing control, he had therefore started a special building fund. By 1798 this had reached sizable proportions. It was augmented by collections which were taken in all local churches when charity sermons were simultaneously preached on a Sunday in Lent. In 1800 the new building was ready, and the Asylum changed its location and its name. It now became the School of Industry for the Blind.

Trade training in the workshops continued for children and adults, but, with the appointment of a full-time sighted teacher, the number of music pupils was increased to ten. John Christie remained two more years, his fee was raised from 6*d.* to 9*d.* per lesson, and when he retired he was given ten guineas by the Committee in recognition of his past services. No sum of money would adequately have recognized Christie's contribution. He was the first in England to advocate that the blind should be taught music. He was the first to teach it to them. In 1799 his first pupil, Thomas Bagley, left to become the organist at the village church in Sidgfield, Durham.

In the new and larger building, all the children became boarders. They came from all parts of the country, and, without exception, they were children of the poor. Their admission depended on the payment of two shillings by friends or by their parish. It also depended upon their capacity for work. In 1800 Samuel Birkenhead, 'being incapable of any labour and very much out of health, was discharged'.[1] The school depended for its income upon the proceeds of the workshops. There was no room for sentiment, or idle hands. There appeared to be no room for love either. George Eaton, a minor, 'declared his determined resolution to be married to Elizabeth Jones, also a minor, and could not be dissuaded'.[2] He was discharged. What happened to Elizabeth Jones is not recorded, but one is tempted to hope that she became Elizabeth Eaton.

[1] Minute Book, 1791–1803, Committee Meeting, September 1800.
[2] *Ibid.*, Committee Meeting, April 1800.

It has been seen that there had been talk of establishing a public school for deaf children while Braidwood was still in Edinburgh. Practical steps were not taken, however, until the mother of one of Braidwood's pupils at Hackney, a Mrs. Creasey, interested John Townsend, a Dissenting minister of Bermondsey, in the idea. With commendable latitudinarianism, Townsend sought out Henry Cox Mason, the Rector of Bermondsey, and together they set about raising funds. The response was good, a small committee was soon formed, and Joseph Watson was invited to leave Hackney and take charge of the new institution. It was with some trepidation that the Committee decided to open the Asylum for the Support and Education of the Deaf and Dumb Children of the Poor, for some of its members, especially Cox Mason, felt that it would not be possible to find enough children to form a school.[1] They need not have worried, for although the school opened in November 1792 with only six children, three boys and three girls, four years later it had twenty, and a waiting list of fifty. The Asylum now grew apace, and in 1809 it moved from Bermondsey to larger premises in the Old Kent Road. By then there were eighty children, trade training had been introduced, and the waiting list was bigger than ever.[2] Within a further ten years the number of children at the Old Kent Road was to reach two hundred, and by 1880 there were three hundred and fifty at the main school and its branch establishment at Margate.[3]

Watson's appointment had been on a strange financial basis. He was paid no salary, but he made, and was expected to make, his living from the profit that he obtained on his contracts from school supplies and from any private pupils that he might take. This was to be a source of trouble for the future, for the superintendents came to care more and more for their fee-paying pupils, and less and less for those admitted free, whose instruction was delegated to assistant teachers. This happened almost from the outset at the London Asylum. One of the original six pupils was a fee-payer who lived in Watson's own house, and not with the other children. By 1795 Watson was concentrating on the pupils who provided his livelihood, and an assistant, Robert Nicholas, was appointed to teach the poor children.[4]

Having been trained at Hackney, Watson had been pledged to the bond of secrecy, but on Braidwood's death in 1806 he felt that he could now publish the method by which he taught. This he did in

---

[1] Ministry of Education Archives, Education Class 14, Piece 5.
[2] Watson, *Instruction of the Deaf and Dumb*, Introduction, p. xxix.
[3] *R.C.B.D.*, Vol. 2, Appx. 2.
[4] Hodgson, *The Deaf and their Problems*, p. 150.

1809 in his *Instruction of the Deaf and Dumb*. Like his uncle, his method was based upon Wallis. He started with articulation, combining speech elements into symbols and then into words. Afterwards the pupil would learn to write and to read. He was prepared to allow the children to use natural signs until the oral system had been mastered.[1] His was therefore a combined system, rather than the pure oralism of the German method, and by his acceptance of signs he opened the way for the decline of the oral and the emergence of the manual method. Nevertheless, like Braidwood, he was undoubtedly an oralist. Arnold, the first historian of the deaf in this country, has written of him: 'Of Dr. Watson himself we have formed a very high estimate. There is a robustness, reasonableness and kindliness in all he says, that prove he had studied and applied his principles so well that he was not much moved away from them by the tide that had crossed the Channel in favour of systematic signs.'[2]

Joseph Watson remained at the Asylum until his death in 1829, a rule of thirty-seven years. He was succeeded by his son, Thomas James, a Cambridge graduate, who had assisted his father during his later years, and had, for a time, been headmaster of the Glasgow Institution. The nepotic tendency continued when, on the death of Thomas James in 1857, the latter's son, a great great nephew of Thomas Braidwood, the Rev. James Watson, also of Cambridge, took over the school. Not until James Watson's resignation in 1878 was the connection with the Braidwood family finally broken. For 118 years the headship of one or other of Britain's schools for the deaf had been in the hands of a member of the family. The connection had not always been for the best, for sons are not necessarily as good as their fathers.

After the London Asylum, no other establishment for deaf children appeared for eighteen years. Provision for the blind was more rapid. Edinburgh and Bristol provided for them in 1793, and London in 1800. As at Liverpool, the inspiration at Edinburgh was provided by a person deprived of sight. Thomas Blacklock was born near Dumfries of poor parents, and became blind at six months. Nevertheless, using the most rudimentary aids, he became a poet, scholar, Doctor of Divinity and a minister of the Scottish Church.[3] In 1783 he drew attention to the plight of the blind in an article in the recently started *Encyclopædia Britannica*. A little later he translated Valentin Haüy's *Essai*,[4] and determining to open a similar school, he

---

[1] Watson, *Instruction of the Deaf and Dumb*, Introduction, pp. xxix–xxxi.
[2] Arnold, *Education of Deaf-Mutes* (1891), Vol. 2, p. 119.
[3] Spence, *An Account of the Life, Character and Poems of Mr. Blacklock* (1754).
[4] Haüy, *An Essay on the Education of the Blind*. Translated by T. Blacklock (1793).

enlisted the aid of David Miller, blind from birth, as an instructor. But in 1791 he died, with his translation still unpublished and the school unopened. Miller interested a Leith minister, David Johnston, in the scheme, and together they raised money, and established the Society for the Relief of the Indigent Blind. Within a matter of months they opened workshops, admitted nine children and changed the title to the Asylum for the Industrious Blind. Blacklock's original aim of a school was lost, and the professed aim of the Asylum became industrial training.[1]

The Asylum for the Blind, at Clifton, Bristol, was also established with the avowed purpose of providing vocational training and subsequent employment. Founded by two members of the Society of Friends, it opened with four boys and two girls. Its main feature was that, like Liverpool, the children at first attended daily. After ten years, however, it conformed with the asylum principle, and its pupils became resident.[2] But it remained small, and after ninety years there were still only twenty-one pupils.

The School for the Indigent Blind, London, is usually considered as the last of the eighteenth-century foundations, as Johns, Anagnos, Bartley and Ritchie all give 1799 as the date of its opening.[3] However, a brochure published by the School in 1813[4] shows that the first children were not admitted until late in 1800, and the first subscriptions were not solicited until December 1799. Even so, it belongs to the eighteenth century, for its four founders, Ware, Bosanquet, Boddington and Houlston, formed their committee well before 1801. Their sole object was to instruct the blind in a trade, in order that they might be wholly or partly self-supporting and benefit from 'the effect which habits of industry must necessarily produce on their feelings and general character'.[5]

The school opened with fifteen resident pupils aged between twelve and eighteen. It had been part of the original plan to establish day schools for the blind in various parts of the Metropolis, but the idea was found to be too expensive. Instead it was decided to have a day school adjoining the main building. Strangely, there were insufficient applicants for admission to warrant its opening, though a few day pupils worked with the residents, and had their dinners with them.

By 1813 there were sixty residents, housed in a new building, especially built, in, the then pleasant, St. George's Fields, Southwark.

[1] Anagnos, *Education of the Blind* (1882), p. 33, and Ritchie, *Concerning the Blind* (1930), pp. 13–14.

[2] Ritchie, *op. cit.*, p. 14, and *R.C.B.D.*, Vol. 2, Appx. 2.

[3] Johns, *Blind People* (1867), p. 7, Anagnos, *op. cit.*, p. 33, Bartley, *The Schools for the People* (1871), p. 344 and Ritchie, *op. cit.*, p. 15.

[4] *An Account of the School for the Indigent Blind*, p. 3.   [5] *Ibid.*, p. 9.

It was 'an extensive and rambling building, containing a large number of rooms, and enclosing two good-sized playgrounds respectively for girls and boys'.[1] Its main features were the chapel, dining-room and basket shop. They were widely separated, and Johns, who was the school Chaplain, has described the last named as being 150 yards long.[2] Even if he meant 150 feet, it was still of prodigious length. Of course, it was the most important room. One-third of the school's income, which in 1812 was £4,500, came from the sale of goods made by the pupils: thread, sash and clothes lines, baskets, and rope and fine mats 'for hearths and carriages'. The life of the school revolved around the workshop. The instruction was devoted to what went on within it. The only exceptions were the twice weekly religious instruction lessons given by the Chaplain, who also conducted the services on Sundays. Of formal school work there was none; and none could there be until books for the blind were produced.[3]

[1] Johns, *Blind People*, p. 7.   [2] *Ibid.*, p. 8.
[3] *An Account of the School*, pp. 1–31.

3

THE PERIOD OF EXPERIMENT:
I. INSTITUTIONAL EDUCATION OF
THE BLIND AND DEAF

ENGLAND in 1800 presented a very different face from that which she showed fifty years earlier. Her population had expanded from six to nine million. Its distribution had changed. The expansion was due not so much to an increase in the birth-rate as a decline in the death-rate. The rise of medical science, the growth of hospital care, and the decrease in the consumption of gin were mainly responsible. Responsible, too, were the Agrarian and Industrial Revolutions, which, though they did bring many evils, brought more food and clothing, albeit expensive and unevenly distributed.

Whereas in 1750 there was no power-driven machinery, and four-fifths of the population was engaged in agricultural pursuits, the marriage of Arkwright's power loom to Watt's steam engine had produced the factory. In its turn the factory brought into being the industrial town—and slum. The migration to the town, and the consequent rural depopulation, was accelerated by both enclosures and the break-down of rural crafts. Cottage spinning and weaving could not withstand the competition of mass production, nor could the craftsman from the small market town, who joined the erst-while agricultural labourer in the sprawling slums.

With the increase and concentration of the population, the opportunity for mass instruction presented itself. The need was also present. Bell and Lancaster, and, later, the National Society and the British and Foreign School Society, took advantage of both opportunity and need. They vied with each other in the building of schools. But large classes and monitors did not lend themselves to the instruction of the handicapped. Neither were there sufficient handicapped to warrant the expense of concentrating on them from a sectarian viewpoint. Consequently, the blind and the deaf were neglected by the two Societies. Moreover, they effectively ensured that the State would not assist the handicapped, while at the same time accepting voluntary subscriptions which might otherwise have gone towards the education of the blind and deaf. Nor were the motives which moved the voluntary subscribers so evident in the case of the handicapped.

The Industrial Revolution, it was felt, had brought the need for social discipline to avoid hooliganism, and much later it brought the need for a literate population. Both these, education could provide. Fear induced by the French Revolution was a further motive, and again education would provide a shield against the onslaught of subversion, and its allies vice and irreligion. The poor should be taught to live upright and industrious lives in the position it had pleased God to place them.

The strongest impetus to the provision of education sprang, however, from religious convictions. Methodism and Evangelicalism both played a part. The former was not confined to the followers of Wesley, but was a way of life devoted to self-discipline and work for others, as well as attendance at Church or Chapel. It was to be found among the trading and professional classes, whose Puritanism impelled them to charitable works, so that God would not be deprived, through the poverty and ignorance of man, of the glory that was justly His. Evangelicalism, too, had an other-worldly ideal. Little concerned with the evils and sufferings of the present life, it was greatly concerned with the salvation of the individual.

Simple, plain humanitarianism also played its part. While Jane Austen was writing *Sense and Sensibility* in 1811, Elizabeth Fry was visiting the prisons. Against the reactionary, anti-revolutionary teachings of Burke, the voices of Wilberforce, Wordsworth, Southey, Coleridge, Owen, Cobbett and Thomas Spence were raised on the other side. While the National Society and the British and Foreign School Society went their own way, humanitarianism combined with Methodism and Evangelicalism to support schools for the blind and deaf.

But the times were not propitious. The first fifteen years of the nineteenth century were taken up by the French Wars. With peace came a succession of bad harvests and a glut of unemployed servicemen. War contracts came to an end, and Europe, as a market for manufactured goods, was impoverished. Wide-spread unemployment brought a lowering of wages, which when added to the increased price of corn brought distress—and discontent. Already in 1811, the Luddites had broken their first machine and burnt their first factory. The good harvest of 1813 put a temporary stop to Luddism, but in 1816 machines were again broken, and the Cambridge village of Littleport was seized by rioters. Later in the year the London mobs pillaged gunsmiths' shops, and attempted to set up a committee of public safety. The Prince Regent was attacked in the following year, the Habeas Corpus Act was suspended, and the Manchester Blanketeers marched on London. 1819 saw the Peterloo Massacre and the passing of the repressive Gag Acts; and the decade ended with the Cato Street Conspiracy to assassinate members of the Government. During this turbulent twenty years, when the isle was full of noises, only one school for the blind was founded in England, in 1805, and one for the deaf in 1812.

Thomas Tawell was responsible for the 1805 establishment. Like Rushton, he had been blind, but had partially regained his sight. A resident of Norwich, he obtained some local support for his scheme. Most of the money, however, he provided himself. The Asylum and School for the Indigent Blind, which he opened, catered for the two extremes—the aged blind and children. Both categories were employed in the workshops, and Tawell in his foundation deed stipulated that the latter should never be more than twice the number of the former. In the event, there were few children throughout the school's existence,[1] and comparatively little education, even when books for the blind became available.[2]

The General Institution for the Instruction of Deaf and Dumb Children, which was established in Birmingham in 1812, had Thomas Braidwood, grandson of the first Thomas Braidwood, as its first principal. Its foundation was due to Dr. de Lys, a Breton refugee from the excesses of the Revolution. While practising at a Birmingham hospital, he treated a young deaf girl. In an endeavour to assist her, he contacted the Braidwood family, and eventually succeeded in teaching her some speech himself. Continuing what was now becoming traditional, he exhibited her prowess to the local Philosophical Society, and raised sufficient funds to start a school. This opened with fifteen children, who for the first seven years attended daily. When the school moved in 1813 to its present site at Edgbaston, it occupied a building large enough to accommodate, in residence, 175 children. Until Braidwood's death in 1825, half-hearted attempts to teach by the oral method were made. The new Superintendent, Louis du Puget, was a Swiss who had no time for oralism. He

---

[1] It closed in 1901 and continued solely as a workshop for the adult blind.
[2] *R.C.B.D.*, Vol. 2, Appx. 2, and Ritchie, *Concerning the Blind*, p. 220.

I. Institutional Education of the Blind and Deaf

immediately introduced the French system of finger spelling and methodical signs.[1]

The change marked the end of oralism in England for close on fifty years. This was greatly to be regretted. It was also easily explained. Unlike the children in Braidwood's academy in Edinburgh, those in the new institutions came from the poorest of families. Many of them were paupers, many were dull. They were crowded into large buildings with insufficient teachers for the individual methods that oralism demanded. Nor were the teachers always as capable as Braidwood had been, either because they lacked the innate skill or because those in the mystery of oralism failed to impart their knowledge to them. Even those in the mystery, the descendants of Braidwood, were not universally possessed of his genius. They basked in his glory, but in their hands his method became a mere drill.

In the decade following 1820, four more schools for the deaf were opened in England.[2] The first of these, at Manchester, was the work of a merchant banker, Robert Phillips. As was the case with Gallaudet, he took an interest in the deaf daughter of a neighbour. Finding her intelligent, he attempted to place her at one of the two existing schools. Both were full, and neither had prospects of vacancies for some time. He therefore decided that Manchester must have a school of its own. At a meeting of bankers, merchants and manufacturers in June 1823 a committee was appointed and capital raised. William Vaughan, who was the first assistant at the London Asylum, was appointed Superintendent, and the School opened in 1825, with fourteen resident children, all taught by the manual method.[3]

At this period the shortage of places in schools for the deaf was so acute that only older children were admitted. Rarely could a child aged below ten find a place, never below seven. However, in 1819, Arrowsmith had published his *The Art of Instructing the Infant Deaf and Dumb*. In it he recounted how his deaf brother aged four had attended an ordinary dame school, and had learnt to speak by imitating the other children and using lip-reading. The little brother, one feels, must have been highly intelligent. Be that as it may, Arrowsmith strongly advocated that the education of the deaf should begin as early as possible. Only in this way could success be achieved before it was time for the child to leave school. His other suggestions

---

[1] Arnold, *Education of Deaf-Mutes*, Vol. 2, pp. 201–3, Hodgson, *The Deaf and their Problems*, pp. 163–4, Bender, *The Conquest of Deafness* (1960), pp. 118–19.

[2] Institutions for the deaf had been established at Edinburgh, Glasgow, Aberdeen and Dublin during the period 1810–19.

[3] Nelson and Lunt, *Royal Residential Schools for the Deaf, Manchester, Historical Survey* (1923).

were not so practical. The deaf should attend ordinary schools where they would soon learn to speak, especially if the instruction they received at school were to be supplemented by their parents at home. Teachers of the deaf should publish their methods, although he felt that there was really little mystery in the teaching of the deaf. Nevertheless, his main point had been made. The infant deaf should be educated.[1]

The appeal was echoed in 1844 by Scott in his *The Deaf and Dumb, their Education and Social Position*, and two years later the Committee of the Manchester School explored the possibility of establishing an infants' department. Even with the best of intentions it was not possible to open the department until 1860. It had its own building and staff, a teacher and two nurses, and thirty children aged four to six. This was certainly the first infants' school for handicapped children in Britain, and probably the first in the world.[2]

The rivalry between Manchester and Liverpool is renowned. It was no less in the early nineteenth century. If Manchester educated her deaf, Liverpool must do so. Again it was a member of the business community, Edward Comer, who took the first step. Unlike his predecessors at Birmingham and Manchester, he had no personal contact with the deaf. His interest was aroused when, on an evening in 1824, he listened to an address by the Superintendent of the Dublin Institution. The traditional public meeting to gather support and finance did not immediately follow. Rather, Comer himself appointed a master to give daily instruction to four children. This plan was soon seen to be a failure. Special residential accommodation was obviously necessary. This Comer provided at his own expense, and twelve children were put in residence. His scheme aroused public enthusiasm, and when at length an inaugural meeting was held, the response was highly satisfactory. So satisfactory that the first Headmaster, John Anderson from the Glasgow Institution, was paid the princely sum of £250 per annum. This prodigality had its effect. Anderson's successor was paid little over £100, and all local children were compelled to become day scholars. There was still enough money, however, to provide the day children with free education and a daily dinner.[3] This is one of the few examples of free education at this period. At most schools for the blind and deaf, the children were paid for by their parents, by friends, or the Guardians of the Poor.

[1] Arrowsmith, *op. cit.*, pp. 25–61.
[2] Nelson and Lunt, *Royal Residential Schools for the Deaf, Manchester.*
[3] *Annual Report for 1852 of Liverpool School for the Deaf and Dumb*, Arnold, *Education of Deaf-Mutes*, Vol. 2, pp. 256–8, and Hodgson, *The Deaf and their Problems*, pp. 166–8.

I. Institutional Education of the Blind and Deaf

As Norwich provided for the blind in rural East Anglia, so Exeter catered for the deaf in the West Country. The establishment of the West of England Institution for the Deaf and Dumb was due to Mrs. Hippisley Tuckfield, who, while on a visit to Paris, heard of and visited De l'Epée's foundation. When, on returning to Exeter, she found that the nearest provision was nearly 200 miles away in London, she felt that Devon children were unnecessarily deprived. Lacking the wealth of a Comer, she could afford neither to pay a schoolmaster nor purchase premises. She could, however, teach the children herself. This she did. Finding the strain too great, in 1826 she appealed to the generosity of the town. Her school became a public charity, and a master from the Birmingham Institution was put in charge.[1]

The last of the four day schools of the 1820's was again in the industrial North. The Rev. Mr. Fenton of Doncaster, feeling that Yorkshire pride demanded an answer to Lancashire's two schools, determined to provide for the deaf. Although a member of the Braidwood family, T. J. Watson, was in charge of the London Asylum, it was not thither that he went for advice. The once high regard in which the family had been held had now declined. It was from the Paris school that Fenton sought guidance. On his return, eager to introduce the French method, he arranged for a group of children from the Manchester school to be brought to Doncaster to demonstrate their ability to converse by the manual method.[2] Distasteful as this public exhibition of handicapped children was, it remained the one certain way of raising money and obtaining publicity. Not only were these public entertainments staged as a preliminary to opening a new school, they were also annual events in most of the blind and deaf school calendars. Speaking at the Conference of Headmasters of Institutions for the Deaf and Dumb in London in 1885, William Sleight, who had taught at Doncaster, and was then Headmaster at Brighton, said, 'If you made a child write a word on a board people were amazed and you got more praise then you deserved. I had public examinations in the Brighton Town Hall forty two years ago. At these examinations anyone might ask a question, and the answers were written on a board.'[3]

William Sleight was Headmaster at Brighton for forty-eight years. This remarkable service was almost equalled by Charles Baker, who was Superintendent at Doncaster from the day the school opened in 1829, until his death forty-four years later. Baker had taught for

[1] R.C.B.D., Vol. 2, Appx. 2, and Arnold, op. cit., Vol. 2, pp. 258–60.
[2] Arnold, op. cit., Vol. 2, pp. 282–4.
[3] Proceedings of the Conference, p. 19.

three years under Du Puget at Birmingham, and there had embraced the French system favoured by the Doncaster Committee. During his long reign at Doncaster, Baker adapted the system so that all children started with natural signs, proceeded to finger spelling, and, finally, memorized long vocabulary lists, arranged in categories, by writing.[1]

England was now entering upon the era of Benthamism. Adam Smith and Bentham himself had taught that economic life should be free and natural, that all should be allowed to find its true level. Added to this, Evangelicalism had embraced that aspect of Puritanism which taught that the elect should be free to prove their justification. Finally, the ideas of Ricardo and Malthus, which had contributed so much to *laisser-faire*, justified to the early Victorians their depression of the poor through a harsh poor law. But the Poor Law Act of 1834 was anything but *laisser-faire*. It was pure Benthamism, authoritarian democracy depending upon a centralized administration. It gave relief in the workhouse only under deterrent conditions. But the disagreeable conditions imposed upon the able-bodied workman were identical for the pauper children who required no such spur.

This depression of the poor, this utilitarianism, was reflected in the charitable institutions which housed handicapped children. At Doncaster, of the first seventy-three children admitted, ten were withdrawn because their parents could not afford the weekly fee of 2s. 6d., and their parishes refused to pay. Others, though paupers, were never admitted for the same reason. The utilitarianism was reflected in Baker's comment: 'Drawing as an art has never been pursued . . . it would add considerably to the expense . . . and would not materially benefit their future life.'[2]

When, in 1833, an almost empty House of Commons voted £20,000 towards the erection of schools, the State made its first contribution to education. At this time there were six institutions for deaf children in England. These were by no means sufficient. But at least they did give education to those who were fortunate enough to be admitted. The education that they gave was frequently poor. The conditions under which it was given were worse. Even so, the deaf were better provided for than the blind. No new institutions had been established for them since 1805. Those that did exist confined themselves to giving industrial training. There was virtually no education in the usual sense. Liverpool gave a little tuition in music; though even this was for vocational purposes. A certain amount of religious instruction was given by the chaplains. Of reading and writing there was none. James Gall, one of those who at this period were attempting

[1] Bender, *The Conquest of Deafness*, pp. 184–5.
[2] Cited by Hodgson, *The Deaf and their Problems*, p. 171.

to produce books in raised type for the blind,[1] recorded that the art of reading and writing by the blind was at a standstill. 'So completely had it been forgotten in this country', he continued, 'that few comparatively, not even excepting the writer, were aware that it had ever been attempted; and no trace of its existence could be found amongst the pupils of any of our blind institutions.'[2]

As the concentration on industrial work increased, and the institutions came to depend to an ever-increasing extent on the profits that came from the workshops, so the ages of the children and the number of the adults in the blind asylums also increased. In 1803, the Liverpool institution raised its lower age of admission from eight to twelve.[3] The School for the Indigent Blind, in London, which had originally stated that it would *prefer* children aged twelve to eighteen, had by 1813 decided that twelve must be the minimum age. There was, however, no age limit at the upper end, 'while the strength remains unimpaired, and the fingers are flexible'.[4] Nevertheless, the children in the asylums were far better off than in the harsh world outside.

In the early nineteenth century street begging, and mendicity in general, was widespread. Children were exhibited by their parents to excite pity by their rags and by sores deliberately produced. Blind and physically handicapped children were particularly susceptible to such abuses. Attempts to reduce the evil were made by the Society for the Suppression of Public Begging established in Edinburgh in 1812, and the London Society for the Suppression of Mendicity a few years later.[5] It was not, however, until 1884, that the Society for the Prevention of Cruelty to Children was established. Nor were the evils confined to begging. At Maidstone in 1831, a thirteen-year-old boy was hanged for theft. Two years later the Old Bailey saw the sentencing to death of a nine-year-old boy for pushing a stick through a shop window. In 1834 two children aged ten and eleven were sentenced to transportation for seven years at Stafford.

In the year that the State made its first contribution to education, William Wilberforce, who had done so much to alleviate suffering, died. His friend and fellow worker for the abolition of slavery, Henry Brougham, felt that the best memorial to him would be found in the establishment of a school for the blind. Wilberforce had been born in the East Riding, and had for long represented the county of York

---

[1] See Chapter 4.
[2] Gall, *A Historical Sketch of the Origin and Progress of Literature for the Blind* (1834), p. 29.
[3] Minute Book, 1790–1803, Committee Meeting, August 1803.
[4] *An Account of the School for the Indigent Blind* (1813), p. 12.
[5] Mowat, *The Charity Organization Society 1869–1913* (1961), pp. 6–7.

in Parliament. Brougham, who, before his elevation to the peerage, had also represented the constituency, took the chair at a public meeting which endorsed the idea of a school. It was to be sited, naturally, at York. Premises, which had once been the house of the Abbot of St. Mary's Abbey, and later the residence of the President of the Council of the North, were obtained. Funds were collected. In 1835 the first two pupils arrived, and the school opened under Anderson from the Edinburgh school for the blind.[1]

Anderson's tenure was brief. He was succeeded after a year by the Rev. William Taylor, who was well acquainted both with Haüy's work in Paris and with the ever-increasing British embossed types for the blind.[2] As books in the new types became available, they were introduced into the school, and soon Taylor himself was printing books at the school. Education was given, therefore, from the outset. But the multiplicity of, and the lack of uniformity in, the number of types available militated against efficiency. As late as 1869 the girls were taught by one system, the boys by another. 'Clearly this was an anomaly,' wrote Buckle, the newly appointed Superintendent, in his report to the Managers.[3]

The introduction of education did not mean the end of industrial training. Throughout the nineteenth century, and well into the twentieth, it remained of paramount importance. One of His Majesty's Inspectors, Dr. Eichholz, describing the appointment in 1908 of a new superintendent to a school for the blind, commented: 'He is unlikely to fall into the common error of superintendents of blind schools which is to neglect the school for the saleroom.'[4] At York, on weekdays, between nine and twelve-thirty in the morning and two to five-thirty in the afternoon, the children were engaged in industrial occupations, save 'when any of them are receiving general instruction from the master'.[5] The general instruction was from nine to twelve and two to four-thirty, when 'the pupils shall be employed, in turns, under the tuition of the master, in arithmetic, reading, writing, and other studies of general improvement'.[6]

There is little doubt that education was given, not for its own sake, but as an aid to securing employment. The *Report* of 1873 states: 'The object of the Institution is to give the pupils such instruction as may enable them to obtain a livelihood; attention being, at the same time, paid to their moral and religious education.'[7] This concentration on industrial work was by no means exceptional. It was to be

[1] *Annual Report of Yorkshire School for the Blind for 1882*, pp. 6–9.
[2] See Chapter 4, pp. 45–6.
[3] *Annual Report of Yorkshire School for the Blind for 1873*, p. 13.
[4] Ministry of Education Archives, Education Class 32, Piece 8.
[5] *Annual Report for 1873*, p. 10.   [6] *Ibid.*, p. 10.   [7] *Ibid.*, p. 5.

found in all the institutions for the blind. In the 1870's, children were admitted to the School for the Indigent Blind at Southwark at the age of ten. A report of the Charity Organization Society described what happened. 'Mental and industrial training commence together. After the first year more time is given to the latter than the former; and after the fourth year, if fair progress has been made in the school-room, almost the whole time is devoted to industrial pursuits.'[1]

There was greater uniformity among the various institutions in the industrial pursuits followed than in the systems of teaching the children to read. Basket,[2] mat and brush making were the most popular. These were closely followed in popularity by rope, sash-lines and netted articles. Describing the sash-lines made at the Southwark school, E. C. Johnson proudly reported: 'Her Majesty's pictures at Buckingham Palace and Windsor are suspended by sash-lines manufactured at this institution.'[3] Occasionally, a once profitable industry would have to be abandoned, as at Hull, where the making of ships' fenders became uneconomical when the institution found itself being undersold by the products of Durham Gaol.[4]

Profiting by the example set by the Liverpool Asylum in the eighteenth century, the teaching of music for vocational reasons was also widespread. The York school established a brass band in 1843.[5] The Southwark school built a band room, 'where a band of thirty players—viola, flutes and brass horns—plays such music as one hears from a good German band'.[6] Among the earliest pupils at York was William Strickland. His name appears in almost every *Annual Report* for fifty years. One of the first references occurs in 1840: 'Wm. Henry Strickland, aged fourteen, who, at the date of the last report, was organist at the Church of Acomb, has been elected organist at St. Martin's, and gained the situation by a contest with two seeing competitors. He has lately been made an assistant teacher of music in the School.'[7] He remained there as music master until 1883.

In the same *Report*, there is mention of another pupil: 'Catherine Haynes, aged thirteen, left the School a few months ago to take the situation of organist at a church near Bawtry.'[8] This reference is more typical. Few children were as successful as Strickland. Many were failures. Sir Francis Campbell, who, during the last thirty years

---

[1] Charity Organization Society, *Report of Special Committee on the Training of the Blind* (1876), p. 31.   [2] York as a refinement made game and wine hampers.
   [3] Johnson, *London International Exhibition, 1871. Report on the Methods of Teaching the Blind and the Deaf and Dumb*, p. 15.   [4] *R.C.B.D.*, Vol. 2, Appx. 2.
   [5] *Annual Report of School for 1882*, p. 10.   [6] Johns, *Blind People* (1867), p. 7.
   [7] *Annual Report of School for 1840*, p. 10.   [8] *Ibid.*, p. 10.

of the nineteenth century, did more for the musical education of the blind in this country than any man before or since, gave as his opinion that prior to 1870, the blind had been poorly taught in music. 'Consequently,' he continued, 'those that applied for organists posts were those who possessed very little education and refinement, who had no knowledge of reading and writing the Braille musical notation, or the ordinary notation used by the seeing, who had no technical development worthy of the name, and who did not understand voice development and choir training . . . of course they failed, but their failure was ascribed to their blindness, not to their lack of education and training.'[1]

A new development in the education of the blind occurred in 1838 with the establishment of a school by the London Society for Teaching the Blind to Read.[2] The avowed aim was no longer vocational training, but education, or, at least, the teaching of reading. Nevertheless, experience showed that the blind could not live by reading alone. The introduction of industrial training produced only a limited conformity, for there were still differences. Pupils were admitted from the age of eight, yet industrial training did not start until the age of fourteen. This was the pattern of the future: a sound education followed by vocational training, not inefficient education parallel with, and subordinate to, industrial work. The pupils, too, at this school were rather different from those elsewhere. They were, according to the *Report of the Charity Organization Society*, 'of a grade superior to that of the indigent classes, the majority contributing towards their own support and education'.[3]

The difference in the background from which the children came was reflected in the lessening of the restrictions placed upon them. They went home for three weeks holiday at Christmas, and five in the summer.[4] Rarely were the poorer children in the other institutions for the blind and deaf granted more than three weeks holiday in a whole year. There were differences, too, of quantity and quality, in the articles of clothing that the children were asked to bring with them to the school. The children at the London Society's School had to bring six handkerchiefs, those at York only two—they must have been immune from colds.[5]

---

[1] Campbell, *The Musical Education of the Blind* (1893), p. 5.

[2] See Chapter 4, p. 47.

[3] *Report of Special Committee on . . . the Blind*, pp. 32–3.

[4] *Thirty-Sixth Annual Report of the London Society for Teaching the Blind to Read* (1874), p. 7.

[5] The list of clothing that the girls had to take to the York school makes interesting reading. Among other items were: 4 Shifts, 2 Flannel Petticoats, 2 Pairs of Stays, 2 Frocks (one a dark Stuff), 2 Night Caps, 2 Black Hats, and 1 Cloak. *Annual Report of School for 1873*, p. 13.

I. Institutional Education of the Blind and Deaf

In the same year as the London Society opened its school, an institution for both deaf and blind children was founded in Newcastle-upon-Tyne. It was the first in England.[1] It was not a success. Its origin was both accidental and acrimonious. A group of Newcastle citizens agreed in the first instance to establish a school for the blind. When this opened, there occurred, in keeping with the spirit of the times, a dispute concerning the form that the religious teaching should take. A rival organization was therefore formed. The blind school, which it also opened, had insufficient children to warrant its continuance. Expediency, therefore, dictated that provision for the deaf should be made in the same school. Thus, for ten years Newcastle had one school purely for the blind, another for both blind and deaf. Gradually the number of blind children in the combined school decreased, and the number of deaf increased. Eventually, reality was faced. The rival organizations came to terms. All the blind were to be educated at the Royal Victoria Asylum for the Industrious Blind, the deaf at the Northern Counties Institution for the Deaf and Dumb, as the rival establishments now came to be named.[2]

Although Manchester had been one of the first cities to provide for the deaf, she still had no school for the blind. For this she was not wholly to blame. An endowment fund, for the purpose of establishing a school for the blind, had been bequeathed by an Oldham merchant, Thomas Henshaw, as far back as 1810. Litigation over the will had delayed matters, as had the poor public response to appeals for land and suitable buildings. When eventually Henshaw's Blind Asylum opened in 1839, interest had swollen the endowment fund to £50,000. Fifty years later the Asylum possessed investments valued at £70,000 and property at £23,000. It was amongst the wealthiest institutions in the land.

Unfortunately, Thomas Henshaw made his bequest, and drew up the foundation deed, at a time when there was little thought of educating, as opposed to giving vocational training to, blind children. It was not therefore possible to utilize the wealth in the way that the changed conditions dictated. The original object of the institution had been twofold: to provide asylum for the impotent and aged blind, and to give instruction to the indigent blind capable of employment. Girls, once they were admitted, remained in the Asylum for life; boys remained until the age of twenty-one. These conditions, allied to the fact that for the first year of the Asylum's existence, only

---

[1] Belfast had established such a school in 1831.
[2] Ritchie, *Concerning the Blind*, p. 222, and Arnold, *Education of Deaf-Mutes*, Vol. 2, pp. 338–40.

industrial training was given, inhibited the reception of children. In 1864 there were only seven children under fourteen. With the increase of the facilities for education, and a request to the Court of Chancery for the amendment of the terms of the endowment, the number of children had by 1888 significantly increased to seventy-nine.[1] Thirty years later Dr. George Newman could report that the school was considered to be equally as important as the trade department.[2]

Chartism, that protest against the conditions described so graphically by Dickens, Kingsley and Disraeli in his *Sybil*, reached its apogee in 1839, and reappeared in 1848. During the intervening period Marx and Engels read at the British Museum and published the *Communist Manifesto*; Rochdale opened the first Co-operative store; and Shaftesbury discovered a room in London with a family in each of its four corners. But life in the institutions for the blind and deaf was untouched by these developments without, and the decade saw the establishment of nine new schools.

These included the first school in England for handicapped children to be established by a religious organization; the first long-term combination of blind and deaf children in the same institution; and the first school for the handicapped in Wales. The first named was the Catholic Blind Asylum at Liverpool. It was opened in 1841 under the Sisters of Charity of St. Vincent de Paul. Elementary education and industrial training was given to children from the outset. There were also sheltered workshops for adults.[3] The school which catered for more than one handicap was the Institution for the Blind and the Deaf and Dumb at Bath. It was for children only. Had it catered for the blind solely, the usual workshops would have been attached. As it was, the presence of the deaf meant that the blind were given more education than was usually the case. Whether for this reason or some other, the blind resented being educated with the deaf. The latter, not unnaturally, objected to this attitude, and in their turn complained of the proximity of the blind. There were a small number of children, however, who felt no resentment. These were the deaf-blind. For them the Bath school did valiant work. But the acrimonious atmosphere which prevailed among the other pupils could not be allowed to continue indefinitely. After fifty-four turbulent years the school closed in 1896.[4]

The first Welsh school was the Royal Cambrian Institution for the Deaf and Dumb. It opened at Aberystwyth in 1847 with two day

---

[1] *R.C.B.D.*, Vol. 2, Appx. 2.
[2] *Annual Report for 1908 of the Chief Medical Officer of the Board of Education*, p. 111.   [3] *R.C.B.D.*, Vol. 2, Appx. 2.   [4] *Ibid.*

I. Institutional Education of the Blind and Deaf

pupils and two boarders. Three years later it moved to more highly populated Swansea. There, in addition to children, it accepted adults whose education had been neglected and who would not have been received by any other institution.[1] After exactly a hundred years it moved again—to Llandrindod Wells, where it still stands.

Bristol, which had long since made provision for the blind, now opened an institution for the deaf. Equally Exeter, where the deaf were already cared for, established a school for the blind. This and the Midland Institution for the Blind at Nottingham were both branch schools of the London Society for Teaching the Blind to Read.[2] From the outset therefore, education commanded as much attention as industrial work. Such was the case, too, at the General Institution for the Blind at Edgbaston, Birmingham.

Though its foundation in 1847 was not directly the work of the London Society, it followed the Society's system and was liberally supplied with its books. The school's establishment was the work, once again, of a merchant. William Harrold had been impressed by the charitable work that he had seen in the United States. On his return to Birmingham, he appealed for funds and made a handsome contribution himself. While money was still being collected, his daughter, Elizabeth, and her friend, Mary Badger, rented a small house and taught the first pupils. As elsewhere, their example fired the public imagination, the venture became a public charity, and the school a public institution. Mary Badger's interest in, and connection with, the school continued, and she was honorary Lady Superintendent from 1848 to 1893.[3]

During the school's first year there were seventeen children, of whom the youngest was only six. Their teacher, Miss Allerton, was given the exalted title of Governess. Each day she instructed them in the Scriptures and in reading. Once weekly she taught them music, geography with the aid of raised maps, arithmetic, both mental and by the means of peg boards, general knowledge and history.[4]

This was by far the most comprehensive education that the blind received at this period. There were still institutions which concentrated almost entirely on industrial training. At the oldest, the School for the Indigent Blind, Liverpool, the teaching of reading was not introduced until 1862. The *Annual Report* for that year stated that the original object of giving instruction in an art or trade was still unchanged, but, in addition, 'all the Pupils capable of learning

---

[1] Ministry of Education Archives, Education Class 32, Piece 227.
[2] Ritchie, *Concerning the Blind*, pp. 222–3.
[3] *First Annual Report of the General Institution for the Blind*, 1848, pp. 3–5, and *The Birmingham Royal Institution for the Blind, 1847–1947* (1948), pp. 4–7.
[4] *First Annual Report*, pp. 5–6.

are taught to read by means of a raised type'.[1] Even this concession was not obtained without the need for an explanation. At the Annual General Meeting of subscribers, the Treasurer, after giving his statement of the accounts, 'spoke more especially as to the amount of time expended in having various books and Newspapers read to the Pupils'.[2] This, of course, was at the expense of time that might have been spent in the workshops. Therefore, moved the Treasurer, the children should be taught to read.

Naturally, the more recently established institutions found it easier to introduce school work. They had not the long-founded tradition of trade instruction. But even Birmingham, with its extensive curriculum, had its industrial training, to which 'a considerable portion of each day' was devoted.[3]

Along with education, industrial training was mentioned among the aims of the school. Included, too, was 'imparting to the children that knowledge which shall bring them their duty to God and man'.[4] A similar phrase was to be found in the aims of most of the institutions for the handicapped. Where not expressed, it was implicit. The worship of God and the study of His Word played an important part in the daily life of each school. The children assembled each morning before breakfast and again in the evening before bed 'to hear a portion of Scripture read by the master, and to join in prayer; and by day they learn to commit to memory, verses from the Psalms, or other religious lessons'.[5] Before Braille was introduced in the last quarter of the century, almost all the books from which the blind learnt to read were reprints of portions of the Bible. On Sundays the amount of time devoted to religion was greater. At Doncaster, even the youngest of the deaf children studied the Gospels from 6.30 to 8 in the morning, 3 to 5 in the afternoon, and 5.30 to 7.30 in the evening. In addition, they attended public worship from 10 to 11.30 a.m. and 11.40 a.m. to 1.[6]

One wonders whether time tables like this one were actually followed, or whether they were included in annual reports to please the subscribers, who, being ardent Christians themselves, would wish to believe that the children were being given adequate religious instruction. If this was the case, there were some entries in the annual reports that must have given them gratification. The Ulster Institution for the Deaf and Dumb, and the Blind, Belfast, recorded

---

[1] *Report for 1862*, p. 2.
[2] Minute Book 1856–1880, manuscript account of Annual General Meeting, 17.1.1862.
[3] *First Annual Report*, p. 5.   [4] *Ibid*, p. 3.
[5] *Annual Report of Yorkshire School for the Blind for 1873*, p. 9.
[6] Hodgson, *The Deaf and their Problems*, p. 172.

I. *Institutional Education of the Blind and Deaf*

that: 'A little mute, in his 8th year, a day scholar, was unfortunately killed at one of the Factories before he could have known the revealed will of God. Very different, however, were the circumstances of a poor blind boy, who died about the same age. He was delicate and deformed; but during a lingering and painful illness, he discovered a vigour of mind, an eagerness for spiritual instruction, a meekness of disposition, which gave satisfactory evidence of a saving change of heart.'[1] Ten years later another institution noted that: 'S.R., a blind Irish girl, suffering from great delicacy of health, was received into the school two years prior to her death, under peculiarly providential circumstances. It was deeply interesting to her Christian friends to remark how gradually she was led from the errors of Romanism to the pure doctrines of the word of God, by a blessing on the power she acquired, to search the Scriptures for herself.'[2] Nor were day pupils exempt from the need to attend religious worship. Those attending the School for the Indigent Blind at Liverpool, be they children or adults, had to produce to the Superintendent certificates of regular attendance at places of worship. Failure to do so entailed dismissal from the school.[3]

The last of the schools built in the first half of the century were both established in the same town, Brighton, in the same year, 1842. They were the Asylum for the Instruction of the Blind, and the Institution for Deaf and Dumb Children. The first deaf-mute clergyman to be ordained in the Church of England, the Rev. R. A. Pearce, was educated at the latter. He became a missionary to the deaf and dumb in the Diocese of Manchester. Also educated there was a girl who, at the age of five, had caught scarlet fever, and had consequently suffered 'a bad discharge from the ear, which had been allowed to go on unchecked under the popular delusion that to stop it would be fatal'.[4] Instead she was allowed to become deaf. This was only a little over seventy years ago. There was still at that time a great deal of deafness which could have been prevented.[5]

The decade 1840–50, which had been so prolific in the foundation of institutions for the blind and deaf, was followed by one which saw the opening of but one school in England and Wales. However, an interesting experiment was attempted in Scotland during the period. James Donaldson, of Edinburgh, bequeathed all his fortune to the

[1] *2nd Annual Report for 1838*, p. 7.
[2] Cited by Ritchie, *Concerning the Blind*, p. 22.
[3] *An Address in favour of the School for the Blind in Liverpool* (1808), p. 16.
[4] *R.C.B.D.*, Vol. 2, Appx. 2, p. 32.
[5] Some of the causes of deafness of children at the Georgia Institution in the United States might not have been prevented, but they were, at least, unusual. They included: taking strong medicine, kicked by a mule, thrown from a horse, and firing a gun while the head was in a kettle. *R.C.B.D.*, Vol. 2, Appx. 30.

establishment of a residential school for the education of destitute children. Housed in a palatial residence, and called Donaldson's Hospital, it accepted, as a deliberate policy, one deaf child to every two hearing destitute children. This proportion was subsequently changed, and the number of deaf children equalled the number of hearing. All the pupils were accommodated in the same building, using the same facilities save classrooms and teachers.[1] The experiment was a success. Donaldson's Hospital continued to cater for the deaf and the hearing until 1938, when the hearing moved to other schools, and the deaf children joined with those from the Royal Institution for the Deaf, also in Edinburgh, to form Donaldson's School.

Although the children at Donaldson's Hospital may have been as isolated from the outside world as the children in other institutions, the handicapped children there did at least have the opportunity for contact with non-handicapped children. It was this lack of contact with normality, this almost complete segregation from ordinary life, that was one of the worst features of the education of the handicapped for the first seventy years of the nineteenth century. It was . significant that many of the earlier institutions included the word asylum in their titles. All too often they were regarded as places of refuge from a cruel and unsympathetic world, rather than schools which trained for an independent life in a hearing and seeing world. Some of the institutions were aware of the danger. The Managers of the Liverpool School for the Blind reported that they had 'continued during each successive year to render it less of an *asylum*, where the ease and comfort of the blind were principally considered, and more approaching to a *school*, where they should be instructed in some useful art or trade, by which they might be enabled to procure for themselves a comfortable livelihood'.[2] Awareness of the danger and good intentions were not in themselves enough. While schools adhered to the practice of confining the children within the walls of the institution, normality of behaviour could not be expected. For seven years no child at the Asylum for the Deaf, in the Old Kent Road, left the school in term time, save to attend church.[3] At the London School for the Indigent Blind, children 'who had friends joined them for a week at Christmas and Midsummer'.[4] Not all had friends.

[1] Arnold, *Education of Deaf-Mutes*, Vol. 2, pp. 358–60, and Watson, T. J., 'A History of Deaf Education in Scotland '. Unpublished Ph.D. Thesis of Edinburgh University (1949).
[2] *An Address in Favour of the School for the Blind in Liverpool*, p. 8.
[3] Hodgson, *The Deaf and their Problems*, p. 204.
[4] Bartley, *The Schools for the People*, p. 348.

I. Institutional Education of the Blind and Deaf

When the children finally left the schools, the transition to the outside world must have presented grave difficulties. Some, of course, never left. They remained on in the sheltered workshops. As the workshops became full, fewer and fewer were allowed to stay on. There was no after-care for those who left, and the position was clearly stated by the Committee of the London School for the Indigent Blind: 'Cases of extreme indigence are not those in which admission to this School is likely to be of most use, for when the pupil is dismissed, the value of the instruction he has received, must entirely depend upon the means he may possess of putting in practice the art in which he has been instructed, and unless his friends shall be in a condition to furnish him with a constant supply of materials for the regular exercise of the skill he may have acquired, the School will have taught, and he will have learned to very little purpose.'[1]

The problem was to some extent alleviated by the work of Elizabeth Gilbert, who in 1853 organized a number of trained blind persons, provided them with materials, and assisted them to sell their products. This was the first home workers' scheme, for the blind were based on their own homes. It led, however, to the formation of sheltered workshops for adults, as distinct from those attached to schools. This was not an ideal solution, since it perpetuated the segregation of the blind, and made their eventual integration with society that much more difficult.

Isolation was not confined to the children within the institutions. The institutions themselves were divorced from the outside world. Thus, the main stream of educational progress passed them by. Secure in their own little worlds, some superintendents cared not what happened elsewhere. Those who did care had little opportunity for finding out. 'I am one of the old school teachers,' said William Sleight;[2] 'I have been Head Master of the Brighton Institution forty-three years tomorrow. I went there from Yorkshire. For a long time I did not see a fellow labourer once in three or four years; we were isolated and alone.'

There was, too, the isolation bred of jealousy. E. C. Johnson, a disinterested worker for the blind, summarized the position in his description of the apparatus for the blind shown at the Paris Exhibition of 1867. 'England which is so rich in institutions for the blind is almost unrepresented at the Exhibition. This is attributable to a want of harmony and concert amongst the various schools and societies in England; to the dread of intrusting their interests to other

---

[1] *Account of the School for the Indigent Blind* (1813), p. 15.
[2] At the Conference of Headmasters of Institutions for the Deaf and Dumb, 1885. *Proceedings of the Conference*, p. 19.

hands than their own; and to the opposition which is so strong an element amongst the lovers of particular systems for teaching the blind to read.'[1]

At first the education in the deaf schools had been superior to that in the blind. As more books for the blind became available, the standard in blind schools improved, but the education of the deaf declined, as the early oralism was replaced by a system of signs. Superintendents, who had previously trained their assistant masters in the oral method, now allowed them to acquire from the children what knowledge they could of signs. Richard Elliott, later to become headmaster of the Old Kent Road Asylum for the Deaf, described the position there when he joined the staff in the middle of the century. 'Mr. Thomas James Watson, the headmaster, rarely came into the school . . . the assistants received no sort of training . . . not a word of direction, advice or encouragement was ever given to me or indeed to any of us . . . provided there was the appearance of work it seemed to be the business of no one in particular to see whether it was efficient or otherwise. . . . The Headmastership seemed a sinecure.'[2]

Under conditions such as these, even the sign and manual system declined and became debased. Children invented their own signs, which were copied by the teachers and passed on to a future generation of deaf children. There was much memorizing and transcribing of written matter that was not understood. Elliott recounts the story of a boy who produced a beautifully written exercise of the conjugation of the verb 'to be'. Asked what 'I am' meant, the boy gave the sign for 'jam'.[3] With the first rush of deaf school building over, promotion for teachers became more difficult. Fewer good men came into the work, and the schools became more dependent upon teachers who were themselves deaf. At one period, out of nine assistants at the London Asylum, six were deaf ex-pupils. Moreover, the conditions of service were severe. In 1832 an assistant articled himself to the Headmaster of the Glasgow Institution 'to serve night and day, Sunday and holiday, for seven years, under a penalty of £50'.[4]

Even when good teachers were secured, there were difficulties in retaining them. The Committee of the Old Kent Road Asylum paid nearly £20 to buy out a teacher drawn for the militia. Another of their assistants, who was deaf, was seized by the Press Gang, and the Committee had to prove his deafness in order to secure his release.[5]

---

[1] Johnson, *Report on Apparatus and Methods used in the Instruction of the Blind, at the Paris Exhibition, 1867*, pp. 30–1.
[2] Cited by Hodgson, *The Deaf and their Problems*, p. 197.
[3] *Ibid.*, p. 200.   [4] *R.C.B.D.*, Vol. 2, Appx. 2, p. 42.
[5] Hodgson, *The Deaf and their Problems*, p. 162.

I. Institutional Education of the Blind and Deaf

Every attempt was made to conceal the decline in teaching standards from the subscribers to the institutions. Blackboards were removed, lest visitors should ask the children awkward questions. Annual reports were full of extracts from children's work which were obviously false.[1] If justification for falsification there can be, it lies in the fact that the subscribers were people who expected to see results for their money. If these were not forthcoming, they would cease to subscribe. Hence, if the schools were to be kept open, the subscribers must be deceived.

If conditions in the schools for the blind and deaf seemed bad, they were no worse, and were in many ways better, than those obtaining in other schools. The ordinary schools, too, suffered from poor teaching and ill-paid teachers, from lax supervision and inadequate equipment. But at least the material conditions in the institutions were good. Although the conditions described by the Commissioners, who enquired into the state of education in Wales in 1847, may not have been universal, they were by no means isolated.

Of a parochial school they reported: 'This school is held in a ruinous hovel of the most squalid and miserable character; the floor is of bare earth, full of deep holes; the windows are all broken; a tattered partition of lath and plaster divides it into two unequal portions; in the larger were a few wretched benches, and a small desk for the master in one corner, in the lesser was an old door, with the hasp still on it, laid crossways upon two benches, . . . to serve for a writing desk. Such of the scholars as write retire in pairs to this part of the room, and kneel on the ground while they write . . . The Vicar's son informed me that he had seen 80 children in this hut. In summer the heat of it is said to be suffocating; and no wonder.'[2] Another parochial school 'was held in a room, part of a dwelling house; the room was so small that a great many of the scholars were obliged to go into the room above, which they reached by means of a ladder, through a hole in the loft; the room was lighted by one small glazed window, half of which was patched up with boards; it was altogether a wretched place; . . . the floor was in a very bad state, there being several large holes in it, some of them nearly a foot deep; the room was so dark that the few children whom I heard read were obliged to go to the door, and open it, to have sufficient light.'[3]

[1] Denmark, 'The New Education Act', *Teacher of the Deaf*, Vol. 42, No. 252, December 1944, p. 151.
[2] *Reports of the Commissioners of Inquiry into the State of Education in Wales*, Vol. 1, p. 238.
[3] *Ibid.*, p. 265.

An Assistant Commissioner who visited a dame school wrote: 'I never shall forget the hot, sickening smell, which struck me on opening the door of that low dark room. . . . It more nearly resembled the smell of the engine on board a steamer, such as it is felt by a sea-sick voyager on passing near the funnel. . . . Everything in the room (i.e. a few benches of various heights and sizes, and a couple of tables) was hidden under and overlaid with children.'[1]

Overcrowding may have occurred in the institutions for the blind and deaf, but on nothing like the scale described by the Commissioners as occurring elsewhere. The handicapped children may have led regimented and isolated lives, but they led them in comparative comfort. They were well housed and well clad, and though their food may have been plain and monotonous, it was wholesome. Those who were admitted were the lucky ones. They were spared the horrors of begging, or the boredom of life in the workhouse. They were given a modicum of education, and some of them were taught a trade. This was all that the institutions set out to do. This was what they did. Of them it might be written, as Newman wrote of the Utilitarians: 'They aimed low, but they achieved their aim.'

[1] *Reports of the Commissioners of Inquiry into the State of Education in Wales*, Vol. 1, p. 238.

4

THE PERIOD OF EXPERIMENT: II. METHODS OF TEACHING THE BLIND TO READ

THE decade which opened in 1832 saw the first development in England of methods of teaching the blind to read. It was singularly unfortunate that after a long, barren period so many different systems should appear at the same time. Thomas Blacklock's translation of Haüy's account of his teaching methods had been available since before the turn of the century, but no effort had been made to produce embossed type, and the children in the earlier schools received virtually no education. In 1823 some of the books produced by Haüy in his type were brought to England by Lady Elizabeth Lowther for her blind son, Charles. Using this type, he was taught to read by the Rev. William Taylor, who became his tutor and later superintendent of the Wilberforce School for the Blind, York. Haüy's type was the ordinary, italic form of the Roman letter, and his pupils wrote ordinary script backwards with a steel pen on thick paper, and so embossed it on the reverse side. The type was therefore legible to both eye and finger, and in 1832 Charles Lowther obtained some types of this kind from Paris, and printed parts of the Bible with his own hand. In the same year the Edinburgh Society of Arts offered a prize for the best type for the blind, which was won by a blind Scot, Alexander Hay, with a completely arbitrary system which bore no relation to the normal letters, and could not therefore be read by a sighted person without instruction. The Society decided, however, that it could not give unqualified recommendation to Hay's type without further investigation, and offered another prize in 1833. In view of the 1832 award, it was not surprising that most of the entries were of the arbitrary kind. Yet the prize went to Dr. Fry of London and his alphabet of plain Roman capitals. The Society was influenced in its recommendation of Fry's system by the advice it sought from William Taylor, who had been favourably impressed by Haüy's type when he was Lowther's tutor.[1]

Despite the Society's recommendation, it appeared to many closely connected with the blind that the Roman characters were not sufficiently distinct to the touch. They did not fulfil to the finger the promise they made to the eye. Yet experiments with, and modifications to, Fry's type continued to be made. John Alston, treasurer of the Glasgow Asylum for the Blind, effected slight changes and from 1837 printed many books in it at the Asylum. He made three tours of British institutions for the blind to publicize his type, which was adopted by three of them.[2] Taylor at York also printed books in it, and by 1870 its use was widespread. Even in 1886 it was still the main system at the Southwark school.[3]

Another protagonist of the non-arbitrary type was the Edinburgh printer, James Gall. He was dissatisfied with the lack of education at the Edinburgh Asylum, and during the 1820's he experimented with various types in order that he might print books for the Asylum. The authorities in charge refused his offer, and so, when in 1833 he introduced a new character, founded upon ordinary Roman capitals but with angles instead of curves, he opened a separate institution for teaching blind children to read. He published his system but it failed to meet with the success of Alston's, since many of his letters were so divorced from the original Roman that he failed to receive the backing of supporters of that type, and his system was confined almost entirely to his own school. Nevertheless, he was an indefatigable advocate of the blind becoming literate, although he was aware of the viewpoint of most institutions. 'It may be argued,' he recorded, 'that the providing of books for the pupils, the fitting up of a schoolroom, the loss of labour during the time necessary for learning to read and write, with other contingent items, would make a very serious inroad upon the funds of the institution, which it could not afford; that the design of the institution is definite, and does not include the pursuits of literature; and therefore it may be urged, with considerable plausibility that reading and writing should not be

---

[1] Gall, *An Account of the Recent Discoveries which have been made for facilitating the Education of the Blind* (1837), pp. 14–18, 41–7.
[2] Alston, *Statements of the Education, Employments, and Internal Arrangements adopted at the Asylum for the Blind, Glasgow* (1842), pp. 3–5, 44–8.
[3] *R.C.B.D.*, Vol. 3, Evidence of Miss Hiscock, 23.1.1886.

II. Methods of Teaching the Blind to Read

taught.'[1] His counter to this argument was that if funds would not run to a school-room it did not follow that there should not be a school, and that there might be a financial gain as literate children would make better and more contented workers.

In 1838 the era of the arbitrary systems opened. Some of these were frankly stenographic; others consisted of a combination of symbols and rudimentary Roman letters. The first of them, Lucas, was of the former kind. Thomas Lucas, like Gall in Edinburgh, was disappointed with the local institution, and in 1830 opened a small school for the blind in Bristol. He was then sixty-six, but during the next seven years he developed his system based, like shorthand, on line, curve and dot. In 1837 he went to London to publicize his method, but died soon after arriving there. He had, however, interested sufficient people in his work, and the following year the London Society for Teaching the Blind to Read was formed. Its aim was the propagation of the Lucas system. It was to be fulfilled by the establishment of a school where Lucas would be taught and books in embossed type produced, and by the encouragement of the opening of similar schools elsewhere. At first the Society was remarkably successful. Its school at Bloomsbury, which later moved to Regent's Park, admitted both day and residential children aged eight and upwards. At the outset their stay was short as it was intended that they should learn to read in six months. Indeed the Society claimed that mastery of Lucas could be obtained within three months.[2] But the length of stay soon increased, and other subjects apart from reading were introduced. Concentration on reading remained, and even in 1886 little girls were taught nothing from the age of eight, save knitting, until they had conquered Lucas.[3] The schoolmaster had the additional duty of embossing books in Lucas, and these were soon produced in large numbers, some being exported as far as Australia. Most of them went far nearer home to the Lucas schools which were opened at Exeter, Bath, Nottingham, Leamington and Plymouth. Some of these schools were short-lived and others changed to different systems. Lucas played a brief, but effective, part in the production of literature for the blind.

The part played by the phonetic system of James Harley Frere was not so important. This again was stenographic, and appearing contemporaneously with the Lucas system became at first a rival. Its complexity led to its failure, for the simple linear signs of which it

[1] Gall, *A Historical Sketch of the Origin and Purpose of Literature for the Blind* (1834), p. 207.
[2] *Thirty-Sixth Annual Report of the London Society for Teaching the Blind to Read* (1874).
[3] *R.C.B.D.*, Vol. 3, Evidence of Miss P. Hamilton, 11.2.1886.

was composed represented, not letters of the alphabet, but vocal sounds. Its importance lies in the fact that parts of it were reproduced in the last of the English systems, Moon's.

While Alston, Gall and Lucas were perfecting their types, William Moon was becoming blind. His sight began to fail when he was four, and by 1839 he was completely blind. He was then twenty-one. Within a year he began to work on behalf of those similarly afflicted. He concerned himself not so much with children at school as with the blind in their own homes, and he did much to found home teaching societies. He described his type, devised in 1847, as 'Composed principally of the Roman letters in their original or in slightly modified forms. . . . Where I could not alter to advantage some of the more complex letters of the Roman Alphabet, I removed them altogether, and substituted new characters in their stead.'[1] The new characters which he substituted were taken straight from Frere, but to avoid any infringement of the latter's system he made the purely arbitrary signs selected represent different letters from those which they represented in Frere's system. This plagiarism can be condoned in view of the outstanding success of Moon's system. It was widely adopted, and of all the English types of this period it is the only one still in use. Moon's selflessness, too, would count in mitigation. He personally printed many of the books in his type at a small workshop adjoining his Brighton home. Although he could have made a profit, there was nothing commercial about the enterprise. The books were sold below cost price; he gave his time both free and freely, and charged nothing for the rent of premises, wear and tear of machinery, or type setting. When he gave evidence before the Royal Commission on the Blind and Deaf in 1887 there were more books in Britain in his type than in any other; the Moon Society, founded to publicize the system, was flourishing; and an honorary doctorate of laws had been conferred upon him by the University of Philadelphia.[2] On his death in 1894 the work was continued by his daughter until her own death in 1914 when the Moon Society was taken over by the National Institute for the Blind, which still publishes some books and periodicals in Moon type for those who have lost their sight in later life and find Braille baffling because of its technical difficulties, or because of work-hardened fingers which lack sensitivity.[3]

Thus by the middle of the nineteenth century a number of different but competing systems were in use. Each had its protagonists; each was followed in one school or another. At a time

[1] Moon cited by Ritchie, *Concerning the Blind*, pp. 55–6.
[2] *R.C.B.D.*, Vol. 3, Evidence of Moon, 19.5.1887.
[3] Thomas, *The Royal National Institute for the Blind, 1868–1956* (1957), p. 61.

when unity was the main necessity, those concerned with the welfare of the blind were divided against each other. There was much bitter controversy, and progress was inhibited. The lack of uniformity meant that institutions worked in solitary isolation with their teachers loth to move elsewhere where the learning of a new system would be necessary. Moreover, there was a tremendous wastage of resources. In the main, the same few books, mostly of a religious character, were reproduced in each different type. Of the 490 books in Moon's type in 1887, 127 were books of the Bible or single chapters. Such duplication meant that there was comparatively little that the literate blind could read. In any case the types themselves were nowhere near being ideal. Some were too complicated, others demanded a high degree of sensitivity of touch, while all were expensive to produce and laborious to reproduce.

Meanwhile, in France, the problem was being solved. In 1812 the three-year-old son of a harness maker at Coupvray blinded himself while playing with one of his father's awls. For Louis Braille this was unfortunate. For the remainder of the blind world the accident was to lead to a happy outcome. At ten, the young Braille entered the Institution Nationale des Jeunes Aveugles at Paris, and by the age of seventeen he had progressed so well that he was invited to remain at the school as a master. At the same time, Charles Barbier, an artillery officer in the post-Revolutionary army, devised a system of embossed dots to enable fire orders to be delivered by written message in the dark. At the suggestion of the Académie des Sciences he brought his system to the notice of the authorities at the Institution Nationale des Jeunes Aveugles. Its significance appears to have been lost upon all save Louis Braille. He realized that whereas the permutations of the twelve dots of Barbier's system might be too complicated for blind fingers, the principle was an excellent one. He therefore reduced the number of dots to six which he arranged in a basic form of three horizontal pairs. Letters of the alphabet, punctuation marks and contractions were represented by the omission of one or more dots from the basic form. For example, for the first ten letters of the alphabet the two lower dots were omitted altogether, and the letters were formed by the two upper pairs or by some further omission from these. In all there were sixty-three possible combinations.

Braille had obvious advantages over all other existing systems. It could be adapted to any written language; be used for musical notation and mathematics; and, with the aid of a stylus, be quickly and easily written by hand. The dot was also easier to feel than the line, and since it took up less space, works in Braille were less bulky. Yet the tradition that the embossed letter had to resemble the printed one was so strong that its inventor had the greatest difficulty in securing its adoption, even by his own school. He first introduced it in 1829, and five years later issued a perfected version. He was not, however, allowed to teach it officially, and for many years Louis Braille taught it to the children at the Institution Nationale in his spare time. It is not therefore surprising that its introduction to Britain was delayed. But prejudice, stubbornness and a lack of unity delayed its introduction far longer than was necessary. Not until 1872 did the first English school teach its pupils by Braille, and twenty years later children were still being taught by Alston and Lucas types.

5

THE PERIOD OF EXPERIMENT:
III. DEVELOPMENTS IN THE
EDUCATION OF THE FEEBLE-MINDED
AND PHYSICALLY HANDICAPPED

IN 1799, the year seven by the new Revolutionary calendar, a boy aged eleven or twelve was seized by hunters in the Caune Woods of Aveyron, Southern France. Naked, dirty, scarred, and unable to speak, he selected food by smell and appeared impervious to heat and cold. He was brought to Paris where he excited much curiosity and interest. Although undoubtedly wild, he bore little resemblance to the picture Rousseau had drawn of the noble savage which was man before he was bound by the conventions of society. Instead he presented a revolting appearance. 'A disgustingly dirty child affected with spasmodic movements and often convulsions who swayed back and forth ceaselessly like certain animals in the menagerie, who bit and scratched those who opposed him, who showed no sort of affection for those who attended him; and who was in short, indifferent to everything and attentive to nothing.'[1]

Among those who saw the boy was the newly appointed medical adviser to De l'Epée's foundation, the Institution Nationale des Sourds-Muets. He was twenty-five, enthusiastic and ambitious. Yet his ambition was tinged with idealism. He was Jean-Marc-Gaspard Itard. He sought, and obtained, permission to care for the boy, whom he called Victor, at the Institution Nationale. Although Pinel, physician-in-chief to the insane at the Bicêtre, was of the opinion

---

[1] Itard, *The Wild Boy of Aveyron*. Translated by G. and M. Humphrey (1932), p. 4.

that Victor was a hopeless idiot, Itard felt that the apparent sub-normality was due to the fact that the boy had lacked the usual experiences which are part of the training of civilized man. Itard knew of Locke's thesis that all knowledge was acquired by experience, and he concluded from this that he only had to give Victor the necessary training to supply the mental content that would make him an ordinary boy. Possibly Itard had only a cursory knowledge of Locke's works, for what he overlooked was that while experience is necessary to produce mental development, so is a mind capable of using the experience. Kant had made this very point some twenty years earlier, but Itard persisted in his view, and with infinite patience he trained Victor for five years. At the end of this period he reluctantly concluded, what for some time he had come to suspect, that Pinel was right. Victor was an idiot.

When Itard gave up his attempt, he regarded the experiment as a failure. Undoubtedly Victor had improved. From a repulsive creature he had developed into an affectionate youth who lived like a human being. Although he had next to no speech, he understood much that was said to him, and could even read a few words. Itard's failure, in so far that there was failure at all, was confined to his inability to substantiate his original diagnosis. In all other aspects he was outstandingly successful. For he demonstrated that by systematic teaching of the right kind, even those of extremely sub-normal intelligence could be educated.

In two reports[1] Itard described his methods. His principles were the triple development of the function of the senses, the intellectual functions and the emotional faculties, and he attempted to achieve this development through what he termed 'the 5 principal aims of the mental and moral education of the Wild Boy of Aveyron'.[2] First, Victor was weaned to social life by making it more pleasant than the previous one, but at the same time keeping as closely as possible to the lines of his previous life. Secondly, his nervous sensibilities were aroused by the most energetic stimulation, and, occasionally, by intense emotion. Thirdly, the boy's knowledge of ideas was broadened by giving him more needs and increasing his reactions to his environment. Fourthly, he was assisted to speak by making it necessary for him to imitate. Lastly, when simple mental activity arose from physical needs, that activity was channelled to educational ends.

This was the first scientific attempt at the education of those of limited intelligence. It showed how psychological principles could be

[1] Published in 1801 and 1806 respectively, and later combined under the title *Rapports et Mémoires sur le Sauvage de l'Aveyron.*
[2] Itard, *The Wild Boy of Aveyron*, p. 10.

applied to the problems of learning. It also showed the need for further research. Finally, it acted as a spur to Edouard Séguin and, much later, inspired Maria Montessori.

Itard's success had brought him renown, and for a period Séguin became his pupil. From Itard's concentration on sense training, Séguin developed what he termed his physiological method, which was based on a neurophysiological hypothesis. He believed that there existed a link between sensation and idea, that the education of the senses would therefore nourish the mind, and that true education was consequently an active response to situations. His method was, therefore, a systematic training of the senses of sight, hearing, taste and smell, and hand-eye co-ordination. Like Itard he had five steps: the training of the muscular system, the training of the nervous system, the education of the senses, the acquisition of general ideas, and finally, the inculcation of the ability to think in the abstract and to understand moral precepts. He believed that feeble-minded children should use pictures, cards, patterns, figures, clay, scissors, colours and even books. He devised a great deal of teaching apparatus, which was designed to train the muscular system and to educate the senses.

Some of his devices were incorporated by Montessori into her method of teaching normal children. Others were used by Binet and Simon in their construction of intelligence tests. The latter were possibly rather ungrateful. Of him they wrote: 'Séguin impresses us as an empiric endowed with great personal talent, which he has not succeeded in embodying clearly in his works. These contain some pages of good sense, with many obscurities, and many absurdities.'[1] They would say of him, as Ingres said to his pupils in the Rubens gallery at the Louvre, 'Salute him, but pay no attention to him.'

This was unnecessarily harsh. Certainly Séguin's methods can be criticized, and probably the most valid criticism is that his approach to sense training was too mechanistic. He introduced many basic principles into the education of the mentally defective, and his own high opinion of himself is nearer the mark than Binet and Simon's. 'Ayant contribué plus que personne à appeler l'attention sur la classe délaissée des Idiots, ayant rendu quelque espoir à beaucoup de familles et donné soulagement à un petit nombre d'autres; ayant obtenu . . . les éloges et les encouragements de l'Académie des sciences, ayant seul et avant tout autre appliqué une méthode et ma méthode à l'éducation des jeunes Idiots des hospices de la ville de Paris, . . . je crois ne pouvoir répondre plus dignement à la bonne opinion

---

[1] Binet and Simon, *Mentally Defective Children*. Translated by W. B. Drummond (1914), pp. 3–4.

que les savants, le ministre et les familles ont eue de mon entreprise, qu'en en publiant les résultats theoriques et pratiques.'[1]

He started his educational work in the hospices of Paris in 1837, and although he was the first to apply a definite method, he was not the first in Paris to attempt the education of idiots. Nine years earlier Ferrus, fired by Itard's example, had opened a school for idiots at the Bicêtre, and in 1842 Séguin became Superintendent of this school.[2] His stay there was not long. In 1848 he emigrated to the United States where he became Superintendent of the newly opened Massachusetts School for Idiots and Feeble-Minded Youths.

This establishment was the work of Samuel Gridley Howe, the American philanthropist, whose work for the handicapped was wide ranging. As a surgeon and soldier he had assisted in the Greek War of Independence, and had earned himself the title of the Lafayette of the Greek Revolution. On his return to Boston he founded, and became Principal of, the Perkins Institute for the Blind where, as a result of his subsequent pioneering work in the education of the deaf-blind, Helen Keller was educated under his successor. He agitated on behalf of the care of the insane, concerned himself with prison reform, and, in the 1840's, turned his attention to those of low intelligence. Impressed by Howe's insistence on the need for a school for idiots, the Massachusetts Legislature appropriated 2,500 dollars for an experimental institution, and Howe persuaded Séguin to become its Superintendent.[3]

In addition to the first American institution, the 1840's saw the opening of establishments in Switzerland, Germany and England. In 1841 Dr. Guggenbühl founded his Institutions for Cretins at Abdendburg, near Interlaken. D. H. Tuke, a member of the family which did a great deal for the insane in England, visited it in 1862, the year before it closed. He was not impressed by what he saw, but realized that the significance of Guggenbühl's work was the example he set to others, 'which undoubtedly did more good in this indirect way than by curing the cretins placed there'.[4] The following year Dr. Saegert, of the Asylum for the Deaf, Berlin, tried to assist mental defectives by using physiological techniques. His success encouraged him to open a small private school for them—the first in Germany.[5]

There followed in 1846, the first provision for idiots in England. A

---

[1] Séguin, *Traitement Moral, Hygiène et Éducation des Idiots et des Autres Enfants Arriérés* (1846), p. 1.
[2] Beach, *The Health Exhibition Literature* (1884), Vol. XI, pp. 534–45.
[3] Richards, *Samuel Gridley Howe* (1935), pp. 10–107, and Schwartz, *Samuel Gridley Howe, Social Reformer, 1801–1876* (1956), pp. 8–90.
[4] Tuke, *Chapters in the History of the Insane in the British Isles* (1882), p. 305.
[5] Beach, *op. cit.*

small, so-called, school for them was opened by the Misses White, at Rock Hall House, Bath, which had previously been used as a hospital for lepers. Little is known of this establishment save that it opened with four patients and continued to remain small.[1] It is highly improbable that it provided more than custodial care. Of medical attention and educational instruction there appear to have been none. This can hardly, therefore, be considered as the real beginning of the care of the mentally defective. This came the following year with the Asylum for Idiots at Park House, Highgate. It should be emphasized that individual defectives would have been cared for before this in madhouses, as they were then called. The difference between the mentally unbalanced and the mentally defective had long been realized, but this was the first attempt at making separate provision for the latter.

Dr. Andrew Reed, who was the moving spirit behind the Park House Asylum, knew nothing of the Bath venture, but he had heard of, and was influenced by, Guggenbühl's institution. He urged the erection of a large building, and was given financial support by Miss Plumb, 'a most philanthropic lady'.[2] The Duke of Cambridge and the Duchess of Gloucester agreed to become patrons, contributions came from the charitably minded, and the Asylum opened with Dr. Millard as its Superintendent. All ages were admitted, but, as far as children were concerned, the earlier efforts were directed to those of the lower grade in intelligence, as it was considered that training and medical treatment could effect a cure. Only when it was realized, as a result of biological and psychological research, that the condition must be accepted and education best suited to it given, did the main effort turn to the higher grade defectives.

In 1855 the Asylum moved to Earlswood Common, Redhill. The large building in which the institution is still housed today was opened by the Prince Consort, and its name changed to the Earlswood Asylum.[3] It was visited in 1887 by members of the Royal Commission on the Blind and Deaf. They found 570 inmates, over half of whom paid no fees. Others paid up to the fantastically high sum of £357 per annum. Of the children present, the Commissioners found two, both deaf, about whose sub-normality they had grave doubts. One could lip-read; the other read by the manual alphabet to some of the Commissioners. This confusion of deafness with idiocy was a constant danger, and only comparatively recently, with the development of audiometric techniques, has the danger finally

---

[1] Tuke, *op. cit.*, p. 304.
[2] *The Health Exhibition Literature* (1884), Vol. XI, p. 525.
[3] Tuke, *Chapters in the History of the Insane*, p. 305.

receded. Nor was the danger confined to the deaf. Tuke, who visited a number of idiot asylums, recorded that mistakes were sometimes made, and children were treated as being of low intelligence when in fact they were retarded for other reasons.[1] On the other hand, there were extremely low grade children present. Since they were all instructed together this presented difficulties. Earlswood overcame the difficulties with ease. 'Those incapable of further instruction are taught merely to sit still in school,' noted the Commissioners.[2] Itard's work of eighty years earlier, if ever known here, was forgotten.

Other idiot asylums were soon opened. The Eastern Counties Asylum at Colchester, also the result of Andrew Reed's initiative, was established in 1859. Five years later two more came into being, the Western Counties at Starcross, Devon and the Royal Albert at Lancaster. Although the foundation date of the latter has been accepted as being 1864,[3] the first patients were not admitted for some years. The procedure leading up to the opening was typical of the period. In 1864 ten local gentlemen met together and accepted the offer of one James Brunton, a member of the Society of Friends, to donate £2,000 to establish the Northern Counties Asylum for Idiots and Imbeciles.[4] Since £2,000 would be nowhere near enough,[5] the next four years were devoted to public meetings and letters to the local press directed to collecting sufficient money. Her Majesty was approached, consented to become a patron, and approved the new title of the Royal Albert Asylum. With finance and patronage now secured, and the Archbishop of York as President, the foundation stone was laid in 1868. Two years later a member of the medical staff at Earlswood, G. E. Shuttleworth, was appointed Superintendent and patients were admitted.[6]

In 1877 Séguin visited the Asylum, and it is to be supposed that the children receiving instruction benefited from his advice. Some of the training of the most inert imbeciles indicated that they did. They sat in a row, and the teacher threw bean bags at them until they put up their hands to protect themselves. They were then persuaded to throw the bags back.[7] It is doubtful, however, whether Séguin's advice would have been necessary in the case of a boy seen by the Commissioners for the Blind and Deaf. 'One pupil attracted the

---

[1] Tuke, *op. cit.* [2] *R.C.B.D.*, Vol. 2, Appx. 2, p. 34.
[3] *Report of Wood Committee*, Vol. 1, Part 2, p. 53.
[4] Jones, in *Lunacy, Law and Conscience*, p. 199, wonders whether the donation of £2,000 was made by D. H. Tuke. Keir in the Institution's own publication, *The Royal Albert Institution, Lancaster* (1929), is quite definite that it was not.
[5] The eventual cost was £50,000.
[6] Keir, *The Royal Albert Institution, Lancaster* (1929).
[7] Shuttleworth, *Proceedings of the Conference on Education under Healthy Conditions* (1885), pp. 217–19.

special attention of the Commissioners by his remarkable power of calculating dates, money, etc., e.g. if asked on what day of the week the second Tuesday in May 1981 [*sic*] would fall he would answer correctly in far less time than the Commissioners could work out the sum on paper. All his calculations were mental.'[1] It is possible that this boy should never have been at Earlswood. On the other hand some dull children can, without the least understanding, work out long mechanical sums. In some Asylums this is what they were asked to do.

By 1870 five asylums for idiots had been established—the Midland Counties Asylum at Knowle, Birmingham had opened in 1868. Of these, adequate arrangements for the education of children were made only at Earlswood, Starcross and the Royal Albert, and even in these the arrangements were not always as adequate as they might have been. All of them admitted adults, and were not, therefore, solely confined to children. Admission was by election or payment, and only Starcross and the Royal Albert would admit pauper children, and then only in small numbers. In addition there were two private institutions at Hampton Wick and Chilcompton, Somerset. They were for the 'higher classes', and admission was by payment only.[2]

The great need, therefore, was for provision for mentally defective pauper children. There were many of these in the workhouses and workhouse infirmaries.[3] Not all of them were the children of paupers in receipt of relief, for if parents had an imbecile child who required institutional care, and they were unable either to pay for the child's admission, or obtain its free election to an existing asylum, the child would be admitted to the workhouse and the parents pauperized. If the parents were not in fact destitute, they were called upon to contribute towards the maintenance of their child. Such partial, or even full contribution, would not, however, remove the stigma and disfranchisement of pauperization.[4]

The Metropolitan Poor Act 1867 empowered the Poor Law Board, later the Local Government Board, to combine into a district the unions and parishes of London, in order to establish an asylum for pauper imbeciles. As a result, the Metropolitan Asylum Board, consisting of representatives of each union and parish, was established,

---

[1] *R.C.B.D.*, Vol. 2, Appx. 2, p. 32.

[2] Tuke, *op. cit.*, pp. 319–20, and *C.D.E.C.*, Vol. 2, Evidence of F. Beach, 10.2.1897.

[3] In 1815 a Lancashire mill-owner contracted with a London workhouse to take **one** idiot to every twenty sound children supplied to his mill. *Hansard*, 6.6.1815, col. 626.

[4] *C.D.E.C.*, Vol. 2, Evidence of T. D. Mann, 24.3.1897, (Mann was a barrister and **clerk** to the Metropolitan Asylum Board), and *C.D.E.C.*, Vol. 1, p. 7.

and in 1870 opened asylums at Caterham and Leavesden, Hertford-shire. In addition, the smallpox hospital at Hampstead was converted into an asylum. In 1873 the first step towards the separation of children was taken by the Leavesden Committee when they transferred some hundred children, previously spread over the wards at Leavesden, to Hampstead. Here they were to be kept apart from the adults, and educated under a school mistress. The following year Caterham took a similar step, and by the end of the year there were 250 children at Hampstead, all receiving education. Hampstead was already too small for this number, and it was decided to erect an entirely new building, purely for children, at Darenth. However, in order to attempt some after-care, it was also decided to build two blocks and workshops on adjoining land, to which the children would move when over sixteen. While the idea itself was admirable, with the passage of time those in the workshop blocks became older and older, so that Darenth, like other asylums, catered for all ages.[1]

The new establishment[2] was opened in 1878, and 354 children moved in from their temporary accommodation at Clapton. As the accommodation was still limited, the original children were all selected, all higher grade and all capable of being educated. But after 1880 more buildings were erected, and the mental capacity of the children admitted became lower. Consequently, the number of children who, in the opinion of the authorities, were helpless and unimprovable increased, and the proportion of children attending the school decreased. Thus, by 1887, of the 600 children on the so-called school side of Darenth only 362 were receiving any form of instruction.[3] Ten years later there were 1,000 persons on the school side of whom 323 actually attended the school. Of the remainder, some were children and some adults, and all were supposedly hopeless cases.[4] This was by no means the case as far as the children were concerned. Miss Hoatson, Headmistress of the school, testified before the Departmental Committee on Defective and Epileptic Children that there were a number of children who could benefit from her school, but who remained permanently in the wards with the lower grade children.[5] In any case, there was complete intermingling in the sleeping blocks and at mealtimes between the children at school and the 'hopeless' cases.

The reason for this state of affairs was not hard to find. There was

---

[1] *C.D.E.C.*, Vol. 2, Evidence of Mann.
[2] It was in two parts, the Darenth School for Imbeciles for children, and the Darenth Asylum for those over sixteen.
[3] *R.C.B.D.*, Vol. 2, Appx. 2, p. 18.
[4] There were a further 1,000 adults in Darenth Asylum.
[5] *C.D.E.C.*, Vol. 2, Evidence of Miss M. Hoatson, 19.2.1897.

an acute shortage of room. The school, with its 300 odd children, consisted of four classrooms and one large school-room. Here nine classes were accommodated, three in the school-room and two in each of two classrooms. There were other shortages, too. The staff was made up of the headmistress, who did not teach, two assistant mistresses, six attendants and three monitors.[1] This staff pupil ratio was worse than it seemed. The mistresses, both uncertificated, were paid £35 and £30 per annum.[2] Yet they were aged thirty-four and thirty and had been at Darenth for fifteen and ten years respectively. The attendants helped in the residential blocks and received £20 per annum, £2 more than the ordinary attendants in the blocks. The monitresses were ex-pupils of the school. They had to be employed, testified Fletcher Beach, because the Committee would not pay for more teachers. The cost of educating a child was extremely low 'because the school staff is starved'.[3]

Mann, clerk to the Metropolitan Asylum Board, believed that ordinary schools had a better teacher child ratio only 'because the children are capable of so much more instruction'.[4] As far as he was concerned, the comparative difficulty of teaching did not arise. Dr. F. H. Walmsley, Medical Superintendent at Darenth, was even more complacent, and, worse, patronizing. He told the Committee on Defective and Epileptic Children that every child at Darenth reached its highest educational potential. Of this he was quite certain. It was put to him that with better classrooms and apparatus, and more teachers the children would do better, but he refused to agree. He thought that everything, including the teaching staff, was sufficient. He appears to have been a most obstinate and difficult witness, constantly saying that it was difficult for him to answer questions in terms that 'the lay mind' could comprehend.[5]

In view of these difficulties, the instruction given to the children was good only in parts. In the preparatory class they did simple manual work: threading reels, grasping balls, putting nails into holes and pins into pin-cushions. All children entered this class when they first came to the school. Some remained there six months, others three years. All, however, when they left the class, started on the formal work of which Itard and Séguin would have disapproved. They were taught to read, to write and to calculate. But very few,

---

[1] These are Miss Hoatson's figures. Fletcher Beach, who had retired as Medical Superintendent the previous year, in his evidence in 1897 gave three mistresses and five attendants. It may well be that a mistress left during the year.
[2] In the board schools uncertificated mistresses started at £50, certificated at £70.
[3] *C.D.E.C.*, Vol. 2, p. 11, Evidence of Beach, 10.2.1897.
[4] *Ibid.*, Vol. 2, p. 172, Evidence of Mann.
[5] *Ibid.*, Vol. 2, Evidence of Walmsley, 5.3.1897.

conceded Miss Hoatson, learnt to read and write properly. As for arithmetic, she continued, they were taught only simple mental arithmetic, addition and subtraction.[1] On the other hand, Dr. Shuttleworth[2] had seen children at Darenth working long mechanical sums which they did not in the least understand, and while Fletcher Beach agreed that they should do nothing that was not understood, he claimed that many did understand compound sums and pence tables.[3] The Commissioners for the Blind and Deaf found a class doing geometrical drawing, and another class of speechless children who were not deaf but who nevertheless were being taught the manual alphabet. A third class was receiving an object lesson. 'The children appear to learn more from one another than from the teacher,' was their comment.[4]

But one must guard against being over critical. The difficulties were tremendous. Beach had seen classes of 100 under an attendant and a monitor.[5] Some children did not enter the school until they were thirteen, having spent the whole of their lives in the workhouse. Miss Hoatson had been there since the school opened, and so undisciplined were the children at the outset that her first six months had been spent in trying to control and govern them.[6] One cannot but admire and praise these devoted, patient and ill-paid women, who despite all handicaps made the lives of the children under their care fuller and happier. Nor should it be forgotten that there were children at Darenth capable of benefiting from the type of education given. Although the majority were imbeciles, there were also some who at the worst would be feeble-minded, and would today be termed educationally sub-normal. Walmsley estimated that some fifty of the children would be capable of holding their own in the special classes which the board schools established in the 1890's.[7] At the Royal Albert, where the children were similar to those at Darenth, Shuttleworth thought that ten per cent were feeble-minded and a larger percentage were capable of learning to read.[8] Certainly some of those at Darenth were reading well from Nelson's Standard IV book. Of the boys who had left, two had joined the Dragoon Guards and a third was in the Marines. Whatever may be thought of the personnel in the nineteenth-century army, obvious imbeciles were quite definitely not accepted.

[1] *C.D.E.C.*, Vol. 2, Evidence of Miss Hoatson.
[2] A member of the Committee on Defective and Epileptic Children.
[3] *C.D.E.C.*, Vol. 2, Evidence of Beach.
[4] *R.C.B.D.*, Vol. 2, Appx. 2, p. 18.   [5] *C.D.E.C.*, Vol. 2, Evidence of Beach.
[6] *Ibid.*, Vol. 2, Evidence of Miss Hoatson.
[7] *Ibid.*, Vol. 2, Evidence of Walmsley.
[8] *Ibid.*, Vol. 2, Evidence of Shuttleworth, 10.2.1897, and Shuttleworth, 'Exceptional School-children', *Teacher's Encyclopaedia* (1912), Vol. 5, pp. 214–38.

III. Education of Feeble-minded and Physically Handicapped

While the idiot asylums and Darenth were making their provisions for the education and training of mentally defective children, the Charity Organization Society was making recommendations as to how the provisions could best be made.[1] The Society was established in 1869. Its purpose was the encouragement of new and the co-ordination of existing charitable efforts. Its members were men of standing; its suggestions carried weight.[2]

One of its Council members was Sir Charles Trevelyan, recently retired with honour from the Governorship of Madras. In 1875 he started campaigning on behalf of what he termed improvable idiots. He felt that pressure should be brought upon the State to provide for their education, and he summarized his views in a pamphlet which he placed before the Council.[3] With Trevelyan as its Secretary, a special Sub-Committee of the Charity Organization Society examined the whole question of the education and care of the metally handicapped. As always, on committees of this kind, the medical profession was well represented. There was no one from the field of education. The members visited the main asylums, and what he saw induced Trevelyan to introduce a motion that 'feeble-minded children ought not to be associated with adult Idiots'.[4] The motion was withdrawn, but the occasion was of importance as being the first recorded mention of the term feeble-minded.

It should be stressed that until towards the close of the nineteenth century the terms idiot, imbecile, feeble-minded and mentally defective were used interchangeably, and bore little or no relation to the degree of mental incapacity of the persons to whom they were applied. Only on one point was there comparative agreement; the class of the mentally defective differed from the class of the mentally unsound. The former was a case of mental incapacity from birth or an early age, the latter insanity in a person who had been sane. Or, in the words of the annotator of the Mental Deficiency Act 1913, 'an idiot was a person who never had a mind; a lunatic a person who had had a mind and lost it'.[5] Nevertheless, the Lunacy Act 1890 confused the issue. ' "Lunatic",' it stated, 'means an idiot or person of unsound mind.'[6] Even in 1961, C. L. Mowat, in his excellent book on the Charity Organization Society, refers to the feeble-minded as 'harmless lunatics'.[7] It is quite evident, however, that Trevelyan

---

[1] Charity Organization Society, *Report of Sub-Committee on the Education and Care of Idiots, Imbeciles and Harmless Lunatics* (1877).
[2] For an account of the Society, see Mowat, *The Charity Organization Society, 1869–1913* (1961), and Bosanquet, *Social Work in London* (1914).
[3] Bosanquet, *op. cit.*, pp. 195–6.   [4] *Ibid.*, p. 196.
[5] Lithiby, *The Education Acts, 1870–1919* (1920), p. 469.
[6] See Section 341.   [7] Mowat, *op. cit.*, p. 59.

employed the word feeble-minded in the sense that it was used until the Mental Health Act, 1959. He employed it to mean a high-grade defective who was not so incapacitated as to be an imbecile or idiot.

When the Sub-Committee reported in 1877, it recommended that the distinction between lunatics and harmless feeble-minded should be emphasized. The latter should mix neither with lunatics in asylums nor paupers in workhouses. Rather, the country should be divided into districts, each sufficiently large to warrant the construction of a special institution containing up to 2,000 adults and a school for 500 children. The State should encourage voluntary effort in this direction and, where encouragement was insufficient, itself give financial aid. The recommendations were presented to the President of the Local Government Board by a deputation led by Shaftesbury.[1] A direct but by no means immediate result was the passing in 1886 of the Idiots Act. This was a poor thing of little value. It merely permitted existing institutions to admit mentally defective children at the wish of their parents without a Magistrate's Order. Of encouragement and aid there was none. The indirect results of the Committee's deliberations, recommendations and protestations were of greater import. They served to draw attention to the needs of the feeble-minded, and ensured that they were included in the eventually wide terms of reference of the Royal Commission on the Blind and Deaf.

No report on physically defective children was to be made until 1893, and little education was available for them until the twentieth century. First attempts at their care, however, dates from the Tudor Poor Laws. These allowed a commission to collect alms for the poor and also for cripples. In addition, crippled children aged five to fourteen were to be apprenticed in order to learn a craft and become self-supporting.[2] It was this aspect of care that came to the forefront in the latter half of the nineteenth century. In the first half of the century revulsion against had turned to pity for the physically handicapped. In England the pity took little practical form. In Germany it was tinged with economic considerations. The more practical Teuton was less moved by charity based on sentiment than by rehabilitation based on retrenchment. Thus, when hospitals for the care of the crippled were established in Germany, schools were attached to them to give the children vocational training. The first of these *Heimschulen* was founded in the eighteenth century, but the best known is that established by the Kurtz Foundation in Munich

---

[1] Bosanquet, *op. cit.*, p. 197.
[2] 26 Henry VIII, 1535, c. 27 and 43 Elizabeth I, 1601, c. 2.

III. Education of Feeble-minded and Physically Handicapped

in 1832. Here, a certain amount of education as well as industrial training was given, and when in 1844 it was subsidized by the State it became the first instance of the education of crippled children by public funds. Industrial schools for cripples continued to be established during the century—at Baden and Potsdam, and in Scandinavia at Copenhagen, Stockholm, Christiania and Gothenburg. Some of them provided a little education, but the emphasis in all of them was on vocational training.[1]

In England the training of cripples in separate institutions dates from the opening of the Cripples' Home and Industrial School for Girls at Marylebone. It was established almost fortuitously. In 1851 several ladies intended to form an ordinary industrial school. It opened with three girls, one of whom chanced to be a cripple. When the ladies of the Committee spoke with this girl, they realized that there was a special need to cater for crippled girls, and so the Cripples' Home was founded in addition to the Industrial School. By 1870 the establishment contained 100 girls, 75 of whom were crippled. The remainder were physically fit, and had been sent to the school by a Magistrate's Order under the Certified Industrial Schools Act, 1866. It had been decided to retain the Industrial School connection, so that the non-handicapped girls could do the heavy housework which was too much for the cripples. Without such a joint plan, the Committee pointed out, the expense of the school would have been much greater.

Encouraged by the success of the venture, the Committee had enlarged itself to include men, and in 1865 opened the National Industrial Home for Crippled Boys, in Kensington. In most respects this was similar to the girls'. There were slightly fewer boys, only 86, but there were more trades available for them to learn. The major difference was that the Kensington establishment was for cripples only. In both institutions the children were given a modicum of school instruction: the basic subjects of reading, writing and arithmetic, plus a little religious education. The teaching was by voluntary teachers. Its extent was an hour or so each morning. For a time, around 1870, the most backward at the girls' school received extra lessons in the evening from a paid certificated teacher, who came from the Home and Colonial Training College.[2] This is the first recorded instance of a special class for backward children, though the board schools were soon to adopt their Standard 0's.

Undoubtedly, however, the aim of both the schools was to teach a trade, and the education was geared to this end. As soon as 'the

---

[1] Frampton and Rowell, *Education of the Handicapped*, pp. 127–42.
[2] Bartley, *The Schools for the People* (1871), p. 363.

lower standards of elementary education' had been mastered the children devoted all their time to industrial work.[1] The girls were taught to make mats, baskets and bonnets, the last named being the major industry, and the boys carpentry, copper-plate printing, saddlery and tailoring. On leaving many of the girls were apprenticed to milliners and drapers, and the boys followed one of the trades taught at the school. Children were admitted between the ages of twelve and eighteen, and remained for three years, whatever the age at admission. If, however, a pupil proved unable to learn a trade, he was immediately discharged and his place taken by another. In order to have as few failures as possible, the Committee insisted that all entrants should have the full use of their arms, hands and eyes. This condition limited entry to the less severely handicapped. Unlike most institutions of the day, admission was not by election but by priority of application or comparative severity of condition.

The children came from many classes, but the majority were from poor homes. Indeed, by 1890, the object of the Kensington school was 'to receive for three years—board, and clothe, and educate on Christian principles—destitute, neglected, or ill-used crippled boys'.[2] The expression 'ill-used' was appropriate. Once a child was admitted to either school, he was not allowed to leave, even for one day, during the whole of the three years. Apart from walking out with the Matron for exercise, he never left the building. He could have a visitor once in three months. He could write a letter once a month. Otherwise he was excluded from the outside world. Bartley, with masterly understatement, commented: 'The rules of the London Institutions are somewhat rigid.'[3]

The regulations would prevent parents, even in needy circumstances, from applying for admission if they had any affection for their children, and were not prepared to lose them for three years. On the other hand, they encouraged parents to neglect their children by admitting them. Sometimes those parents who parted with their child experienced a loss other than that engendered by love and affection. The Charity Organization Society Report of 1893 tells of a boy admitted to Kensington, whose mother owned a small sweet shop. 'Whilst he lived at home he was generally placed in a prominent position in the shop, rather for exhibition than utility, for he was only required to look miserable.' Soon after admission the mother complained that receipts were falling rapidly, as customers had been attracted to the shop by sympathy for the boy, and that now he had

[1] Charity Organization Society, *The Epileptic and Crippled Child and Adult* (1893), p. 129.
[2] *Ibid.*, p. 119.   [3] Bartley, *op. cit.*, p. 365.

left, many of them ceased to deal with her.[1] From parents like these, incarceration for three years may have been a pleasant change.

Criticism can obviously be levelled at the schools at Marylebone and Kensington: children kept under rigorous discipline, a Committee preoccupied with industrial occupation, so preoccupied that a shop was established in Baker Street, where goods made at the schools were sold. The income from this was so good that the total annual cost of each child to the institutions was only £28. On the other hand, the vast majority of the children they received, not having attended any school, could neither read nor write, and one must endorse the judgement of the Charity Organization Society: 'Had they not been received into some Home, they would probably, owing to their crippled state, have never received even the most elementary instruction.'[2] Nevertheless it might be said of the nineteenth-century education of the physically handicapped as was said of Munich: 'Every man should be glad but no man proud.'

[1] Charity Organization Society, *The Epileptic and Crippled Child*, pp. 106-7.
[2] *Ibid.*, p. 129.

6

THE PERIOD OF TRANSITION:
I. CHANGES IN THE EDUCATION
OF THE BLIND

IN the social history of the nineteenth century, the decade after 1865 marks a turning point. The cherished beliefs of earlier days were under attack, and marked changes were occurring. Darwinism was rife, and the iconoclastic teachings of John Stuart Mill's *Liberty* were leading to an examination of hitherto accepted conventions. The Tests Act removed most of the remaining religious discriminations at Oxford and Cambridge, and Girton and Newnham were established. Cardwell's army reforms abolished the purchase of commissions and flogging in peacetime, and the Commander-in-Chief became subordinate to the War Office. Entry to the Civil Service was determined by examination, and patronage lost more ground. The Reform Act of 1867 extended the franchise, and voting by ballot was introduced. Reform of licensed premises was achieved by the Licensing Act and of the courts of law by the Judicature Act. The T.U.C. was founded, and the unions themselves were given wider rights, including the right to picket. Booth established the Salvation Army, Marx wrote *Das Kapital*, and the miners, Burt and Macdonald, became Members of Parliament.

Most of these measures were concerned with the demolition of the old. Apart from Forster's brave Education Act in 1870, little was done during Gladstone's first Ministry to build anew. But with the death, in 1873, of the arch-exponent of Utilitarianism, J. S. Mill, and the advent, the following year, of Disraeli's second Administration, *laisser-faire* ceased to be a force in the land. Hitherto, social reform had been achieved only through the patient work of small groups, and much against the will of the major parties. Now it was introduced by Disraeli, both because, as his novels had shown, he sincerely believed in it, and because of the undoubted appeal it would make to the newly enfranchised electors, and the consequent electoral advantage it would bring. Therefore to the statute book were added the Public Health Act, which established a sanitary authority in each area; the Artisans' Dwelling Act, the first serious attempt at housing legislation; the Merchant Shipping Act, which guarded against overloading; the Food and Drugs Act, to prevent adulteration; the Land Transfer, the Agricultural Holdings and Friendly Societies Acts.

Henceforth it would be realized that government had a new purpose, and reform a new meaning. No longer would it be sufficient for a government to govern. No longer would reform mean only parliamentary or political reform. To win a general election a party must now have a programme of social reform, and it would be seen that the duty of the legislature would be to legislate, and of the government to provide facilities for it to do so. This was the beginning of social democracy and the end of Utilitarianism, the beginning of collectivism and the end of Samuel Smiles' individualist self-help, the beginning of the *savoir-faire* of Socialism and the end of the *laisser-faire* of Liberalism. This was the beginning of the harnessing of bureaucracy to democracy, as advocated by J. S. Mill despite his Utilitarianism.

This seminal decade, partly because of Forster's Act and partly because of the change in the social climate, was equally important in the history of special education. Worcester College, the first, and for long the only, school to prepare boys who were blind for the Universities and the liberal professions, was established. The forerunner of the Royal National Institute for the Blind, the British and Foreign Blind Association, passed judgement upon the rival methods of teaching, and its strong advocacy of Braille led at last to the adoption of a uniform method. The first training college for blind teachers, the Royal Normal College and Academy of Music at Norwood, opened its doors. The Charity Organization Society, itself founded in the decade, appointed special committees to report on the welfare and instruction of the blind and the provision for improvable idiots—the first such investigations in an age given to Royal Commissions and Committees of Enquiry. The London School Board organized special classes for its deaf children, and appointed a special teacher for the blind. The first of many abortive bills calling upon the State to educate the deaf was introduced, and the first memorial on behalf of the education of the blind was presented to the Government. The first European Congress of Teachers of the Blind was held in Vienna, and a public school for the deaf returned at long last to the oral methods of Thomas Braidwood. The Association for the Oral Instruction of the Deaf and Dumb was formed, and its training college accepted its first students. Germany organized day classes for feeble-minded children, and a pioneer institution for epileptics. The Metropolitan Asylum Board separated pauper imbecile children from the adults, and provided education for them. The first school for crippled boys was opened, and Séguin published his renowned work on idiocy.

The College for the Blind Sons of Gentlemen, at Worcester, was the brain child of William Taylor, former Superintendent of the Wilberforce School for the Blind, York. In 1866 he persuaded a fellow clergyman, Hugh Blair, to open the school as a private venture. Blair's experience of the blind had been gained while he was tutor to the blind son of the Dean of Ripon, but more valuable was his friendship with S. S. Forster, who had been a colleague on the staff of the King's School, Worcester. It was to Forster that he turned for assistance, two years after the school's foundation. In reply to Blair's telegram to join him, the thirty-six-year-old Forster, who was tutoring in Rome, telegraphed succinctly, 'I will be with you in two days.'[1] The school soon became a proprietary institution, and equally soon was in financial difficulties.

Blair left in 1872 on his appointment as Rector of St. Martin's, Worcester, and Forster agreed, despite the apparent imminence of its closure, to take over the school with its thirteen boys. By dint of hard work, personal sacrifice, and constant appeals for financial assistance, Forster succeeded in keeping the College open. But the original aim that 'blind children of opulent parents might obtain an education suitable to their station in life'[2] would obviously have to be modified, since the cost of giving a public school type of education was higher than most parents of blind boys could afford. They were not opulent, or at least not opulent enough to pay the fees of £110 per annum, for in 1871 Blair had reported that 'as wealth is but seldom the accompaniment of blindness we have been reluctantly compelled to decline admitting students whose position entitled them to the advantages of the College but whose want of adequate fortune made their entrance impossible'.[3] Forster's plea for the endowments of scholarships was slowly becoming effective. By 1873

[1] Medhurst, *The Rev. Samuel Strong Forster* (1891), p. 6.
[2] Thomas, *The Royal National Institute for the Blind, 1868-1956* (1957).
[3] Johnson, *London International Exhibition, 1871. Report on the Methods of Teaching the Blind and the Deaf and Dumb*, p. 12.

I. Changes in the Education of the Blind

£1,000 had been collected, and fifteen years later the trust fund had been doubled, and scholarships had been endowed by the Clothworkers' Company, Uppingham School and Gardner's Trust.[1] Forster could then write that 'whenever we are sure that a child has been carefully and tenderly nurtured, though not in affluence, we are willing to admit him';[2] the needy could at last be admitted and one in three of the boys was needy.

It was now time for the College to become a semi-public institution. Indeed the Clothworkers and Gardner's Trustees had threatened to withdraw their support unless it did.[3] In 1889 it therefore became controlled by a Trust Deed, and administered by a Board of Governors. It was still, however, small, with only fourteen boys. Two of these were sighted, for it had now become the policy to admit clergymen's sons 'at a moderate sum to assist the blind boys about thus doing a service to the clergy and our own boys'.[4] Like the boys the staff was mixed. Of the four masters, apart from Forster, three were blind. This excellent pupil teacher ratio enabled the College to obtain good results. In the first twenty years of its existence, four of its old boys gained Firsts and seven others obtained honours degrees.[5] The emphasis was on Classics, Divinity, English Literature and Mathematics. French, History and Music were also taught, and one must ascribe to Medhurst the exaggeration of a biographer when he claims that Forster introduced Chemistry, Physiology, Botany and Geology,[6] for the Commissioners who visited the College three years before Forster's death in 1891 made no reference to these subjects in their comprehensive report on the curriculum.[7]

Nevertheless, Forster undoubtedly did magnificent work. The boys played hockey with a wicker ball with a bell inside, walked on stilts, bathed and rowed, had the usual drill of those days, and went for walks in the beautiful Worcester countryside. There was here little of the incarceration so typical of institutions for the blind. Naturally the small numbers helped, but this in itself was a hindrance, for with an age range of seven to nineteen, teaching, albeit individual, must have been very difficult. As elsewhere there was a shortage of books, especially books of the kind required at Worcester. This difficulty the College overcame by printing its own. Blair introduced Roman type, 'I am wholly in favour of that respectable

---

[1] *R.C.B.D.*, Vol. 2, Appx. 2. Gardner's Trust for the Blind was established in 1879 when Henry Gardner left £300,000 for the relief of the blind.

[2] Forster, *A Plea for the Higher Culture of the Blind* (1883), p. 8.

[3] *R.C.B.D.*, Vol. 3, Evidence of Forster, 9.3.1888.

[4] *Ibid.*, Vol. 3, Evidence of Forster.   [5] *Ibid.*, Vol. 2, Appx. 2.

[6] Medhurst, *The Rev. Samuel Strong Forster*, p. 15.

[7] *R.C.B.D.*, Vol. 2, Appx. 11.

and universally-used system of blind typography,' he wrote;[1] and Forster followed his predilection.

Although Forster's work was confined to his careful nurturing of Worcester, his influence was widely felt. He showed that the blind could be humanely as well as liberally educated, and his constant advocacy of the higher education of the blind ensured a continuation of his work, at least as far as boys were concerned. Blair, as early as 1869 at a meeting at Worcester Guildhall, had expressed his ambition to found a similar school for girls, but half a century was to pass before such a school was to open.

In the year that Forster joined Blair at Worcester, Thomas Rhodes Armitage founded the British and Foreign Society for Improving the Embossed Literature of the Blind. Armitage, of a wealthy Irish family, lived as a child in France and Germany. He was educated at the Sorbonne, and later read medicine in London. After serving as a surgeon in the Crimean War, he worked in German hospitals, and finally became a general practitioner in London. His sight had been failing for some years, and in 1860, at the age of thirty-six, he gave up his practice and retired to his country seat in Ireland to recover his health. His sight, however, continued to deteriorate, and in 1866 he joined the Committee of the Indigent Blind Visiting Society, and for two years visited the blind of London in their homes.[2] He found many living in squalor and by begging. Those who had as children learnt to read at one institution could not use the system of reading taught at another. Equally, those who had been taught the rudiments of a trade were unable to follow it when left to fend for themselves without materials and a market for their product. What was required, he realized, was not monetary relief but efficient education and training leading to secure employment.

He determined to concentrate first on the improvement of their education. The first necessity was for a uniform system in order that a plentiful supply of literature might be produced. Moreover, this system was to be selected by men themselves blind, who would try out each system but would have no pecuniary interest in any.[3] Armitage obtained the collaboration of four others, all well educated, of whom the most colourful was James Gale. Known as the Blind Inventor and the Gunpowder Tamer, he had discovered a method of making gunpowder explosive or non-explosive at will. He volunteered to give a demonstration on Wimbledon Common by sitting on a

---

[1] Blair, *Education of the Blind* (1876), p. 8.
[2] Illingworth, *History of the Education of the Blind* (1910), pp. 90–9, and Ritchie, *Concerning the Blind*, p. 84.
[3] *R.C.B.D.*, Vol. 3, Evidence of Armitage, 14.5.1886.

I. Changes in the Education of the Blind

barrel of gunpowder mixed with his secret substance, and allowing a red-hot poker to be thrust into its side. Fortunately perhaps, his offer was not accepted, although he did successfully demonstrate his invention by less flamboyant methods.[1]

These five became the Executive Council of the Society whose name they soon changed to the British and Foreign Blind Association for Promoting the Education and Employment of the Blind. After two years of research and correspondence with leading associations and institutions at home and abroad, they reached their decision: 'The Council recommend Braille as the educational system for all blind children, and for the every-day wants of all blind persons whose touch has not been seriously impaired by manual labour. For the old and the dull of brain and touch they recommend a simple line system approaching as near the Roman as is compatible with perfect tangibility.'[2] The simple line system that they had in mind was Moon, and they advocated 'that steps should be taken to introduce Braille to this country and discourage all others save Moon'.[3]

This was a momentous decision. Although it was unfortunate that they had to recommend two systems, for this contained the seeds of future controversy. It probably also delayed the universal acceptance of Braille by the schools. For though the first and most important step had been taken, it was to be some years before the institutions would be prepared to discard their own well-tried systems. Conservatism and inertia played their part, but so, with greater cogency, did the fact that they were loth to discard the few books they had so laboriously collected or printed. Their views were summarized by E. C. Johnson, of the Blind Man's Friend Charity, who wrote, 'Although the lovers of Braille in England are few, their pretentions are great, and they seem to ignore the fact that the fullest literature for the blind in this country, America, and Germany, has issued from societies which advocate the employment of the ordinary type of the seeing, or the Moon modification of the alphabetical system.'[4] The Association endeavoured to meet this objection by printing Braille books, but it was a long and slow task, and by 1886 only sixty different works had been printed. Among these was the series used in many board schools, Nelson's Royal Readers, so that blind children could read the same books and be taught alongside sighted children.[5]

[1] Thomas, *The Royal National Institute for the Blind, 1868–1956*.
[2] *Report of the British and Foreign Blind Association, 1871*, p. 4.
[3] *R.C.B.D.*, Vol. 3, Evidence of J. L. Shadwell, 5.2.1886.
[4] Johnson, *London International Exhibition, 1871. Report on the Methods of Teaching the Blind and the Deaf and Dumb*, pp. 5–6.
[5] *R.C.B.D.*, Vol. 3, Evidence of Shadwell.

Armitage gave liberally of his time and money. 'The belief that I have been able to take my share in this great work,' he wrote, 'has gone far to reconcile me to the abandonment of a profession, to the scientific prosecution of which I had hoped to devote my life; but the very defect of sight which proved an insuperable obstacle in the career which I had chalked out for myself, has peculiarly fitted me for a new and more extended sphere of usefulness.'[1]

Armitage's sphere of usefulness was wide. Having dealt with the unification of systems, he now turned his attention to the employment of the blind. In 1869 he had visited the Institution Nationale des Jeunes Aveugles where Louis Braille had taught music, and found that whereas in England but one half per cent of the blind lived by music, in Paris thirty per cent supported themselves in this way. He became convinced that music would be the best occupation for the blind. But in order to train them, it would be necessary to give them a better education than was possible at the time in existing institutions. 'It was not easy,' he recorded, 'to find a person, fitted by nature and education, to undertake this work; many qualities besides thorough knowledge of music must be united in such a man, as great power of imparting information, love of his work, zeal, faith in success, and tact in managing pupils and teachers.'[2] The difficulty of finding such a man inclined him to think in terms of extending an existing institution. But the hour produced the man.

F. J. Campbell had been born in Tennessee thirty-seven years earlier, and was 'trained up in the good domestic school of a farmhouse'.[3] He was blinded by accident at the age of six, and had to wait four years before admission to the Nashville Blind School. He made such good use of his six years there that he was able to think in terms of going to university. He taught music in order to raise the necessary funds, but shortly after his admission to Harvard the firm in which he had placed his savings went into liquidation. He then taught music at the Perkins Institution under Howe, and in 1871 on his way back to Boston after studying music at Leipzig, he visited London.[4] There Campbell and Armitage met. After the first half hour, Armitage knew he had the right man; 'he seemed to be exactly the person suited for this work, and this opinion was confirmed by the answers to enquiries from Dr. Howe'.[5] Campbell in his turn was impressed by Armitage, and together they planned the Royal Normal College.

[1] Armitage, *The Education and Employment of the Blind* (1871), Preface, p. v.
[2] *Ibid.*, p. 51.   [3] Richards, *Samuel Gridley Howe*, p. 265.
[4] *R.C.B.D.*, Vol. 3, Evidence of Campbell, 7.5.1886.
[5] Armitage, *op. cit.*, p. 51.

I. Changes in the Education of the Blind

It was necessary, as always, to raise money. Armitage himself gave £1,000,[1] and members of the British and Foreign Blind Association and the Charity Organization Society were active in raising a further £2,000. The Queen consented to become a patron, the Duke of Westminster invited guests to Grosvenor House for fund raising purposes, and Shaftesbury wrote to *The Times*.[2] With such backing, the enthusiasm of Armitage, and the efficiency of Campbell the College could not but succeed. It opened with two children in March 1872, with the object of affording 'the youthful blind of this country a thorough general and musical education . . . so as to qualify them to earn a living as organists, teachers and pianoforte tuners'.[3] Such was the poor standard of blind teaching in Britain, that Campbell staffed the school with teachers from blind schools in the United States, and as these moved, with the encouragement of Campbell, to the new school board classes for the blind,[4] he replaced them with teachers from the States, without blind experience, whom he trained himself.

The College was in three departments, general education, the science and practice of music, and piano tuning, and was sited at Norwood, near the Crystal Palace, as this was one of the few places where the children could have 'constant opportunities of hearing the standard vocal and instrumental works of the Great Masters'.[5] Children were admitted for general education at seven, and at thirteen those who were suitable proceeded to the upper school, where their general education was continued alongside their tuition in one of the other departments. At seventeen an advanced course was available to those wishing to be teachers of music.[6] Within a year there were fifty-two children, and as the reputation of the school increased and spread, children were sent and paid for by local committees in the larger cities. Others were admitted on scholarships, and by 1875 the majority of the children were from outside the Metropolis.[7] Ten years later there were 170 pupils. There was much emphasis on P.T., and soon there were two gymnasia, two roller skating rinks and a swimming bath.

The school won high praise from J. Rice Byrne, H.M.I., who at Campbell's request carried out an unofficial inspection. 'I noted the presence of what I may call the proper Educational furor, that passion

---

[1] He was later to give 1,000 guineas to build a swimming pool.
[2] *Report of the Royal Normal College, 1873.*
[3] Letter to *The Times*, 10.5.1873.
[4] By 1886 five had gone to the London School Board, one to Cardiff, and one to Bradford.
[5] *Report of the Royal Normal College, 1873*, p. 9.
[6] *R.C.B.D.*, Vol. 2, Appx. 2.
[7] *Report of the Special Committee of the Charity Organization Society on the Training of the Blind* (1876), p. 38.

for teaching on the part of the teachers, for learning on that of the students. . . . In this respect you contrast but too favourably with a very large proportion of our schools, moving as they are accustomed to do mechanically in a groove, within the narrow lines prescribed by the new Code of Education.'[1] Commenting on the thoroughness of the teaching he continued: 'Here again I may compare you to the disadvantage of too many of the charitable institutions of this country, in which the instruction given is at once pretentious and desultory.'[2] On a subsequent inspection he reported that the College 'can be recommended as a model for all institutions in this country which have for their object not merely to teach the Blind to read the Bible and to make mats and baskets, but to generally educate them'.[3]

The Royal Normal College was a success. Ninety years after Valentin Haüy's children had shown their attainments to Louis XVI at Versailles, and but two years after the College opened, Campbell's pupils gave a musical performance before Victoria at Windsor. 'Dr. Campbell having the go ahead principles of the Americans went a great deal faster, and a great deal further than I was at first inclined to go,' said Armitage, 'but I am quite sure he was right.'[4] He was certainly right. The school at Norwood became an example of how the blind should be educated. It showed the value of Braille, of music and of liberal studies; and like Worcester it foreshadowed a new trend in institutional care.[5] Its influence was wide, and Campbell's part was acknowledged by Glasgow with a doctorate of law and by the State with a knighthood.

It is evident that the Charity Organization Society's Special Committee on the education of the blind was influenced by the establishment of the Normal College. The main finding in its 1876 *Report* was that the new foundation had emphasized the serious lack of adequate vocational training for children, and the need for securing for them suitable subsequent employment. It also advocated that the blind should be educated from the age of five; no institution at the time would accept them under seven. The Sunshine Homes of fifty years later were foreshadowed in the recommendation that the blind child should receive training in habits of self-confidence and in the development of the senses of hearing and touch from a very early age, that parents be encouraged to give this at home, and that where this was

[1] Royal Normal College, *Historical Statement of the Higher Education of the Blind* (1873), p. 6.

[2] *Ibid.*, p. 6.   [3] *2nd Report of the Royal Normal College, 1874–5*, p. 17.

[4] *R.C.B.D.*, Vol. 3, p. 380, Evidence of Armitage, 14.5.1886.

[5] One phrase in the terms of admission savoured of the old institutionalism. Two householders were required to guarantee that in the event of a pupil's death, the funeral expenses would be paid.

I. Changes in the Education of the Blind

not possible, special preparatory schools should be established. The Committee felt that a Royal Commission should investigate the whole question of State aid to the blind. It also expressed the view that the blind should be educated with the sighted in the public elementary schools, and that they should remain there until they were fifteen, at which age industrial training would begin. Where necessary children should go for a year's preliminary training to an institution before starting in an ordinary day school. But this should be exceptional.[1] On the other hand the First International Conference of Teachers of the Blind at Vienna in 1873 had resolved that the blind should only be educated with the sighted in the absence of something better.[2] In the event, when the London School Board first catered for the blind, it was the way of the C.O.S. and not Vienna that they followed.

[1] *Report of the Special Committee of the Charity Organization Society on the Training of the Blind.*
[2] Ritchie, *Concerning the Blind*, pp. 90–3.

7

THE PERIOD OF TRANSITION:
II. SCHOOL BOARD CLASSES FOR
THE DEAF AND BLIND

THE 1870 Education Act, which gave powers to form school boards to provide elementary education for all children, contained no exceptions, and probably none were intended. Certainly the deaf and the blind were neither specifically included nor excluded, despite efforts on behalf of the blind in the form of a memorial and a deputation to W. E. Forster,[1] and on behalf of the deaf by the introduction by St. John Wheelhouse of a Bill allowing the Exchequer to make grants to institutions. However, in the Act's interpretation by the London School Board, on its formation in 1872, their ineligibility was illustrated by the fact that in the classification, deaf, blind and idiot children were united under the heading 'permanently disabled'.[2]

Sir Charles Reed, the second Chairman of the London School Board, took a different view, and in 1874 he initiated enquiries concerning the means by which the deaf and blind could be educated. He contacted William Stainer, Chaplain of the deaf and dumb church in Oxford Street and one time assistant at the Old Kent Road, who agreed to accept the post of Superintendent of the instruction of the deaf.

Stainer found that most of the deaf appeared to be in Bethnal Green. He therefore requested a room in a public elementary school

---

[1] These were organized by Elizabeth Gilbert, blind daughter of the Bishop of Chichester. Nevertheless, such was the position of women in 1870 that she could not participate in the deputation, and had to await its result in the Westminster Palace Hotel.

[2] Stainer, *The Powers of the School Board and the Poor Law Guardians* (1888).

there, and parents of deaf children were instructed to bring them there at a certain time. From these he selected five considered suitable for instruction, and in September the class opened. There is some conflict as to the method he adopted. Stainer himself averred that he gave oral instruction. But as the number of children increased he advertised for an assistant. The only applicants were teachers who were deaf themselves, and appointing one of these, he naturally found it impossible to continue with the oral system. He continued to give a little oral instruction as he had always been convinced that it was the best way, though he confessed that it was difficult to employ the oral system with children who were in school for only five days a week.[1] On the other hand, Mrs. Westlake, a member of the London School Board's special committee for deaf and blind children, believed that Stainer only became an oralist after attending the 1880 International Congress at Milan, where he found that the oral system was widespread in Europe and the United States. 'It was,' testified Mrs. Westlake, 'a very sudden conversion.'[2] Be that as it may, it is evident that Stainer had been originally trained in the manual system at Old Kent Road. Equally, Mrs. Westlake's testimony regarding Stainer's method in 1874 is suspect, as she did not join the Board until 1876. Certainly the Board in 1879 appointed a pure oral teacher, Mrs. Dancy, who taught a class at Bermondsey under the superintendence not of Stainer, but of Van Praagh, of the Association for the Oral Instruction of the Deaf and Dumb.[3]

This in fact was the turning point. All the Board's future teachers were oralists trained at either Fitzroy Square or Ealing,[4] and even Stainer attended Ealing for a short time. The Board adopted a policy of training pupil teachers, who gave part of their time to the special classes, and part to being trained at one of the two oralist colleges. By 1888 there were 373 children in fourteen centres, all now under Stainer, and all in the classrooms of ordinary schools.[5] Some of the bigger centres containing up to fifty children were in fact autonomous special day schools. But the fact that they were day schools had been one of Stainer's arguments against introducing oralism. Now that the oral system had been introduced he determined to overcome this difficulty by establishing boarding homes for some of the poorest children, who would still continue to attend the centres. The homes had the additional advantage of decreasing the distance that many of the children would have to travel to the

[1] *R.C.B.D.*, Vol. 3, Evidence of Stainer, 4.3.1886.
[2] *Ibid.*, Vol. 3, p. 192, Evidence of Mrs. Westlake, 4.3.1886.
[3] *Ibid.*, Vol. 3, Evidence of Mrs. Dancy, 24.3.1886.
[4] See Chapter 8.   [5] *R.C.B.D.*, Vol. 2, Appx. 26.

special classes. The homes had no connection with the Board, were non-profit making, and were maintained by the contributions from Guardians or charitable sources. K. W. Hodgson thinks highly of Stainer. 'He and his Homes had rendered great service for an exceptionally difficult period of over twenty years.'[1] But the Commissioners who visited the homes in 1888 were not so easily pleased. The food was poor, and many of the children were suffering from skin complaints. Moreover Schöntheil, headmaster of a London institution which employed oral methods, was asked by the Board to inspect its centres. His report, submitted in 1888, stated that 'the attendance is so irregular as in itself to preclude satisfactory results, but when we add to this the unwashed, half-clad, and unfed condition in which the children often come to school, we cannot marvel that teaching them to any purpose is found impossible.'[2] Allowing for some exaggeration on Schöntheil's part, one must conclude that the Board's experiment was not an outstanding success. Stainer certainly gave liberally of his time, energy and money.[3] It would be best for him to be remembered for this, and not for any educational results that he achieved.

Whereas the provision by the London School Board for the deaf was the first occasion on which the education of these children was assisted by public funds, their provision for the blind was anticipated in Scotland and also in London itself. During 1868 a blind boy was admitted to the Mid Parish School at Greenock, and taught by Alston's by the schoolmaster alongside, and with the assistance of, sighted children.[4] By 1874, fifty blind children were being taught thus in Scotland. The previous year, the London Home Teaching Society arranged for some of its teachers to visit London's National Schools twice weekly to teach Moon to any blind children who should be admitted. A few were then admitted for the first time.[5]

In 1875 the School Board also enlisted the aid of the Home Teaching Society. One of its blind teachers, 'not a very high class individual'[6] according to Mrs. Westlake, was appointed by the Board. He was assisted by a young teacher, who had lost her sight while in the service of the Board, and together they visited and taught

---

[1] Hodgson, *The Deaf and their Problems*, p. 251.
[2] *R.C.B.D.*, Vol. 3, p. 870, Evidence of Major-General Moberly, 17.7.1888.
[3] He claimed that he lost £2,000 on the homes in thirteen years.
[4] An attempt on the same lines had been made as early as 1834, when the Directors of the Edinburgh Institution for the Blind sent a number of boys to the Sessional School. No record exists of the system of instruction used, and the attempt was short-lived.
[5] Barnhill, *A New Era in the Education of Blind Children* (1875), pp. 32–44.
[6] Not really to be wondered at on a wage of 30s. per week. His successor, a woman, received twice as much.

II. School Board Classes for the Deaf and Blind

blind children in the Board's schools. The initiative for this move came from Martin Tait, Secretary of the Home Teaching Society, who suggested it to John MacGregor, a member of the Board. As in the case of the National Schools, Moon's system was used, and Tait was satisfied with the quality of the teaching.[1] Others were not; and Marchant Williams, one of the Board's Inspectors, was asked to, and made a report. Published in 1878, this stated that the instruction was 'as bad as it could possibly be',[2] and recommended the appointment of a sighted superintendent with blind teachers to teach the children in special classes. The children would spend only part of their time in the special classes, and for the remainder of the day would be educated in the ordinary schools nearest their homes.[3] The recommendation was implemented, and in 1879 Campbell was persuaded to relinquish one of his most efficient teachers, Miss M. C. Greene, as Superintendent. An American, she had taught at Norwood since its opening.[4] With her came two Norwood-trained blind teachers. They found thirty-four children being taught very indifferently by the Moon system.[5]

Meanwhile the Board had convened a Conference to examine the various systems. Supporters of each type were present. Armitage and Campbell advocated Braille; Forster spoke for the Roman; and Moon, naturally, recommended his own system. At the time, the Board had in mind that their blind children should be educated in the ordinary schools, alongside ordinary children, reading the same books, and taught by the same teacher. For this purpose, and as a result of the opinions expressed at the Conference, they decided that Roman was the best, but as books in Roman type were imperfectly produced, and as books in Moon were already partially adopted, the latter should be retained for the time being, and books in Roman acquired for experimental use.[6] However, as a result of Marchant Williams' report and Miss Greene's appointment, the Board changed its mind, and Braille was introduced.

Centres similar to those for the deaf were now rapidly opened. By 1888 there were 133 children under the instruction of Miss Greene and five blind teachers at twenty-three centres, all attached to ordinary schools. At the larger centres, up to fifteen children attended for half of each day, but at some of the smaller ones they attended for only two half days per week. The remainder of the time was spent in the

---

[1] *R.C.B.D.*, Vol. 3, Evidence of Tait, 18.12.1885.
[2] *Ibid.*, Vol. 3, p. 5, Evidence of Mrs. Westlake, 17.12.1885.
[3] *School Board Chronicle*, Vol. 20, No. 406, 23.11.1878.
[4] *R.C.B.D.*, Vol. 3, Evidence of Mrs. Westlake.
[5] *Ibid.*, Vol. 3, Evidence of Miss Greene, 17.12.1885.
[6] *Report of Conference on the Instruction of Blind Children, 1876.*

ordinary school, sharing as far as possible the education there, and mixing completely with the sighted children both in the classroom and the playground. The Board received the same grant from the Education Department for a blind child as it did for a sighted one, though, like the sighted, the blind had to pass the annual examination. In 1887 the Commissioners visited a class of eighty children in an Infants' Department, in which there were four blind children. In the following March all four passed 'the Government examination as well as any in their class'.[1]

After an indifferent start the London School Board had more success in its early efforts for the blind than for the deaf, despite the fact that they had less special education, and that like the deaf they were from the poorest class whose parents had not managed to send them to institutions. In any case success was comparative. The accommodation was makeshift and minimal. The instruction, based on the Code, was uninteresting and confined mainly to the three R's. Social and vocational education was almost non-existent. Discipline was sometimes harsh and often repressive. These conditions were merely in keeping with those in the ordinary school, where there was so much mechanical teaching, and learning of books by heart, that inspectors changed the order of words in books when giving dictation, and even made pupils read backwards. Children attended very irregularly. Their excuses were varied, and included: 'Fetching the gin and no boots.' When they attended, they were dressed in a variety of garments. One girl in 1891 appeared absolutely naked except for an old gown. Nevertheless, good and enlightened work was often done, and the deaf and blind were certainly far better off than had they been at home.

Other school boards followed London's example. Sunderland (1882) and Bradford (1885) established special classes for the blind, where, unlike London, the children were completely segregated from the sighted. Cardiff, on the other hand, appointed a blind teacher to visit the ordinary schools attended by blind children. Sheffield opened a class for the deaf in 1879, and so during the following ten years did Leeds, Nottingham, Bradford, Bristol, Leicester and Oldham. The majority used the oral method. Some of the classes were considered by H.M.I.'s to be grant earning. In other cases the Boards claimed no grants as they feared that what they were doing might be judged illegal by the Education Department. They need not have worried. Patrick Cumin, Secretary to the Department, giving evidence before the Royal Commission in 1888, stated that he knew of no School Board, save London, that had done anything for the

[1] *R.C.B.D.*, Vol. 2, Appx. 2, p. 15.

blind or deaf![1] Indeed, considerable confusion existed. Croydon School Board considered that the deaf could not be educated at the expense of the rates, rather the matter was one for private charity.[2] London was offered grants for its deaf classes on certain conditions, but the Board found the conditions, entailing, as they did, examinations, completely unacceptable. Birmingham sent a delegation to visit London's special classes, and subsequently decided that education in day classes was impracticable. The children should go to institutions, but the Board had no power to pay for their maintenance. Hull encouraged parents to send their children to the local deaf institution,[3] and the local Guardians to pay their maintenance. The latter reluctantly paid for one child, despite pleas that other deaf children 'might be tempted by this example to claim assistance for their education'.[4]

[1] *Ibid.*, Vol. 3, Evidence of Cumin, 15.2.1888.
[2] *School Board Chronicle*, Vol. 25, No. 535, 14.5.1881.
[3] It was at this Institution that the Commissioners found a boy who, with trimmer-like impartiality, drew excellent portraits from memory of Salisbury and Gladstone.
[4] *R.C.B.D.*, Vol. 2, Appx. 2, p. 40.

8

THE PERIOD OF TRANSITION:
III. THE RETURN OF THE ORAL
EDUCATION OF THE DEAF

MOST of the early teachers of the deaf had endeavoured to give their pupils speech. De l'Epée's successful experiment with signs, however, induced many of the institutions, which were subsequently founded, to follow his system. As has been seen, Gallaudet took it to the United States, and du Puget introduced it to Britain. By the middle of the nineteenth century its use was widespread. Oralism had correspondingly declined. It was still in use in Germany, though even there it had lost some of its pristine greatness. It was challenged now, not only by the sign and manual system, but also by the combined method.

This had been first employed by the wig-maker, Pfingsten, a man of great versatility, who opened a small school for the deaf in Lübeck in 1787. Lübeck at that time was under the control of Denmark, whose King, Frederick VI, favoured the school. He favoured it to such an extent that in 1805 he charged local authorities with the responsibility for educating the deaf.[1] Pfingsten's method was to teach signs to all the children in the school, and to give speech and lip-reading only to a selected few—the brightest. This was the combined system. Its disadvantage was obvious. Children who were taught speech would only practise and use it when they could make their meaning clear by no other means. In a school where signs were also in use, they naturally used these.

That the pure oralism of Heinicke remained alive at all was due in large part to the work of Friedrich Moritz Hill. Hill, who owed his

---

[1] *R.C.B.D.*, Vol. 2, Appx. 3.

III. The Return of the Oral Education of the Deaf

name to his English grandfather, was a German, born near Breslau in 1805. He had been trained as a teacher by Pestalozzi himself, and had embraced his master's methods. These he adapted to the needs of deaf children, especially Pestalozzi's tenet that young children learnt best in the natural environment of the home. Deaf children, therefore contended Hill, should be taught language as ordinary children acquire it, at their mothers' knees. Grammar and lists of words to be learnt by heart had no place in his method. The children would be assisted to speak through constant daily contact with common objects. Natural actions would be used to the same purpose, and lessons in schools for the deaf would be composed of spontaneous conversations between teacher and child. In 1830 Hill became a teacher at the school Heinicke had founded near Leipzig. There he remained until his death in 1874, publicizing his method and practising what he preached.[1]

His work was taken up by another pure oralist, David Hirsch, Headmaster of the Rotterdam school for the deaf, which had opened in 1853. Hirsch was neither prolific in writings nor original in ideas. But he emphasized the idea he had inherited from Moritz Hill, the idea that speech was not to be acquired as an accomplishment merely to please the subscribers, but as a vehicle of communication to be used on all occasions. Once a child mastered speech he would feel no need for signs. Hirsch was a natural teacher. Under him deaf-born children acquired the ability to speak clearly. Under him, too, other teachers learnt his art. For this, England had reason to be grateful.

Thomas Arnold has related[2] that when he was a young teacher at the deaf school in Liverpool, during the 1840's, a certain amount of oral teaching was attempted there. The main method, however, was the manual. Even the little speech that was acquired was not used in practice. Elsewhere it is doubtful whether there was any attempt at all to teach speech. In England, oralism, as such, was dead. Phoenix-like it was to rise again. The renaissance stemmed from two sources.

Susannah Hull, the daughter of a London doctor, became interested in one of her father's patients. This was a young deaf-blind girl whose affliction was due to scarlet fever. Susannah determined to teach her. She read what she could on the subject, and in 1862 opened a school in a room in her father's house. Her original intention was to cater for children who had acquired speech before losing their hearing through illness. The object, therefore, was the preservation of their speech. When, during the course of her reading, she learnt of the work of Moritz Hill and Hirsch, she realized that even

---

[1] Arnold, *Education of Deaf-Mutes*, Vol. 2, pp. 327–38.
[2] *Ibid.*, Vol. 2, pp. 256–8.

deaf-born children could be taught to speak. She therefore extended her aim and her school. To the enlarged premises came children deaf from birth. These she taught, as she had taught those who already had speech, by the pure oral method.[1]

The other source through which oralism returned was not quite so fortuitously found. Gerrit Van Asch was one of the teachers trained at the Rotterdam school by Hirsch. He was twenty-three years of age when he came to England in 1859.[2] He came as private tutor to the deaf child of the wealthy Solomonson family in Manchester. He came with the avowed intention of teaching by the oral system. His success brought requests from other wealthy Mancunians that he should educate their deaf children.[3] Thus, at the same time as Susannah Hull started her school in London, another private school was opened in Manchester. Both employed the oral method. Both charged high fees. Eventually, too, both schools were sited in London.[4]

While Susannah Hull and Van Asch were establishing their respective schools, Baroness Mayer de Rothschild was considering what might be done for deaf Jewish children in London. She was a Rothschild by both birth and marriage. Her father was Baron Charles Rothschild of Naples; her husband, a first cousin, was Baron Lionel de Rothschild. Banker and philanthropist, he was head of the Rothschild financial house in England. He it was who advanced Disraeli four million pounds to complete the purchase of the shares in the Suez Canal from the Khedive of Egypt. His wife needed rather less money for her project. This was to establish a home and school for deaf Jewish children. Both were opened in Whitechapel in 1864.

At the outset the children were taught by the usual sign and manual method. However, Sir Henry Isaacs, a friend of the Baroness, had earlier sent his two deaf children to Rotterdam to be educated by Hirsch. The results had very much impressed him, and he convinced the Baroness of the superiority of the oral system. Accordingly, Hirsch was approached and requested to release a teacher. Thus another young Dutch teacher crossed the North Sea.[5]

---

[1] Hodgson, *The Deaf and their Problems*, pp. 207–8, and Bender, *The Conquest of Deafness*, p. 144.

[2] There is some discrepancy over the date of his arrival. Hodgson and Bender both give 1860, the *First Annual Report of the Society for Training Teachers of the Deaf for the year 1878* gives 1857, and Van Praagh says 1859—*R.C.B.D.*, Vol. 3, Evidence, 11.3.1886. Van Praagh is likely to be the most reliable since he was a colleague of Van Asch at Rotterdam.

[3] Arnold, *op. cit.*, Vol. 2, pp. 409–12.

[4] Van Asch remained in London until 1879 when he went to New Zealand as Principal of the Sumner Institution for the Deaf and Dumb.

[5] *R.C.B.D.*, Vol. 3, Evidence of J. De Castro, 12.3.1886.

III. The Return of the Oral Education of the Deaf

William Van Praagh was only twenty-two when he arrived to take over the direction of the school in 1867. Unlike the children at the private schools of Susannah Hull and Van Asch, the majority at the Whitechapel school came from poor homes. Some were paupers paid for by Guardians, some were poor children educated and housed free of charge by the school. Only four were fee-paying. With this unpromising material, Van Praagh showed beyond doubt that the oral method could work. So successful was he, and so pleased was the Baroness that she 'determined to extend the benefits of the oral system to the afflicted of every race and creed'.[1] To this end, she canvassed her idea among 'people of influence and high position'.[2] In 1871 two meetings were held at her house in Piccadilly. The list of those invited to attend is not extant, but good wishes and apologies for non-attendance were received from Gladstone, Matthew Arnold, W. E. Forster and William Cowper-Temple. At all events sufficient support was forthcoming to warrant the establishment of the Association for the Oral Instruction of the Deaf and Dumb in the same year.

The Association had three aims. The first, as the name implied, was the publicizing of the oral system. Secondly, it was intended to establish a college in which teachers of the deaf would be trained. Lastly, there would also be founded a school where the students might learn the art of teaching by the oral method. The first aim had been implemented to a certain extent before the establishment of the Association. The last was achieved when the school opened in July 1872, with Van Praagh as the Principal of both it and the, as yet unopened, training college. Within two years the school had thirty-three pupils, all of them day scholars.[3] The break with the tradition of residential schools was deliberate, for Van Praagh believed that the deaf should be encouraged to associate with the hearing, and was highly critical of the asylum system.[4]

By now Van Praagh had an assistant, whom he had trained at the school during the first two years of its existence. This was Mrs. Dancy, who prior to joining Van Praagh, had no knowledge of the education of the deaf, but who, in 1879, transferred to the London School Board to introduce the oral system to its classes.[5] Mrs. Dancy was the first, and until 1874 the only, student at the college part of the Association. Indeed, during its early years the college

---

[1] *Second Annual Report of the Association for the Oral Instruction of the Deaf and Dumb* (1875), p. 13.
[2] *Ibid.*, p. 13.   [3] *First Annual Report* (1874).
[4] Later, when the school became better known, some children came from a distance, and these were boarded out in nearby houses.
[5] See Chapter 7.

was nothing more than a number of student teachers attending the school. For the first six months of their training they observed; for the second six months they taught under supervision. Training could last for either twelve or eighteen months. Those who opted for the shorter course were charged £50, those for the longer £30. This paradoxical situation arose because the students on the eighteen-month course taught free of charge for the last six months.[1]

Van Praagh both defended and advocated his system. 'Every good school presided over by a competent principal or head-master ought to be in reality a Training College,' he wrote. '. . . The best training for a Deaf and Dumb teacher is actual work in a school.'[2] Apart from a few lectures from Van Praagh, this was the training they got—actual work in a school. By this method, twenty-three teachers were successfully trained in the first seventeen years of the school's life. Seven failed and a further seven did not complete the course.[3] It is easy to criticize the training method which the Association employed, the fees it charged and the grandiose name of training college which it adopted. But it did good work. Prior to its establishment, very few teachers in schools for the deaf had received any training at all. Nor was it interested only in fees. Its own students were allowed to pay their fees after they had started teaching. Moreover, it accepted and trained, free of charge, any teacher from an existing institution for the deaf wishing to adopt the oral method.[4]

Better though this training was than no training at all, a comparison with what took place in Germany showed it in its true insignificance. Schöntheil, who had succeeded Van Praagh at the Jewish school in Whitechapel, was a German. He described to the Royal Commission on the Blind and Deaf the training which teachers of the deaf had to undergo in Germany. All must have passed through a Real-schule or Gymnasium. Then followed three years at a training college. After obtaining a teaching certificate, the newly qualified teacher was attached to a particular school for the deaf for two years, the first of which was spent in observation and instruction by the headmaster. Only then would he become a fully qualified teacher of the deaf. The whole of this training was paid for by the State.[5]

Meanwhile, apart from the training college, the practising school itself was growing. Its growth, and the move to larger premises in Fitzroy Square, demanded money. The influential connections, which the Rothschilds had secured for it, now stood it in good stead.

[1] *R.C.B.D.*, Vol. 3, Evidence of Van Praagh, 11.3.1886.
[2] Van Praagh, *On Training Colleges for Teachers of the Deaf and Dumb* (1882), pp. 4–5.
[3] *R.C.B.D.*, Vol. 2, Appx. 2.   [4] *Annual Report for 1882*.
[5] *R.C.B.D.*, Vol. 3, Evidence of S. Schöntheil, 12.3.1886.

III. The Return of the Oral Education of the Deaf

Papers on the oral method were read to the Social Science Congress and to the Society of Arts by eminent aural surgeons; Grosvenor House was lent, as it had been lent to the Royal Normal College, for the annual public examination of the children; the Princess of Wales and the Royal Princes attended the examinations; and the future Edward VII presided at one of the Association's annual banquets. Before doing so, he was conducted over the school. His after-dinner address was full of praise for what he had seen. 'It was astonishing', he stated, 'to hear a little child, who had received only three months' instruction, articulate sounds to me so positively distinct.'[1]

The comment was echoed in 1896 by one of Her Majesty's Inspectors who visited the school: 'This is an excellent School; the teaching is throughout thorough and intelligent, and the articulation very clear.'[2] By then the school had sixty boys and girls aged seven to sixteen. All were day pupils paying fees of £50 per annum. But the school could not support itself on the fees it received. It still depended on subscriptions from the general public, and the annual reports from this time onwards stress more and more its financial difficulties. It suffered from the competition of the School Board classes. It suffered, too, from the improvements made in the old residential institutions for the deaf, improvements for which the inspiration and example it had given were largely responsible. Gradually the number of its pupils declined.

But its work had been done. When William Van Praagh, teaching until the end, died in 1907, oralism was well established, though not as yet universal in England. His had been an important contribution. To him belongs a great deal of the credit for the re-introduction of the oral system. It was his work at the Jewish school in White-chapel that led to the formation of the Association for the Oral Instruction of the Deaf and Dumb, of which he himself was a founder member. Subsequently, the teachers he trained, and the publicity for which he was responsible, assisted in the spread of oralism. Like many great teachers, however, he had his blind spot. Dr. Eichholz, H.M.I., pinpointed it: 'He was an enthusiastic and capable exponent of his art, but lacked power of organization, and but for capable assistance from his subordinates the institution would have fallen into chaos.'[3]

Indications that oralism was breaching the hitherto impregnable defences of inertia and conservatism in the institutions for the deaf were already evident by 1877. In that year a Conference of headmasters of institutions was held in London. It was not convened

---

[1] *Annual Report for 1877*, p. 4.   [2] *Annual Report for 1896*, p. 6.
[3] Ministry of Education Archives, Education Class 32, Piece 121.

without difficulty. Nor was it the first. The headmasters had earlier met in 1851 and 1852. The touch of the dead hand of stagnation permeates the account of their proceedings. Twelve were present at the first meeting, seven at the second. They decided against articulation. They decided little else.[1] The Conference of 1877 was a different affair. It was the work of Richard Elliott, whose description of conditions at the Old Kent Road school, when he first went there in 1857, has already been mentioned. By now he was Headmaster of the branch school at Margate. He had long been dissatisfied with both the attitude of the old established schools towards oralism, and the lot of the children therein. Knowing that James Howard, Baker's successor at Doncaster, was teaching some speech, he enlisted his support, and together they organized the meeting. Watson, Elliott's titular head at Old Kent Road, was invited but refused to attend, and the Committee which controlled both schools criticized Elliott's part in convening the Conference.

Nevertheless, it was a success. Its members visited the Jewish deaf school to observe the effects of good oral teaching. The visit, combined with the pleadings of Elliott and Howard, persuaded the Conference to resolve that reforms in schools for the deaf were necessary.[2] Such a resolution must have seemed like heresy to old James Watson in his citadel at the Old Kent Road. Rather than be responsible for leading his school into the new era, he resigned the following year. He was the first of his family, which had ruled the school for eighty-six years to do so. The others had died in harness. With him went the last link with the Braidwoods. The change, in Churchill's words, marked, if not the beginning of the end, the end of the beginning. Elliott became Headmaster of both schools and the Committee withdrew its condemnation of the previous year.[3]

Apart from Elliott's, another name was becoming prominent at this time. Thomas Arnold was born the son of a cabinet maker in County Antrim in 1816. As a child he was precocious, and with the help of his Minister he became a schoolmaster. In his twenties he taught for a few years at the deaf schools at Doncaster and Liverpool. Leaving teaching, he was ordained as a Congregational Minister, and took over a chapel in Australia. He returned to a pastorate in Northampton. There, in 1868, he took seven-year-old Abraham Farrar, deaf from the age of three, as a pupil. Farrar remained with Arnold until he was twenty, when he sat for, and

---

[1] *Transactions of the First and Second Conferences of Principals of Institutions for the Deaf and Dumb* (1852).
[2] *Proceedings of the Conference of Head Masters of Institutions for the Education of the Deaf and Dumb* (1877).
[3] Bender, *op. cit.*, pp. 145–6, and Hodgson, *op. cit.*, pp. 234–5.

passed, the matriculation examination of London University. This was the first occasion on which a deaf English child achieved success in a public examination. Nor was this Farrar's only achievement. He subsequently qualified, though he never practised, as an architect and surveyor. His tuition throughout had been by the oral method. With his success with Farrar already becoming apparent, Arnold, who had for long been convinced of the superiority of oralism, published, in 1872, his first pamphlet condemning the artificiality of the conventional sign system.[1] At the same time he gave up his Ministry and concentrated entirely upon teaching the deaf. Farrar was joined by other private pupils, and before long Arnold was calling his small establishment the Northampton High School for the Deaf. Never was it as important as its name implied, but for nearly eighty years it remained the only school which purported to cater for the higher education of the deaf. It was always small. Even after Arnold's publications had made him well known, he had only one assistant, and at the height of its achievement under one of his successors, Ince-Jones, the school had only twenty boys.[2] The publication which brought Arnold renown was his *The Method of Teaching the Deaf and Dumb Speech, Lip-reading, and Language* which appeared in 1881. It was republished seven years later by the College of Teachers of the Deaf and Dumb under the title *Education of Deaf-Mutes: A Manual for Teachers*. The revising and rewriting of this book became part of the life work of Abraham Farrar, and *Arnold on the Education of the Deaf* was reprinted as recently as 1954.

Three lines of development by which oralism re-emerged have already been traced: the training of teachers by Van Praagh, the movement for reform within the old established schools led by Elliott, and Arnold's publications. There was a fourth. St. John Ackers, barrister and squire of Huntley, Gloucestershire, had a deaf daughter. When he enquired about the possibility of her being educated, he found a profound divergence of opinion as to the best method. With the object of discovering for himself what was being done for the deaf elsewhere, he visited schools on the Continent and in the United States. He returned from his tour convinced of the superiority of the German method; convinced, too, that his duty lay in securing for the youthful deaf in England the opportunity of being educated by this method. Accordingly, he founded in 1877 the Society for the Training of Teachers of the Deaf and the Diffusion

[1] Arnold, *A Review of the French and German Systems*.
[2] Greenaway, 'Higher Education for the Deaf: its Origins and Possible Developments', *Teacher of the Deaf*, Vol. 47, No. 282, December 1949, pp. 188–92.

of the German System in the United Kingdom.[1] It will be seen that there was little difference between the Society and Baroness Roths-child's Association. Indeed, the Society also had the intention of founding a school, in addition to the objects expressed in its title. In the event, neither the school nor the training of teachers was of great importance. What was important was the propaganda disseminated by the Society, and the prestige with which it was backed. That St. John Ackers was a Member of Parliament was also a matter of importance.

Prior to launching the Society, St. John Ackers had sought the assistance of a young teacher, Arthur Kinsey, whom he instructed to acquaint himself thoroughly with the oral method. To this end, Kinsey visited, and studied at, some of the best foreign schools. He spent a year at Osnabrück,[2] and visited Heinicke's old school at Leipzig, the Vienna school, the school at Hildesheim, and a Swiss school at Basle. The tour ended with a visit to the United States. For all this, St. John Ackers paid.[3] It may be wondered why he did not throw in his lot with the Fitzroy Square school and training college. St. John Ackers himself never supplied an adequate answer. There were suggestions that at Fitzroy Square the German articula-tion had not been adapted to the English language, and that the teachers at Fitzroy Square were being trained for the use of the school there.[4] But this was a smoke screen. The true reason was that St. John Ackers was conservative in both senses of the word. He was ready to adopt the method of the Germans, but he was unable to accept the idea of importing a foreign teacher.[5]

It was Kinsey, therefore, who was appointed Principal of the college and school at Ealing in 1878. The latter was formed by taking over an existing private school, together with its owner—Susannah Hull, who joined the staff as Vice-Principal. Miss Hull's school had always been small, and its incorporation into the Society did nothing to increase its numbers. In 1887 there were seventeen children, by 1895 fourteen, and in 1907 the average attendance was only six.[6] The number of students showed greater uniformity. Some ten were trained each year, although not all succeeded in obtaining a certificate of competence from the college. As at Fitzroy Square, almost all the

[1] *R.C.B.D.*, Vol. 3, Evidence of D. Buxton, 17.3.1886.
[2] Kinsey had received part of his education in Germany, so there were no language difficulties.
[3] *R.C.B.D.*, Vol. 3, Evidence of A. Kinsey, 17.3.1886.
[4] This criticism could never be levelled at the Society. Its school was so small that it rarely needed more than one teacher.
[5] *R.C.B.D.*, Vol. 3, Evidence of Kinsey.
[6] *R.C.B.D.*, Vol. 2, Appx. 2, and *18th Annual Report of the Society for Training Teachers of the Deaf* (1895), p. 7.

students were women. In the first ten years there were only two men students, and both were paid a small salary while they received their training. The women, on the other hand, paid fees, and were given the choice of being resident or not. For the residents a scale of fees was published which included the odd phrase: 'Washing, Beer, Wine, etc, etc, extra.'[1] It is possibly no wonder that of the first ninety students, forty-nine failed to obtain a certificate.[2] The training they received was much the same as that given at Fitzroy Square. It lasted for a year, and after the first term almost all the time was spent in the school.

It has already been indicated that the value of the Society's work lay in the pressure that it brought to bear to secure improvements in the education of the deaf. The fact that it had the Archbishop of Canterbury as its President assisted it in this task. Also active on the Society's behalf, organizing meetings, reading papers, publishing pamphlets, were St. John Ackers, Kinsey and the Society's Secretary, David Buxton. The last named had taught at the Old Kent Road Asylum for ten years before becoming Headmaster of the Liverpool deaf school in 1851. There he had remained until being appointed the Ealing Society's paid Secretary in 1877. He claimed that, even while he was at Liverpool, he had been a supporter of the oral method, but that as headmaster of a combined system school he could not publicly advocate it.[3] Be that as it may, as the ex-head-master of a deaf institution, he was in a good position to know the views of the institutions on the oral method. These he expounded in a paper read to a meeting of the British Association at Sheffield in 1879. Opponents of the oral system, he claimed, did not deny that it was better, but claimed that their own system was good enough for its purpose, especially as it was cheaper. ' "Good enough!", "Cheaper!" ', he continued. 'Is this great country content to be put off with an inferior system, in the matter of education, to that which poorer countries are determined to have? Is so important a matter to be governed by so paltry a consideration as that of Pounds, Shillings, and Pence?'[4] There was a great deal of truth in Buxton's claim. Economics played a large part in the argument, but so, too, did a natural disinclination for change.

So impressed was the British Association by Buxton's views that it appointed a Committee, under A. J. Mundella, to consider and report on the existing systems of teaching the deaf. The Committee

---

[1] *Prospectus of the Society for Training Teachers of the Deaf and Diffusion of the German System* (1878), p. 2.
[2] *R.C.B.D.*, Vol. 2, Appx. 2.   [3] *Ibid.*, Vol. 3, Evidence of Buxton. 17.3.1886.
[4] Buxton, *The German System of Teaching the Deaf* (1879), p. 12.

reported in 1880. It recommended that parliamentary grants should be made for the education of the deaf on the German system, and that either State aid should be given to training colleges for teachers of the deaf, or grants be paid to approved students.[1]

In the same year the oralists were given further encouragement. An International Congress on the Deaf and Dumb was held at Milan. Papers were read by St. John Ackers, his wife, Kinsey, Buxton and Miss Hull. The official French representative, an officer of the Ministry of the Interior, expressed his complete conversion from the sign to the oral system.[2] Finally, the Congress passed the following resolutions:

'This Congress considering the incontestable superiority of speech over signs in restoring the deaf-mute to society, and in giving him a more perfect knowledge of the language, declares that the oral method ought to be preferred to that of signs for the education and instruction of the deaf and dumb . . . and considering that the simultaneous use of speech and signs has the disadvantage of injuring speech, lip-reading, and precision of ideas, declares that the pure oral method ought to be preferred . . . and considering that a great number of the deaf and dumb are not receiving the benefit of instruction recommends that Governments should take the necessary steps that all the deaf and dumb may be educated.'[3]

Of the Milan resolutions, *The Times* commented: 'The result is a virtual unanimity of preference for oral teaching which might seem to overbear all possibility of opposition.'[4] Of equal importance as the resolution concerning oralism was the one calling for State intervention. Armed with this resolution and the recommendation of the British Association, the Ealing Society now campaigned for State assistance in the education of the deaf. Accordingly, in 1881, a deputation waited upon Mundella, Vice-President of the Education Department, and presented a memorial. This stated that in most other civilized countries the education of the deaf was the concern of the State, and requested that the Government should therefore ensure that all the deaf were educated, and their teachers trained.[5] Strangely,

[1] *Report of the Fiftieth Meeting of the British Association for the Advancement of Science* (1880), pp. 216–19.

[2] The Headmaster of De l'Epée's old school in Paris had been converted some years earlier. However, the Franco Prussian War of 1870 had made all things German anathema to the French, and he was dismissed. After the Milan Congress he was reinstated. *R.C.B.D.*, Vol. 3, Evidence of Kinsey.

[3] Buxton, *Speech for the Deaf, Essays, Proceedings and Resolutions of the International Congress on the Education of the Deaf* (1880), pp. 4–5.

[4] *The Times*, September 28th, 1880.

[5] *Proceedings of the Conference of Head Masters of Institutions for the Education of the Deaf and Dumb, London, 1885*, p. 108.

the action of the Ealing Society did not meet with universal support. Many of the older institutions were immovably opposed to State aid. Their motives were mixed. Some feared State aid since it would bring State inspection. Some rejected it on the grounds that it would involve participation in the system of payment by results. Some felt that it was an encroachment upon their independence. All, however, needed money. The Conference of Headmasters at Doncaster in 1882 was, nevertheless, able to pass a compromise resolution. This stated that since charity was generally unable to meet the needs of the education of the deaf, individual institutions should be free to seek supplementary assistance from the State. In this form the resolution did not bind any particular institution to ask for aid.[1]

Towards the end of 1884, there was talk that the Government was about to give assistance towards the education of the blind. The idea of being left behind by the blind served to bring about a temporary unity in the deaf camp. Organized by the Ealing Society, a meeting in Manchester at the beginning of 1885 agreed to memorialize the Government.[2] Once again Mundella received the deputation, led this time by Lord Egerton of Tatton, Chairman of the Manchester school for the deaf. The demands they made were precise. They sought three things: State aid in the form of capitation grants, authority for School Boards to contribute towards existing institutions or else establish their own, and compulsory education for the deaf.[3] Mundella made no specific promise;[4] nor could he in fact have made one, for the deputation was received when Gladstone's second Ministry was tottering under the onslaught of the Irish Members. Between questions on Home Rule, St. John Ackers rose in the Commons and asked Mundella whether the Government would grant an enquiry. In reply he was told that the question of an enquiry into the education of both the blind and the deaf was under consideration, 'and I expect that a decision will shortly be arrived at'.[5] This was on May 18th. On June 8th a decision of a different kind was arrived at. The Government fell.

St. John Ackers did not, in fact, want an enquiry. There was, he felt, no necessity for one; but an enquiry would be better than no action at all. When the Headmasters next met in the July, the possibility of an enquiry was put before them. Also put to them was the

[1] *Report of the Proceedings of the Conference of Head Masters of Institutions for the Education of the Deaf and Dumb* (1882), p. 60.
[2] *Proceedings of the Conference in the Mayor's Parlour on the subject of State Aid for the Deaf and Dumb, Town Hall, Manchester, 1885.*
[3] *Proceedings of the Conference of Head Masters, London, 1885*, pp. 110–11.
[4] *Record of the Proceedings at the Interview of the Deputation appointed to wait on the Committee of Her Majesty's Privy Council for Education* (1885).
[5] *Hansard*, 18.5.1885, col. 701.

point that if they wished to achieve anything, there must be more unanimity. In a rousing speech, Lord Egerton declared that any resolution should be taken direct to the Prime Minister. 'But,' he warned, 'there must be none of this difference of opinion before the Prime Minister. We must not be divided as to how education is to be carried out. We must be united as to the desirability of education being given.'[1]

Egerton did not appeal wholly in vain. On one point, at least, there was agreement. Without dissent, the Conference resolved that State aid was essential, and 'that Lord Egerton of Tatton be respectfully requested to urge upon the Prime Minister, the Marquess of Salisbury, the importance of steps being taken, without delay, to give effect to this Resolution, either by immediate legislation or by the appointment of a Commission of Enquiry'.[2]

[1] *Proceedings of the Conference of Head Masters, 1885*, p. 115.
[2] *Ibid.*, p. 126.

9

THE PERIOD OF STATE INTERVENTION: I. THE ROYAL COMMISSION ON THE BLIND AND DEAF[1]

TEN days after the Conference of Headmasters had passed its resolution, in July 1885, calling for either State aid for the deaf or the establishment of a Commission of Enquiry, the Government took its first official step in relation to the education of handicapped children. It appointed a Royal Commission. Its terms of reference were confined to the blind. For this the workers for the deaf were grateful. They had no desire for an enquiry which embraced both blind and deaf, since they felt that the problems of the blind were not only vastly dissimilar to, but that they would merely serve to distract attention from, the even more complex problems of the deaf. This feeling was reciprocated by the friends of the blind. As recently as 1930, Dr. J. M. Ritchie, a sincere and selfless worker on behalf of the blind, described the extension of the terms of the Royal Commission to include the deaf as 'unfortunate in that it gave State recognition to the vicious bracketing of blind with deaf'.[2]

That the Royal Commission had been appointed for the blind, only, was due to the fact that an investigation into their education had been sought at an earlier date than that on behalf of the deaf. A Conference on the education of the blind at York in July 1883 had recognized the need for an enquiry.[3] This was followed in 1884

---

[1] Material in this chapter is taken from the *Report of the Commission*, Vol. 1, unless otherwise stated.
[2] Ritchie, *Concerning the Blind*, p. 95.
[3] *Report of the Conference of Managers, Teachers, and Friends of the Blind* (1889).

by a meeting at Grosvenor House, convened by the Duke of Westminster. There, it was unanimously resolved to ask the Government to initiate an investigation into the educational needs of the blind. As a result, the Royal Commission was appointed with the Duke of Westminster as its Chairman. Of course, the fact that the work of Armitage and the British and Foreign Blind Association had produced more harmony among institutions for the blind than existed between those for the deaf also contributed to the Government's earlier recognition of the needs of the former.

The earlier recognition was short-lived. At the beginning of 1886 Salisbury, as a result of the representations made to him by Egerton's deputation, decided that an investigation into the needs of the deaf was also warranted. Rather than initiate a separate enquiry, the terms of reference of the Royal Commission were changed. Changed, too, was the composition of its members. Lord Egerton of Tatton replaced Westminster as Chairman, and workers in the field of the deaf were added to those representing the blind. The latter included Campbell, of the Royal Normal College, E. C. Johnson, of the Blind Man's Friend Charity, and Armitage. Among the newcomers were St. John Ackers and Van Oven, both supporters of oralism, and the Revs. W. B. Sleight and C. M. Owen, who, as missionaries to the adult deaf, were wedded to the old sign and manual system. While the Government was to be congratulated on the impartiality thus shown, the presence on the Commission of outspoken protagonists of the opposing methods of teaching the deaf effectively prevented any unanimity of opinion. Also appointed Commissioners were the Members of Parliament, Mundella, William Woodall and Lyon Playfair,[1] the Bishop of London, Admiral Sir Edward Sotheby, and two doctors, Robertson and McDonnell.

The original terms of reference approved by Her Majesty had been to 'report upon the condition of the Blind in Our United Kingdom, the various systems of education of the blind, elementary, technical, and professional, at home and abroad, and the existing institutions for that purpose, the employment open to and suitable for the blind, and the means by which education may be extended so as to increase the number of blind persons qualified for such employment'. With the inclusion of the deaf, these were extended 'to investigate and report similarly upon the condition and education of the Deaf and Dumb as well as such other cases as from special circumstances would seem to require exceptional methods of education'. This last

---

[1] Woodall was Chairman of the Conference of Headmasters of the deaf schools in London in 1885. Playfair was for five months in 1886 Vice-President of the Education Department. He was also Chairman of the Royal Normal College, Norwood.

phrase was something of a surprise. No representations on behalf of the physically or mentally handicapped had been made. Unlike the blind and deaf, there existed no organizations to champion their cause. Of the philanthropic bodies, only the Charity Organization Society with its *Report on the Education and Care of Idiots, Imbeciles and Harmless Lunatics* had paid any attention to them. Admittedly the Royal Commission on the Elementary Education Acts, the Cross Commission, recommended that the feeble-minded in the public elementary schools should be excluded from its terms of reference, and come within those of the Egerton Commission. But the Cross Commission was not appointed until later in 1886, and its recommendation was, therefore, an effect not a cause of the inclusion of the phrase. Rather, the inclusion of 'such other cases as from special circumstances would seem to require exceptional methods of education' was forced upon the Government, for with the introduction of universal education had come the realization that the mentally handicapped constituted an educational problem.

The Commission, whatever else may be said of it, was thorough. It took evidence at 116 sittings, sent out numerous questionnaires, and visited the better known institutions in France, Germany, Switzerland and Italy, and almost all in the United Kingdom. The accounts of these visits, contained in the appendices to the *Report*, contain valuable information for the historian.

Many of the Commissioners were active workers on behalf of the handicapped, all of them had their best interests at heart. But they tempered their views with discretion. From the opening paragraphs of the *Report* they set out to disarm suspicion. What should have been presented as an ethical duty, they showed as a mundane necessity. What should have been revealed as an inalienable right, they concealed as an economic expedient. The blind, the deaf and educable imbeciles, they argued, would, if left uneducated, become a weighty burden on the State. It was, therefore, in the interests of the State to educate them, 'so as to dry up as far as possible the minor streams which ultimately swell the great torrent of pauperism'. It was unfortunate that a *Report* which in so many ways was excellent and enlightened should have lacked the stamp of idealism. The interest of the State was frequently mentioned, the interest of the children rarely.

After its prefatory remarks, the *Report* dealt first with the blind. Guardians of the Poor, it pointed out, were empowered by the Poor Law Act 1862[1] to pay for the maintenance and education of blind pauper children in institutions for the blind. By a further Act,[2] the

[1] 25 and 26 Victoria, c. 43, s. 1.   [2] 42 and 43 Victoria, 1879, c. 54, s. 10.

Guardians were also empowered to subscribe towards any institutions for the blind which rendered aid in relief of the poor. On paper these powers looked good. But they were only powers. The Guardians were not compelled to educate the blind. Moreover, the 1862 Act stipulated that the amount that the Guardians were allowed to pay to the school for both education and maintenance should not exceed the cost of maintaining the child in the workhouse. This was very low. Shortly before the Commission sat, the Act had been amended to permit payment to the school of an amount sanctioned by the Local Government Board, but, in practice, the amount sanctioned was rarely greater than the equivalent cost of workhouse maintenance. Consequently, one of two things happened. Either the school for the blind accepted the child at considerable underpayment, or the child was not admitted since the Guardians would not pay the fee asked by the school.

There were also, of course, Guardians who rarely, if ever, exercised their power to educate the blind in special institutions. The Catholic Blind Asylum at Liverpool complained that when the Guardians did send children, they did not send them soon enough. The case was instanced of a girl admitted at the age of nineteen, who had spent the previous nine years at a workhouse school in which, as she was totally blind, she had learnt nothing. Other Guardians refused to assist needy cases on the grounds that the parents were not truly paupers, though the Act itself made no such distinction. Liverpool again provided an example. A girl, both of whose parents were deaf and dumb, and the father blind as well, was refused assistance. There were four other children in the family, two of whom were deaf, and the father only earned half a guinea a week at ship caulking. The Guardians, however, claimed that as the grandfather, a retired chimney sweep, had put by some savings, the grandchild was not entitled to relief.[1]

On the question of parish relief, the *Report* recommended that parents should be assisted with the maintenance charges at institutions for the blind without having to apply to the Guardians. For though the Guardians had the power to pay even if the parent was not a pauper, many parents were disinclined to make application. Moreover, stressed the *Report*, not all Guardians gave aid. The grant in aid should, therefore, be made by the school authority, and not by the Guardians under whom it assumed (and here the Commissioners allow their true feelings to show) 'the form of a charitable concession rather than an educational duty'.[2]

Passing to the actual education of the blind, the Commissioners

---

[1] *R.C.B.D.*, Vol. 2, Appx. 2.   [2] *Ibid.*, Vol. 1, p. 39.

stated that all their recommendations were based on the idea that the blind should as far as possible be treated like the sighted, and that the objects of education should be to compensate for their defects and train them to earn a living. This admirable statement of principle was completely spoilt by the next sentence: 'It is better for the State to use funds on elementary and technical education for the blind for a few years rather than to have to support them through life in idleness, or to allow them to obtain their livelihood from public or private charity.'[1]

The Commissioners envisaged a division in the education of the blind between elementary and technical and higher. Elementary education, they suggested, might be given in one of three different ways. Children living in rural areas should attend the local village school. There they would be taught by the same teacher, and in the same class, as sighted children. Rather optimistically, the Commissioners felt that the objections of teachers to having blind children in their classes could easily be overcome if the teachers took the trouble to learn Braille. In fact, this part of their scheme depended on the teachers having some knowledge of Braille, though they would not be expected to instruct the children in its use. The child would have been taught the rudiments of Braille before it ever entered the school—by its parents or a district visitor. Despite this emphasis on Braille, and the presence on the Commission of Armitage and Campbell, the Commissioners were not completely wedded to the system. Roman type, too, they believed, should be taught to the blind. If then the ordinary text-books were made available in embossed Roman type, there would be little difficulty in teaching the blind with the sighted.[2]

For children living in towns, a similar scheme was proposed. Again they would attend the ordinary school. But instead of receiving all their instruction from the class teacher, they would, in the first instance, be taught to read the various embossed types by a special peripatetic teacher of the blind. If there were sufficient children they would be taught together at a centre on certain days of the week. Once the children had mastered the types, they could participate completely in the work of the ordinary class.

This idealistic and ambitious scheme was completely impracticable. The Commissioners were moved by the laudable desire not to

---

[1] *Ibid.*, Vol. 1, p. 38.

[2] Although Armitage and Campbell signed the *Report*, they both made reservations. While they believed that the *Report* was the best compromise under the circumstances, they disagreed with certain points that it made. The points of disagreement were not specified, but it is highly probable that the advocacy of Roman type was one of them.

segregate the blind. Free intercourse with the seeing, they believed, produced self-reliance in the blind.[1] But they underestimated both the difficulty of teaching the types to the blind,[2] and the extent of educational retardation induced by blindness. Moreover, their desire that the blind should be educated with the sighted led to the dichotomy in the recommendation concerning types. Their awareness of the superiority of Braille was clouded by their wish to advocate a type that could be taught by a sighted person, and would also allow the blind to communicate the more easily with the seeing world.

The third way in which elementary education might be given was in special boarding schools. These would be for the blind who were delicate, neglected, or, whether they lived in town or country, would have too great a distance to travel to the nearest ordinary school. Most of the blind at this time were, of course, being educated in this way. It was, however, the intention of the Commissioners that the existing institutions should concentrate less on elementary education and more on vocational training. This, many schools were already doing.

The suggestion, therefore, was that the blind should be given elementary education until the age of twelve at either the ordinary schools or institutions. At that age they would enter upon a course of technical instruction or, if they had revealed academic inclinations, they would be given secondary education at what was described as a 'high class college'. Compulsory education, which would have started at the same age as for ordinary children, five, would continue until sixteen. The school authorities should be empowered, and have the duty, to give grants even after the age of sixteen to assist the blind in maintaining themselves while becoming established in their trade.

The technical instruction would be given in the existing institutions, and, where these were insufficient, a school authority should have the power to establish an institution of its own or else to join with other authorities in establishing one. Although the emphasis in the institutions for children over twelve would be on vocational training, education was not to be completely neglected, but should continue alongside the technical training. Of the existing institutions, the *Report* was in some ways critical. Where a school and a sheltered

---

[1] The Commissioners were greatly influenced by the integration of the blind with the seeing which had been attempted in Scotland and by the London School Board (see Chapter 7) and by Barnhill's book which advocated such a system: *A New Era in the Education of Blind Children* (1875).

[2] They felt that no special Code of Regulations for the blind would be necessary, since there was no difficulty in teaching reading, writing and arithmetic to them.

workshop for adults existed on the same premises, it deprecated the policy of allowing the children and adults to mix freely. In such cases, it insisted, there should be a separate educational department for children under sixteen. There was criticism, too, of the parsimony of some of the institutions. Their total investments exceeded half a million pounds, their property was valued at over £300,000. Yet they were not prepared to use their wealth. The annual cost to Worcester College of educating a boy was £90, at the Royal Normal College it was £60, but the average cost at the other institutions was only £23. Since the Commissioners were now recommending that school authorities should pay the schools the cost of educating and maintaining any children they sent to them, they also hoped that the education and maintenance would be at a higher standard than hitherto. In addition, it was expected that the institutions would employ some of the funds thus liberated from educational purposes to improve their workshop facilities and to establish after-care schemes for their old pupils.

With regard to the high class college which had been recommended, the *Report*, while recognizing the value of, and praising the work done at, Worcester College, stated that it was too small and too much of a private venture to justify State recognition and aid. Nevertheless, such a college was required. It should be grant aided, and should prepare its pupils for University entrance.

The *Report* itself had little to say on the training of teachers of the blind. There was a recommendation that teachers should be certificated, and a commendation for the work being done at the Royal Normal College. As for teachers who were themselves blind, there was some doubt as to their value, and they should on all occasions have 'such sighted assistance as may be necessary to insure the efficiency of their teaching'.[1] Far more valuable comment on the training of teachers was to be found in the report of an unofficial inspection of the Royal Normal College:

'The teachers have been attracted to this particular work by a strong sympathy with an afflicted class, and by a consciousness of a special faculty for helping that class. They have gained their success partly through experience, but mainly by means of enthusiasm and self-devotion. For work of this very exceptional character, these appear to me to be the highest qualifications. Other training might add to them, but it could never be an efficient substitute for them. . . . Therefore conditions for the training of teachers should avoid all rigid and inelastic rules, . . . and for the present, and until experience shall have suggested a better course, should encourage liberally any

[1] *R.C.B.D.*, Vol. 1, p. 42.

approved methods of training, and judge their efficacy mainly by their results.'[1]

For the blind, therefore, the Commissioners' main recommendations were that there should be compulsory education from five to sixteen, that school authorities should be responsible for providing it, either directly themselves or paying for it elsewhere, and that parents should not be expected to contribute more towards the education than they would have had it been given in the ordinary school.

The first problem that confronted the Commissioners when they turned their attention to the deaf was their number. A census had been taken in 1881, and this had provided valuable information as far as the blind were concerned. This was not so in the case of the deaf. Parents of a deaf child were unwilling to acknowledge the fact until the child was at least five, and, consequently, young deaf children were rarely entered as such on the return. Apart from the inaccuracy so produced, there were other factors which made the census figures misleading and unreliable. In one district of Ireland the figures for the deaf were so widely at variance with the usual proportion that the returns were sent back for investigation. It was then found that every child too young to speak had been returned as deaf and dumb. However, despite the unreliability of the census figures, it was estimated that in 1888 only a little over half of all deaf children aged five to thirteen were being educated.

The second problem was not disposed of so easily. The Commissioners found, and they could hardly have done otherwise, that there was considerable difference of opinion regarding the best system of teaching. Protagonists of all methods gave evidence. Those supporting the sign and manual system claimed that it was the natural way for the deaf to express themselves, and it also allowed them to communicate with their fellow deaf. The oralists, on the other hand, asserted that the most important thing was for the deaf to be able to communicate with the hearing world; consequently they aimed at making the deaf conversant with their own language and able to express themselves through speech. Finally, supporters of the combined system held the view that the deaf should have the advantages of both sign and manual and oralism, though the Commissioners felt that all too frequently the manual alphabet prevailed, and the pupils relinquished the use of speech.

This minor judgement was almost as far as the Commissioners were prepared to go on the question of systems. It would be unwise, they felt, while so much difference of opinion existed, for the State to

[1] *R.C.B.D.*, Vol. 3, p. 723.

insist on one method. However, they did think that attempts should be made to teach all children, with certain exceptions, to speak and to lip-read. The exceptions would consist of children mentally unsuited for oralism. These, the less intelligent, might be taught by either of the other methods. Care should be exercised, however, to ensure that these children should have no contact at school or at play with those being taught on the oral system. Schools for the deaf, therefore, would have to be divided into two separate, self-contained departments. Such was the unhappy compromise suggested in the *Report*. Even this was not contained in the form of a recommendation. Little wonder then that it had but slight influence upon the institutions. That the change to oralism did eventually take place was due more to the work of St. John Ackers, Van Praagh, Elliott and Arnold than anything the Commissioners had to say.[1] Nor did the compromise satisfy the rival views existing within the Commission itself. St. John Ackers and Van Oven signed a reservation to the effect that they believed that the oral system, and only the oral system, should have been recommended. The Revs. Owen and Sleight, by contrast, felt that the sign and manual, and combined systems had been too lightly dismissed.

On other aspects of teaching the deaf, the *Report* contained enlightened recommendations. The London School Board had, in 1884, requested the Education Department to allow their special classes for the deaf to be grant earning. In reply the Department stated it would be prepared to give grants on condition that children 'sufficiently advanced for any standard will be presented for examination. H.M.I. will be assisted by the teachers in examining them'. Children unable to reach any standard would be seen at work in their class, and the Inspector would 'add to his report his opinion as to the efficiency of the instruction'. The School Board could not agree to these conditions, and requested that the Department appoint a special examiner on whose report a grant might be awarded. The Department then withdrew its earlier offer. 'My Lords,' its letter ran, 'are not prepared to offer any special grants for deaf and dumb children till the Royal Commission inquiring into the education of such children have reported.'[2] The Commission favoured neither the Department's nor the Board's solution. Grants should be given automatically to special classes for the deaf. Equally, the School

---

[1] The change was well under way even before the Royal Commission reported. In the School Board classes in 1888, 507 children were taught by the oral method, 22 by the manual and 48 by the combined. At the institutions, 980 children were being taught orally, 1,004 by the manual method and 497 by the combined.

[2] The whole of the correspondence is reproduced in Vol. 1 of the Commission's *Report*, p. 53.

Boards should be authorized to pay the fees of children they sent to any institutions which had been certified by the Department as suitable for the reception of deaf children. All the children would have to be educated in separate schools or classes. There was no suggestion, as there had been in the case of the blind, that they could be taught in the ordinary classes. Consequently, most of the deaf would have to go to institutions. Only in favourable circumstances, in large towns, would it be possible to establish day schools. However, School Boards should consider the feasibility of boarding out in private houses some of the children they sent to institutions.

As had been recommended for the blind, compulsory education should extend until sixteen. But the reasons for the recommendation were different. In the case of the blind, it was necessary in order that they might be given industrial training. Such training need not be given to the deaf, although there should be an emphasis on drawing, as this was an essential part of the occupations for which they were best fitted: artists, draughtsmen, engravers and sculptors.[1] But the deaf needed to be educated until sixteen in order to complete eight years of schooling, for the Commissioners believed that they need not attend school until they were seven. Systematic teaching of language, they argued, could not begin with deaf children below that age, 'since they are not so forward then as other children of 4 or 5'. Hence, compulsory education of the deaf should be from seven to sixteen. This was muddled thinking. The sooner a deaf child starts to learn speech, the sooner he acquires it, and the less is the degree of his retardation. Nevertheless, the fact that compulsory education was advocated was a considerable advance, and, although based on a false premise, the recommendation to raise the school-leaving age was also to be welcomed.

Welcome suggestions were made, too, regarding the size of classes. In oral schools there should be one teacher to every eight children, and one to every fourteen in schools using the manual system. Evidence was placed before the Commission which showed that the children of congenitally deaf parents were frequently congenitally deaf themselves. It was therefore recommended that boys and girls should be educated separately in order that the chances of intermarriage might be lessened. Not only should the sexes be educated separately, but it was also undesirable that the blind and

[1] In support of this contention the Department quoted figures that showed that fifty-one per cent of deaf children who sat the examinations of the Science and Art Department were successful, as opposed to forty-seven per cent of those from ordinary schools.

deaf should be educated together. Those who were both blind and deaf should be taught in schools for the former. There were also children with residual speech or hearing who required special attention. If they were in schools which used the manual system, they should be taught orally in separate classes, and not mixed with the other children as was then the case.

The Commissioners found a lack of both good teachers and good teaching in schools for the deaf. This they attributed partly to the low salaries compared with those received by the teachers in the ordinary schools, and partly to the inadequacy of the training colleges at Fitzroy Square and Ealing. Absence of State aid prevented the existing schools from paying salaries which would induce good men teachers to come forward, and the women teachers 'are seldom such as would obtain good appointments in schools for the hearing'.[1] Major-General F. J. Moberly, Chairman of the Sub-Committee for the education of the blind and deaf under the London School Board, enlarged upon this: 'None of our teachers who think themselves capable of any ordinary elementary teaching have taken to teaching these defective classes.'[2] To the Commissioners the remedy was obvious. Teachers of the deaf should be paid higher salaries, salaries higher even than those received by teachers of hearing children. Institutions should be aided so that they could meet the increased salary bill. Training colleges for teachers of the deaf should be under Government supervision, and should receive a bigger subsidy than that given to the ordinary colleges. Finally, students entering such colleges should already be qualified teachers.

Having dealt with the blind and the deaf, the Commissioners turned their attention to the third class mentioned in their terms of reference—those requiring, from special circumstances, exceptional methods of education. They considered that this class contained not only the feeble-minded but also idiots and imbeciles. Their first difficulty was to define terms. They had little to go by, and none of their witnesses could frame an adequate definition. Eventually, they decided that the difference between an idiot and an imbecile was one of degree not of kind; that 'idiocy means a greater deficiency of intellect, and imbecility means a lesser degree of such deficiency'.[3] Of the imbeciles, there were some, though it was not known how many, who required special educational arrangements to develop such faculties as they had. With considerable insight the Commissioners

---

[1] *R.C.B.D.*, Vol. 1, p. 77.
[2] *Ibid.*, Vol. 3, p. 871, Evidence of Moberly, 17.7.1888.
[3] *Ibid.*, Vol. 1, p. 95.

suggested the form that these arrangements might take.[1] Although education was possible, the ordinary means of giving it would be quite unsuitable. Some of the children might eventually aspire to the three R's, but of greater importance were the essential preliminaries, sense and muscle training. There should be much physical activity designed to correct the low vitality and generally poor physical condition of the children. In the classroom itself, emphasis would be laid on the improvement of speech and the perceptive faculties, while simple manual exercises would be used to overcome imperfections in muscular co-ordination.

Imbeciles could not be educated in a special class in the ordinary school because there were too few of them to form a class, and the vast majority would require residential training. Their teachers, however, should be drawn from the ordinary schools, since the Commissioners felt that it was necessary 'to be a good teacher of ordinary children to be a good teacher of imbecile children'.[2] On the application of parents, school authorities would be responsible for ensuring the admission of educable imbecile children to institutions, and contributing towards their education, as in the case of the blind and the deaf. On no account should they be allowed to remain in workhouses or lunatic asylums. Where there were insufficient institutions for their reception, local authorities were to be empowered jointly or severally to establish them.[3] Their education should be continued, if necessary, until they were twenty-one, and every effort should be made in the institutions to ensure that the educable imbeciles were separated from those of lower grade.

All this was most enlightened. The application of the term educable to imbecile children, the suggestion that their education should come within the purview of the school authorities, and the recommendation that they should be taught by fully trained teachers, were all ahead of the practice of the time. For that matter they were ahead of the practice today. Children excluded from school are still too frequently termed ineducable; responsibility for their education lies with the local health rather than the local education authority; their

---

[1] For much of their wisdom the Commissioners were indebted to the evidence of G. E. Shuttleworth, Medical Superintendent of the Royal Albert Asylum, Lancaster, who was an assiduous worker on behalf of the mentally handicapped. He was one of the first to advocate the establishment of auxiliary classes for feeble-minded children. See Shuttleworth, 'The Health and Physical Development of Idiots' in *Health Exhibition Literature* (1884), Vol. XI, pp. 526–33, Shuttleworth, 'The Education of Children of Abnormally Weak Mental Capacity' in *The Journal of Mental Science*, Vol. XXXIV, No. 145, 1888, pp. 80–4 and *Proceedings of Conference on Education under Healthy Conditions* (1885), pp. 217–19.

[2] *R.C.B.D.*, Vol. 1, p. 100.

[3] County Councils had been formed under the Local Government Act, 1888.

teachers, admirable though they are, have neither the qualifications nor the salary of ordinary teachers.

Regarding the feeble-minded, the Commissioners had rather less to say. Although the Cross Commission had suggested that their education should be considered by the Egerton Commission, it was felt that only those children who were excluded from the operation of the Education Acts fell within their terms of reference. Since feeble-minded children were not so excluded, the Commission did little more than repeat Shuttleworth's view that they should be educated in auxiliary schools. Its one firm recommendation was that feeble-minded children should be separated from ordinary children, so that they might be given special instruction. What form the instruction was to take, and where it was to be given, they did not specify. They merely suggested that the attention of school authorities should be particularly directed towards their recommendation.

When the Commission's *Report* was published in 1889, it was well received by those most immediately concerned. Headmasters and representatives of governing bodies and School Boards concerned with the education of the deaf met at Manchester Town Hall, under the chairmanship of Lord Egerton. They approved many of the Commission's recommendations, urged that the establishment of a training college for teachers of the deaf should be treated as of paramount importance, and appointed a deputation to wait upon the Lord President of the Council. Viscount Cranbrook received them on the last day of November 1889. To the Memorial that they presented he attached a memorandum. It read: 'Education of Blind, Deaf and Dumb. Let a Bill be drafted for consideration on the lines of the Resolutions annexed so far as legislation is needed to carry them into effect.'[1] On the same day representatives of institutions for the blind met at the Society of Arts with Lyon Playfair in the chair. While not agreeing with everything in the *Report*, they nevertheless called upon the Government to take immediate action to implement its recommendations.[2]

Implementation of recommendations depends not only upon members of the Government, but also upon the permanent officials in Whitehall. It was perhaps fortunate that in 1890 George Kekewich became Secretary to the Education Department. This far-sighted man had the interests of the handicapped at heart. When he received from the Treasury Counsel the draft of the proposed Blind and Deaf Bill, he was dissatisfied. The object of the measure, he felt, should be twofold. First, the blind and the deaf should be compelled to attend school. Secondly, school authorities should make provision

[1] Ministry of Education Archives, Education Class 31, Piece 8. [2] *Ibid.*

for them to do so. But the Bill, as drawn, failed, in that it made provision permissive not compulsory, and, consequently, attendance would only be compelled where provision had been made. Moreover, the first clause in the draft dealt with payments which the school authority could make for the education of a child. 'But,' wrote Kekewich, 'the keynote of the Bill is the compulsion to attend school. Therefore I should suggest that it be placed first.'[1] And first it was placed.

Since the recommendations of the Royal Commission had applied to Scotland, as much as to England and Wales, the Marquis of Lothian in May 1890 introduced the Education of Blind and Deaf Mute Children (Scotland) Bill. It met no opposition in the Lords, and was given its First Reading in the Commons in July. Some slight amendments were agreed to, and it received the Royal Assent four days before the Session ended on August 18th. However, no equivalent Bill for England and Wales was introduced in May, although this had been the Government's expressed intention.[2] Irked by the delay, Egerton, Playfair and Mundella questioned the Government. In June the answer came. 'It will be introduced as soon as certain questions of some difficulty that have risen in connection with it are disposed of.'[3] What the difficult questions were was not revealed. The Bill was eventually presented for its First Reading in July. At the Second Reading the difficult question came to light. 'The expense necessary,' said Cranbrook, 'for the education of the blind and deaf is necessarily on a very different scale to that which is necessary in the case of ordinary children. Therefore there has been some difficulty in England in endeavouring to frame a measure to deal with that point.'[4] It was, therefore, the financial aspects of the Bill that had caused difficulty, and these were to continue to impede its progress. While it was unfortunate that monetary considerations should appear to be of such importance in a measure designed to assist the handicapped, this was perhaps inevitable in view of the Royal Commission's emphasis on the economic advantages of educating them.

Although the Bill passed through its stages in the Lords, it reached the Commons too late, and the 1890 Session ended before it could be debated. Before the Bill was re-introduced in 1891, the Government was memorialized by a number of interested bodies. The headmasters of schools for the deaf and dumb, meeting at Doncaster, protested against the fact that education was made compulsory only

---

[1] Ministry of Education Archives, Education Class 24, Piece 3.
[2] *Hansard*, 21.2.1890, cols. 893–4.   [3] *Ibid.*, 12.6.1890, col. 701.
[4] *Ibid.*, 10.7.1890, cols. 1255–6.

to fourteen, and permissive from fourteen to sixteen. The Local Government Board objected to the intention to repeal the powers of the Boards of Guardians in respect of the education of the blind and deaf. The anti-sectarian National Education Association had strong comment to make:

'The Bill endows from the rates, to an indefinite extent, privately managed denominational institutions,without any control by the representatives of the ratepayers. . . . It stimulates sectarianism, by giving preference to ecclesiastical organizations in the establishment and maintenance of these institutions at public cost. . . . While imposing on public bodies the obligation to support these schools, it does not give them the right to demand admission for any child they may wish to send to them. . . . In short the Bill contains proposals of a highly controversial and reactionary character, of no educational advantage.'[1]

This was hardly fair comment. Scarcely fairer was the criticism advanced in the Lords by Lord Norton during the Second Reading in the 1891 Session. His objections were financial. First, by giving the blind industrial training, tradesmen would be getting apprentices trained at the public expense. Secondly, parents were to be asked to pay no more for the education of a blind or deaf child than for education in an ordinary school. 'It is a great affliction, of course,' he stated, 'to have a blind or deaf child, but you are not in consequence of that to make the unfortunate ratepayers pay more for its education. It is introducing a pauper principle if you only charge the ordinary fee to cover the much greater expense of education at one of these special schools.'[2] Egerton supported the recommendation of the Commission, and gave the obvious answer: 'Parents should not be taxed in any way because they happen to have children suffering under these infirmities of blindness and deafness.'[3] Norton's amendment was negatived.

In his turn, Egerton moved an amendment. He claimed that compulsory education to sixteen, and not fourteen as was in the Bill, was necessary if the children were to finish their education. Cranbrook, the Lord President, replied for the Government: 'I do not say that they will have received by that time [14] a thoroughly finished education, but that is not the duty of the State. If it were the duty of the State to turn out, so to speak, a thoroughly finished article, then all children would have to be kept in training until they were perfectly fitted for their position in life. We do not do that.'[4]

---

[1] Ministry of Education Archives, Education Class 31, Piece 8.
[2] *Hansard*, 16.2.1891, col. 654.   [3] *Ibid.*, 16.2.1891, col. 657.
[4] *Ibid.*, 16.2.1891, col. 661.

This thoroughly specious argument carried the day, though the Bill was subsequently to be amended in Committee to raise the compulsory age to sixteen.

As in the previous year, the Bill reached the Commons shortly before the end of the Session, and it was allowed to lapse. Reintroduced in 1892, it passed the Lords without debate. Its downfall this time came because Salisbury chose to ask for a dissolution, and was subsequently defeated at the polls. In 1893 the Bill was introduced for the fourth time. Ably steered through the Commons by Arthur Acland, the new Vice-President of the Education Department in Gladstone's Liberal Administration, it soon reached its final stages. There was still time, however, for a last protest. Despite the fact that it was now a Liberal measure, one of the members of that Party, Carvell Williams, could not forbear to point out that 'it embodies a principle to which all Liberals should be strenuously opposed—namely, the granting of money out of public rates for the support of privately-managed denominational institutions'.[1] Since, however, the case was exceptional, it should not be regarded as a precedent, and he would not, therefore, oppose the Bill. Together, finance and religion had conspired to delay its passage. On September 12th, 1893, over three years after it was first introduced, the Bill received the Royal Assent.

There was much to commend in the Elementary Education (Blind and Deaf Children) Act. It laid squarely upon school authorities the duty of enabling blind and deaf children 'for whose elementary education efficient and suitable provision is not otherwise made, to obtain such education in some school for the time being certified by the Education Department'.[2] For that purpose the authorities could either establish a school of their own or contribute towards an existing one. In any case, they were responsible for both the education and maintenance of the children. Blind children were to receive such education from the age of five to sixteen, deaf from seven to sixteen. To qualify for recognition by the Education Department, an institution would have to be open to inspection by Her Majesty's Inspectors. In return for this indignity, certified schools would be paid a Parliamentary grant, at the rate of £5 5s. annually for every child. This figure was smaller than that recommended by the Egerton Commission, and much smaller than the actual cost to the authority concerned.

The position, therefore, was that if a school authority educated a child in one of its own schools, it would receive the grant. On the other hand, if it sent the child to an institution, not only would the

[1] *Hansard*, 24.7.1893, col. 408.   [2] 56 and 57 Victoria, c. 42, s. 2.

grant be paid to the institution, and so be lost to the authority, but the authority would also be responsible for paying to the institution the difference between the amount of the grant and the actual cost of education and maintenance. The result was that many of the poorer and less progressive authorities, especially those in rural areas, became only too ready to acquiesce in the wishes of parents that their child should not be sent to an institution. This in itself would not have been heinous. What made it so, was when the authorities neglected to make adequate provision themselves for such a child. The question of the grants continued to present problems for many years to come. As the cost of education increased, so the amount of the grant rose. By 1919 it was £16 10s. In that year a change occurred. No longer would an institution receive a grant in respect of a pupil sent to it by a local education authority. Rather, the authority would pay the whole cost, and be re-imbursed for half the amount by the Board of Education. However, a grant would still be made in respect of those pupils at the institutions who were not sent by a local education authority.

In the main, however, the Act produced good results. Whereas, prior to 1894, only children in the large cities, and those who could secure election or pay to go to an institution were educated, after that date almost all blind and deaf children were sent to school. The exceptions were the few children referred to above, and some of the younger blind children, since attendance officers were loth to compel the seemingly helpless five-year-olds to go to school. Moreover, the children received education as of right, and not as a matter of charity as previously. The greater part of the extra places were found by enlarging existing schools, and with far more young children in the institutions, the difficulties of teaching increased. In addition, now that almost all blind and deaf children were entitled to be educated, the institutions could no longer select for admission the most promising children. Consequently, for a few years after 1894 the standard of attainment in the schools fell. Governmental inspection, however, soon reversed this tendency, for many improvements were wrought in the institutions, and, with the higher salaries it was now possible to pay, the schools were able to secure the services of better teachers.

It has been mentioned that most of the children who were now being educated for the first time were catered for by the institutions. Very few new schools were opened. London and some of the larger industrial towns in the North opened day schools. Only one School Board, Leeds, opened a residential school, and this, against the advice of the Royal Commission, was for both blind and deaf children. Part of the difficulty, of course, lay in the fact that the Education Acts of 1870 and 1876 had created a multiplicity of small school authorities—School Boards and School Attendance Committees.[1] Some of the School Boards, those representing the county boroughs, were prosperous, powerful and progressive. On the other hand, a Board could be so tiny that the parish it represented could 'hardly furnish five members competent to join a Board'.[2] It was out of the question to expect such a Board itself to provide for a handicapped child. It was, of course, open to it to join with others in making provision. But a large number of small school authorities would be needed before there would be sufficient children to warrant the establishment of a residential school. Five School Boards in North Staffordshire did, in fact, combine to open a school. Even then the school had to be for both blind and deaf children.[3]

Commendable efforts were made by some small school authorities. The School Attendance Committee for North Bierley, Yorkshire, provided a special class in a hired room for four blind children. Wellington, Somerset, School Board went one better and established a class for only three blind children.[4] These were exceptional cases. All too frequently small authorities evaded their responsibilities. Only when the 1902 Act changed the basis of local educational administration were the children in the smaller towns and rural areas provided for adequately.

The Education Act of 1902 brought a further benefit to the blind. It had been recommended by the Egerton Commission that school authorities should give grants to the blind even after the age of sixteen, either to assist them in establishing themselves in a trade or to complete their technical training. In view of the opposition which the extension of the school-leaving age to sixteen had aroused, it was hardly to be expected that the 1893 Blind and Deaf Act would have included any reference to grants beyond that age. But the 137 counties and county boroughs which now became local education authorities, L.E.A.s,[5] were required by the 1902 Act to supply not only elementary education but also, in the wonderful language of the Act, 'education other than elementary'. Technical training of both blind and deaf was included in this wide definition, and the training departments of a number of institutions for the blind were certified

---

[1] At their abolition in 1902 there were over 2,500 of them.
[2] *Report of Committee of Council on Education, 1875–1876*, p. 289.
[3] *Report of Committee of Council on Education on Schools for the Blind and Deaf, 1896–1897*, p. 5.
[4] *C.D.E.C.*, Vol. 2, Evidence of H. F. Pooley.
[5] There were also 191 boroughs and urban districts which became L.E.A.s. Their responsibility extended only to elementary education.

by the Board of Education (as, in 1899, the Education Department had become) as day technical classes for those aged over sixteen.

The definition also would, and did, permit the establishment of training colleges and grammar schools. Attention had been drawn by the Egerton Commission to the need of these for the blind and deaf. A few deaf boys were being given secondary education at Northampton under Arnold. Worcester College prepared some of the blind for the Universities. But neither school was completely a public venture; neither could expect immediate aid from the State; neither had been recommended for it by the Commission. Consequently, both charged high fees. Both, too, were for boys only. There was, therefore, room for a mixed grammar school for the blind, and another for the deaf. Which of the 137 L.E.A.s with the power to do so would establish one? Not one of them could fairly be expected to take the lead; not one of them had sufficient suitable children to fill a class; not many of them felt the need to be urgent. Much the same arguments could be advanced in the case of training colleges for teachers of the blind and deaf. Ealing and Fitzroy Square existed, but they had been severely criticized by the Commission. The Royal Normal College at Norwood had been praised, but it trained blind teachers, not teachers of the blind. Again, no L.E.A. would take the initiative. As far as some aspects of special education were concerned, there were still too many authorities.

The Act giving State aid to institutions for the blind and deaf was passed almost exactly a century after the first public blind and deaf schools had opened their doors. During that time the institutions did valiant work. As their number increased, more and more children received education, and when the Government did eventually intervene, well over half of all blind and deaf children were being educated at the twenty deaf and twenty-four blind institutions in England and Wales. Braille on the one hand, oralism on the other, were becoming ever more widely adopted. Gradually the ground that had been lost in the disputes over types and methods was regained. On the matter of oralism, however, the Education Department still refused to commit itself, as witness an extract from one of its last reports:

'The oral system has been adopted in nearly all the schools for the deaf, but inasmuch as eight years' continuous and skilful instruction is generally required to enable the scholars to attain efficient command of oral speech, no trustworthy estimate of the success of the method in this country can yet be formed; and certainly there is no reason to give up the attempt as hopeless.'[1]

[1] *Report of the Committee of Council on Education on Schools for the Blind and Deaf, 1898–1899*, p. 13.

113

Strange that by 1899 there was no trustworthy estimate of the value of oralism, when ten years earlier half the deaf pupils were being taught by it. Confronted with such an argument, the Department would probably have replied that they were not necessarily receiving skilful instruction. This, of course, was the important point, as skilful instruction by the oral method entailed, among other things, tuition by the oral method only. This was far from being the case. Most of the children taught orally used or understood the manual alphabet, but since the latter was not officially taught, the system was known as the oral, not the combined.

10

THE PERIOD OF STATE INTERVENTION: II. SCHOOL BOARD CLASSES FOR THE MENTALLY HANDICAPPED

WHEN, in 1899, the Royal Commission on the Blind and Deaf made its recommendations concerning the mentally handicapped, a number of feeble-minded children were already receiving education of one form or another. Some were being taught in the ordinary schools, others in the idiot asylums or at Darenth. But from an educational point of view they were not recognized as feeble-minded. Those at the elementary schools were treated as normal children, those at Darenth and the asylums as imbeciles.

The first official provision for them was made in Prussia when, in 1867, Dresden established a day auxiliary school. Other German towns, including Elberfeld, which became a model for English day special schools, followed suit. In 1880, Von Gossler, the German Minister of Education, impressed by the success of the schools, called upon all towns with a population of over 20,000 to open an auxiliary school. By 1894 there were thirty-two such schools with nearly 2,500 children. Similar schools had also opened in Austria, Switzerland, Denmark and Norway.[1] The German auxiliary schools were for children who, having spent at least two years in the ordinary schools, had failed to be promoted. Such children, who would not, therefore, in two years have completed the work normally done in one year, were examined by a panel consisting of the head teachers of the ordinary school and the special school and a doctor. They would not be

---

[1] *Special Reports on Educational Subjects* (1898), Vol. 3, pp. 695–700.

admitted if they suffered from a severe bodily infirmity, nor if their mental capacity was too low. Ideally the children would be 'the intellectually weak ones, who, though in possession of the organic five senses, were poorly endowed in perception, memory and reason'.[1]

Although education in Germany was compulsory, attendance at the auxiliary schools was voluntary. Nevertheless, such was the esteem in which the schools were held that they all had waiting lists. When a new school was built at Hanover in 1892, there were sixty applications from parents even before it was open. The school at Elberfeld was so successful that wealthy parents sent their children there, and its prestige became even higher.[2] The schools aimed at training the children 'to useful activity, mannerly living and elevated enjoyments',[3] and to this end they had a free hand in planning their time-tables. In general, however, lessons were of twenty minutes duration, and were 'frequently diversified by the introduction of a song or drill'.[4] There was much concentration on manual work, and many of Froebel's exercises were employed, particularly those that assisted in cultivating the senses. Children entered at the age of eight, they could not enter earlier because of the necessity of spending two years in the ordinary school, and left at sixteen when the majority of them were successful in obtaining employment. If England was to be late in providing for her feeble-minded children, she was at least fortunate to have such an excellent model to copy.

The Education Acts of 1870, 1876 and 1880 brought universal, compulsory education to England. They also brought to the schools a larger number of dull children, and others, who, though not dull, had equal difficulty in learning. These children clogged the lower classes of the schools. Children of ten years of age and upwards should have been in Standard IV or higher, yet in 1880 only forty-seven per cent of such children were in the upper standards. Since dull children could gain exemption and leave at the legal minimum age by good attendance over five years, many of them left school without passing beyond or even into Standard III.

As more and more of them congregated at the lower ends of the schools, the device was sometimes attempted of establishing a Standard O. Here, since a qualified teacher could rarely be spared, the children were put in the charge of a pupil teacher. In fact, the

---

[1] Klemm, *European Schools* (1891), p. 78.

[2] In order to avoid any stigma the name of the school was changed from school for feeble-minded children to *hilfs-schule*, help-school, a title which all the schools eventually adopted.

[3] Shuttleworth, 'The Education of Children of Abnormally Weak Mental Capacity', *The Journal of Mental Science*, Vol. 34, No. 145, April 1888, p. 80.

[4] *C.D.E.C.*, Vol. 2, p. 132, Evidence of Miss M. Hodge, 5.3.1897.

II. School Board Classes for the Mentally Handicapped

Standard O was frequently conducted in part of the Standard I classroom. In the Standard O the feeble-minded were joined by physically handicapped, partially sighted and delicate children, and sometimes, even imbeciles.[1] Their ages varied from eight to thirteen. Together they stagnated. Where no Standard O was formed, a similar group of children would be found in Standard I. Dr. F. D. Harris, a Medical Officer to the London School Board, reported that almost every London school had seventy children in the Standard I. Of these, some twenty-five were almost entirely ignorant. The result was that the teacher concentrated on the brighter children and ignored the twenty-five, who, learning nothing, either misbehaved or became truants.[2] This, then, was the problem that confronted the larger School Boards. In rural areas, of course, the problem was nothing like as acute.

In May 1884 the International Health Exhibition opened in London. At it, papers on the special needs of feeble-minded children were read by G. E. Shuttleworth, Medical Superintendent at the Royal Albert Asylum, and Fletcher Beach, Medical Superintendent at Darenth.[3] In the following year Shuttleworth again read a paper, which was of far greater import as far as special education was concerned. In it he suggested that it would be advisable to establish in all large towns, for children who because of 'physical or mental abnormality were unable to meet the requirements of the Code',[4] either a central school or special school departments, where the children could be taught by special methods. He would not call such a school a school for backward children or a school for imbeciles, but something like a sanatorial gymnasium (this was very like the *hilfs-schule*), where the time-table and the regime could be adapted to the needs of the children.[5]

Shuttleworth followed this up with an article in *The Journal of Mental Science*. After praising the auxiliary schools in Germany and Norway, he repeated his appeal for the establishment of special schools in England. He realized that the expense of such schools would be high since the teaching, to be effective, must be individual,

---

[1] In 1888 there were twenty 'educable idiots' attending the London Board schools. *R.C.B.D.*, Vol. 3, Evidence of Moberly, 17.7.1888. In one class, not a Standard O, in a London school in 1885 there were two paralysed children, one idiot who was unable to walk, eight so delicate that they were constantly attending hospital, and fifteen who could not see the blackboard from the back row of the class. *Second Report of the Royal Commission on the Elementary Education Acts* (1887), Evidence of Mrs. E. M. Burgwin, 24.11.1886.

[2] *C.D.E.C.*, Vol. 2, Evidence of Harris, 17.2.1897.

[3] *The Health Exhibition Literature*, Vol. XI, pp. 526–33 and pp. 534–45.

[4] *Proceedings of Conference on Education under Healthy Conditions* (1885), p. 219.

[5] *Ibid.*, pp. 217–19.

and to be good, must be given by well-trained teachers who must be well paid. But what poor Norway could do, surely wealthy England could afford. In any case it might in the long run be economical in view of the 'remunerative industry of restored pupils'. But he avoids too much emphasis on the financial justification, and thoroughly redeems himself by ending that apart from this, it was a Christian duty to do the best for them.[1]

In the same year, 1888, Francis Warner, consultant paediatrician to a number of children's hospitals in London, advocated the same course to the Egerton Commission. Warner was convinced that there were far more children requiring education in a special school than any of the school authorities imagined.[2] He set out to find how many. The Royal Society and the British Association backed his work, the Charity Organization Society promised to publish his results. Warner felt that there was a close correlation between physical and mental defects. He was, therefore, of the opinion that weak-minded children could be detected purely by physical indications. By 1890 he had examined 50,000 children in London's Board and Poor Law schools. One per cent, he found, had physical or nervous defects, and, in addition, were reported by their teachers to be of very low intelligence. All these children, Warner maintained, demanded special education in separate schools. Copies of the report were sent to the London School Board and the Local Government Board.[3]

The Charity Organization Society did not immediately publish Warner's results, for that body had in 1890 appointed a Sub-Committee to recommend upon the educational needs of feeble-minded children. The Sub-Committee reported in 1892, and its views, together with the results of Warner's survey, were published by the Society. Warner's contention that a large number of children required special education was warmly supported. The education should be given in separate special schools which it should be the duty of the School Boards, as opposed to voluntary organizations, to establish. Moreover, if circumstances dictated that a child required residential care, it was again the duty of the School Board to provide for its maintenance. As matters stood at the time, payment for maintenance could only be made by the Guardians, and that at the cost of the pauperization of the parents.[4]

The tide was now running strongly in favour of special schools for the feeble-minded. For, in addition to Shuttleworth's advocacy,

[1] Shuttleworth, 'The Education of Children of Abnormally Weak Mental Capacity', *The Journal of Mental Science*, Vol. 34, No. 145, April 1888, pp. 80–4.
[2] *R.C.B.D.*, Vol. 3, Evidence of Warner, 7.2.1888.
[3] *C.D.E.C.*, Vol. 2, Evidence of Warner, 12.2.1897.
[4] Charity Organization Society, *The Feeble-minded Child and Adult* (1893).

II. School Board Classes for the Mentally Handicapped

Warner's investigation and the Charity Organization Society's report, the Egerton Commission itself had recommended that School Boards should separate feeble-minded from ordinary children. It was, therefore, natural that, even without a directive from the Education Department, some of the more progressive School Boards should be thinking in terms of forming special schools or classes. Nor must it be thought that the School Boards were acting entirely under external pressure. Certainly this was not the case in the London School Board. Major-General Moberly, who, since his retirement from the Army in 1880, had devoted much of his time to working among London's poor, had in 1887 become Chairman of the Board's Sub-Committee on the education of the blind and deaf. Since he was also a member of a Board of Guardians, and secretary of a branch of the Charity Organization Society, he was fully conversant with the problem of the education of the mentally handicapped. Before the Egerton Commission reported, he had felt the need for special schools. 'I was aroused to the idea generally that we were responsible for all the children of London,' he later told the Committee on Defective and Epileptic Children.[1] Without special schools, that responsibility could not be fulfilled, for although there were many feeble-minded children in the elementary schools, there were many more excused school as being permanently disabled.

He was confirmed in this view when he found a girl, apparently an imbecile, at Harrow Road school. She was learning nothing there, and he sought to have her admitted to Darenth. The Medical Officer of the Board of Guardians refused to certify her, and since it was useless returning her to Harrow Road, Moberly had her sent to a private school where she improved greatly in a short time. It was, therefore, clear that even if the School Board ensured that all their feeble-minded children attended school, the Board would still not be fulfilling their responsibility. What they had to ensure was that the children attended the right kind of school. They could only do this by establishing special schools. Moberly, therefore, in 1890 persuaded the Board's School Management Committee to accept a motion to establish a special school. The Committee soon regretted its decision and dropped the project 'very quickly'.[2]

Moberly, however, persevered. On December 18th, 1890 the School Board resolved 'that the School Management Committee be instructed to prepare a scheme by which special instruction may be provided in separate schools or classes, for those children who, by reason of physical or mental defects, cannot be properly taught in the

[1] C.D.E.C., Vol. 2, p. 101, Evidence of Moberly, 3.3.1897.
[2] Ibid.

ordinary standards or by ordinary methods'.[1] L. R. Klemm published at this moment his *European Schools* in which he described a number of notable schools which he had visited. Among them was the *hilfs-schule* at Elberfeld. In preparing their scheme, the School Management Committee drew extensively on Klemm's account of the Elberfeld school. In March 1891 the School Board approved their Committee's scheme and the following resolutions.[2]

As an experiment three special schools were to be established in the first instance in the poorest districts containing a large number of schools. These schools should be called Schools for Special Instruction. They should contain sufficient rooms for the children 'to be properly classified, in order to meet their individual capacity for mental development, so that they may ere long be enabled to assume their places in the ordinary schools'. There should not be more than thirty children to one teacher. An extended Kindergarten system was the most likely to succeed, 'a free hand being allowed to each teacher to obtain the principal object—the opening of the mind of the pupil'. In general the schools would be staffed by women, although men might occasionally be required for the more advanced manual work. Children deemed suitable for admission were to be nominated by the head teachers of ordinary schools 'as intellectually weak, poorly endowed with perception, memory, reasoning, etc.',[3] and before admission examined by a committee composed of one of the Board's inspectors, the Board's Medical Officer and the head teacher of the special school. The final resolution was that the attention of the Education Department should be directed to the recommendations of the Royal Commission on the Blind and Deaf concerning the education of feeble-minded children. One would have supposed that it would have been the Department's duty to draw the Board's attention to such a matter, and not vice versa. Certainly the impression is given that the Department would have been perfectly content if no School Board had taken action to implement the recommendation of the Egerton Commission.

The Board's resolution was passed to the Department with a request in the covering letter that provision be made in the Code for recognizing schools of special instruction, and 'providing that any course of instruction may be followed which is reported at the end of the 1st and each succeeding year by the Chief Inspector to be for the children's advantage'. This was a revolutionary suggestion and a

[1] Public Record Office, Education Class 14, Piece 43.

[2] The Committee's scheme, the resolutions and the resulting correspondence between the Board and the Education Department are to be found in Education Class 14, Piece 43 at the Public Record Office.

[3] This phrase was taken direct from Klemm, *European Schools*, p. 78.

far cry from payments by results. It was also extremely sound educational policy. But the Department was tied to its past. Would the children, its letter asked, 'be taught according to the Standards and would the curriculum include the three branches of instruction for Infants given in Article 98 of the Code?' Almost disdainfully the reply came: 'The Board do not deem it desirable that they should be under an obligation to follow any definite curriculum for these special schools.' They did, however, suggest a conference between the Rev. T. W. Sharpe, Her Majesty's Chief Inspector, and a committee of the Board concerning the general lines of the scheme of instruction. To its credit the Department broke with its past, and in July sanctioned the establishment of three schools of special instruction.

In October the School Board made its first appointment, which was also the first in the country, in connection with the education of feeble-minded children. Mrs. E. M. Burgwin, a teacher for twenty-seven years, was appointed Superintendent in charge of the organization of the special schools. Shortly afterwards she visited the German schools upon whose organization the School Board had already extensively drawn.[1] It was intended that she should return in time to open the first school in the following summer.

In the event, it was not in London, but in Leicester, that the first school opened. Two differing accounts of the steps leading to its establishment exist. Francis Warner claimed that the movement for the education of the feeble-minded in Leicester started with one boy. Ellis, Chairman of the School Board, became interested in the boy, who could neither be sent to an asylum because no doctor would certify him as an imbecile, nor on the other hand be kept at the ordinary school, where he was most troublesome and would not learn.[2] The boy was taken to London to be seen by Warner. 'I,' testified Warner before the Committee on Defective and Epileptic Children, 'gave a report on him, and said that it would be well to look for other cases in the town.'[3] The other account was given by Major, the Leicester School Board Inspector. He asserted that he became aware of the existence of a number of feeble-minded children in the schools, and requested the Board to take up the matter. Teachers were asked to send to his office children suitable for a special school. Four hundred were sent, and seen by a panel of five members of the Board who reduced the number to twelve. A classroom at Milton

---

[1] Public Record Office, Education Class 14, Piece 43.
[2] The case is similar to the one which impelled Moberly to action in the London School Board.
[3] *C.D.E.C.*, Vol. 2, Evidence of Warner, 12.2.1897.

Street Board School was made available, and at Easter 1892 these twelve feeble-minded, Leicester children became the first in Great Britain for whom special provision was made.[1] The two accounts are not incompatible. One thing, however, is definite. There was very little previous planning, no advice was taken from abroad, and there was no protracted correspondence with the Education Department. Indeed, it is very doubtful whether the Department knew of the existence of the class for the first few years. The first reference to it in the files of the Department occurs in 1895, when the School Board was authorized to treat the children in the special class as infants for grant earning purposes.[2]

Whether or no the class was official at the outset, it was certainly successful. Initial opposition from parents was overcome so effectively that five of them moved house to be nearer the school. In order to avoid giving offence to parents, the class, for it was little more than a class for the first few years, was called simply the special class. Its hours approximated to those of the ordinary school, save that the children attended for only four and a half instead of five hours. The lessons, however, were very much shorter in length, and there was a great deal more manual and industrial work than in the ordinary school. There was a great deal less reading. Only one and a half hours were devoted to it each week. The progress of the children in this aspect of education was not very marked. When they left at the age of fourteen, some, but not all, could read the simplest book, the Standard I book, while the best could only read the Standard III book. This is not to criticize the class. On the contrary, the children, long inured to failure in the ordinary school, would require activities far removed from reading to assist them in regaining their confidence. They would also need sense training exercises to prepare them for reading. In any case, since the children in the class were all of extremely low intelligence, for a fourteen-year-old child to read a book designed for a nine-year-old would be quite an achievement. It would certainly be far in excess of anything he would have achieved in the ordinary school.

Major agreed that the children in the special class were probably of a lower grade than those in the London special schools. 'We say in Leicester,' he continued, 'that in London the child is sent away, and not taken care of by the Board, but that the Leicester Board does take care of him. The London Board deals with him in another direction.'[3] The direction which Major had in mind was Darenth, where,

---

[1] *C.D.E.C.*, Vol. 2, Evidence of H. Major, 10.3.1897.
[2] Ministry of Education Archives, Education Class 32, Piece 69.
[3] *C.D.E.C.*, Vol. 2, Evidence of Major.

II. School Board Classes for the Mentally Handicapped

as has been seen, there were a certain number of feeble-minded children who might well have been at a special school. On the other hand, there was no Darenth at Leicester, and there were undoubtedly some children in the special class who would have been better placed in a school for educable imbeciles, had one existed.

Selection of children for admission to the Milton Street class was made by Major alone. Any child aged six or over who might be considered suitable for the special class was referred to him. If the child was at the ordinary school, he was referred by the teacher; if at home, by the school attendance officer. Major examined each child from a reading book, not to see if the child could read, but whether he could interpret pictures and answer social questions relevant to his environment.[1] Here was a rudimentary intelligence test. Its importance lies in the fact that it was given not by a doctor but an educationist. The admission procedure of the first special class in England was based on educational criteria, and no medical officer had any say in it whatsoever.

Before the establishment of the Milton Street school, Leicester had depended upon the Standard O system. When, under the admission procedure to the special class, Major started seeing most of the slow learning children, he was in a position to control the size of the Standard O's. This he did in two ways. He retained in the infants' school for an extra year all those of low intellectual ability. Secondly, they were not allowed to remain in Standard O for longer than two years. Hence, Standard O came to contain children aged eight to ten, who were taught writing, arithmetic and other subjects with Standard I, and only for reading were taught separately. This insistence, that no child stayed in the same class for more than two years, at least had the advantage of ensuring that children did not leave school from the lowest class. There were also considerable disadvantages, and even an enlightened administrator like Major was compelled to give most unenlightened answers in an attempt to defend the system, as the following cross-questioning by the Chairman of the Committee on Defective and Epileptic Children shows:

'How long does a child stay in one standard?'

'—If a child is deficient when he has been in the same standard 2 years, it is no good keeping the child in that standard any longer.'

'You would teach him something more difficult?'

'— Yes. . . . I have had a case where a boy has failed in arithmetic 5 years running in 5 successive standards, but I should not have liked to have kept that lad down in one standard for 5 years.'

'Did he know anything of arithmetic at the end of his course?'

[1] *Ibid.*, Vol. 2, Evidence of Major.

'— He was always uncertain.'

'One important thing in arithmetic is accuracy?'

'—Yes. He was always inaccurate throughout his course, and I take it would have been just the same if I had kept him at Standard I all through.'

'Would he never have learned accuracy in doing simple sums?'

'—Not to be certain of them.'[1]

In 1895 the class moved from Milton Street to a room at Willow Street Board School. The number of children attending increased very slowly, and by 1911 there were only forty-five. After the turn of the century, when the school was certified by the Board of Education, there were constant criticisms of it in the Inspectors' reports. The premises were poor, the children were badly behaved, even the teaching was lacking in efficiency. 'Leicester,' read one report, 'was the first town to establish special provision for M.D. children, but its interest appears to have been arrested as soon as it was aroused.'[2]

Three months after the first children had entered the special class at Milton Street, London opened the first of its special schools. The Board had been authorized to erect new premises for 150 children in the playground of the Hugh Myddleton School, Finsbury.[3] The building would not be ready until 1895, so the Hugh Myddleton school of special instruction was accommodated temporarily in empty classrooms in the main buildings. The number of the children grew rapidly, and soon there were eighty under three teachers, all women. From the outset, London adopted the policy of appointing good teachers to its schools of special instruction. At the Hugh Myddleton, each of the teachers was certificated and each of them was paid £15 more per annum than the certificated teachers in the ordinary schools.

Their appointment in the first instance was for five years, as the Board felt that they should be given the opportunity of returning to ordinary schools after that time should they so desire. However, there was no intention of refusing to re-appoint them should they wish to stay on. The object of the regulation was simply to safeguard the health of the teachers, and to relieve them from strain.[4] There was an idea prevalent at this period that too prolonged a contact with feeble-minded children would have unfortunate effects upon the teacher concerned. The theory was supported by one of His Majesty's

---

[1] *C.D.E.C.*, Vol. 2, p. 139, Evidence of Major.

[2] Ministry of Education Archives, Education Class 32, Piece 69.

[3] This school contained 2,000 children and was the largest under the London School Board.

[4] *C.D.E.C.*, Vol. 2, Evidence of Moberly, 3.3.1897 and Evidence of Miss R. Whenman, 26.2.1897. Miss Whenman was teacher in charge of the school.

II. School Board Classes for the Mentally Handicapped

Inspectors, who soon after the turn of the century wrote: 'She is a somewhat extraordinary individual and who illustrates well that it is not safe to keep a woman at this class of work continuously and without a break (say for a year) when she might be engaged in ordinary school work.'[1] Today, a return to the ordinary school for a year is still advocated.[2] The reason, however, is different. It is now felt that the teacher in the special school sometimes tends to lower his standards, and that a year with ordinary children will help him to re-establish them.

Not all the children at the Hugh Myddleton school were feeble-minded. Fifteen of them were crippled or delicate children of average intelligence. In addition, there were two partially sighted and three partially deaf children. All these children were backward, and despite their superior intelligence they mixed happily with the dull children. Nor did the teachers experience any particular difficulty in teaching children whose basic ability differed so widely. Distribution into classes was by attainment. In the lowest class were twenty-three children. The youngest was six, the oldest was fifteen. This was also the age range within the school. The fifteen-year-old girl was one of the partially deaf children. She was described as being very innocent and gentle and a great help with the little ones in the class.[3]

Children in this class threaded beads, pricked the outlines of objects with pins, learnt to count, added objects, sang, marched and drilled. Of formal work there was very little. For this the School Board, the Superintendent, Mrs. Burgwin, and the class teacher, Miss Anderson, were to be congratulated. The twenty-two children in the middle class did more formal work. In arithmetic, the better children were capable of adding and subtracting thousands. According to their teacher they had insight into what they were doing: 'I take all concrete till they really understand it.'[4] All the children had passed the stage of one syllable words and were reading books suitable for six-year-olds. In the third class there were five children who could read at the Standard III level. All five were delicate or epileptic children of normal intelligence. No feeble-minded child read better than Standard II level. Throughout the school there was much emphasis on what was termed occupations. Needlework, crochet work, macramé work, clay modelling, painting and basket weaving were all attempted.[5]

[1] Ministry of Education Archives, Education Class 32, Piece 69.
[2] *Training and Supply of Teachers of Handicapped Pupils* (1954), p. 5.
[3] C.D.E.C., Vol. 2, Evidence of Miss F. Anderson, 26.2.1897. Miss Anderson was the class teacher.
[4] *Ibid.*, Vol. 2, p. 81, Evidence of Miss Whenman.
[5] *Ibid.*, Vol. 2, Evidence of Miss Cattle, 26.2.1897.

A cane was kept in the school, but was rarely used. Instead, the three ladies preferred to punish the children by making them stand in isolation in the hall, or read or write when the other children were being given occupations. At times other forms of punishment were employed:

'In the case of a child who takes her boots off and throws them at other children and occasionally at the teacher, sometimes we keep her boots for the rest of the morning until she goes home, because it is really dangerous to allow her to have them; we have little forms of punishment like that.'[1]

Despite such little forms of punishment the children were very contented. The Vicar of Clerkenwell, the Rev. J. H. Rose, had been a Manager of the main Hugh Myddleton school since 1870, and had constituted himself an informal manager of the special school.[2] He was a frequent visitor. 'You can see the changed happy look on the children's faces,' he said in evidence before the Committee on Defective and Epileptic Children. 'In the olden time, when we had to put all the children to the same standard, these defective children always had such a hopeless look, and did not understand in the least what the teachers were trying to do. . . . School was a drudgery, and a hopeless kind of business to them. But now there is no happier looking class in the Hugh Myddleton Schools than you will find in the defective school.'[3] Two girls, he recalled, had been transferred back to the main school and were working successfully in Standard V. By 1906, there were 120 children in the school, and in that year His Majesty's Inspector confirmed the Vicar's report: 'The instruction and discipline of this large school are commendable. The numbers of children yearly transferred to ordinary schools indicates the practical value of the teaching.'[4]

Once the success of the Hugh Myddleton school became known, General Moberly, who had experienced some difficulty in securing agreement to its establishment, found little opposition to his suggestion that more such schools should be opened. By 1896, four years after the first school started, London had twenty-four special schools attended by over 900 pupils.[5]

During the same period five other School Boards, Nottingham, Birmingham, Bradford, Brighton and Bristol established special schools for defective children. The school at Nottingham was

[1] *C.D.E.C.*, Vol. 2, p. 82, Evidence of Miss Whenman.
[2] The official Managers of the special school were the members of the School Board Sub-Committee on the education of blind, deaf and other handicapped children.
[3] *C.D.E.C.*, Vol. 2, p. 132, Evidence of Rose, 3.3.1897.
[4] Ministry of Education Archives, Education Class 32, Piece 91.
[5] Public Record Office, Education Class 14, Piece 43.

II. School Board Classes for the Mentally Handicapped

opened in April 1893. As at Leicester, children for admission were selected by the local inspector from among those suggested as being suitable by teachers in the ordinary schools. Admission was confined to children aged eight or over, since 'defective children below this age appear to be adequately provided for in infants' schools, which are organized and taught in accordance with enlightened kindergarten principles'.[1] Birmingham also selected its children without recourse to a medical officer. Instead of a special school, the City established two special classes, each for twenty children and each on the site of, but completely separate from, an ordinary school. The teachers of the special classes decided which children were suitable for admission by visiting the ordinary schools or the homes of the children concerned. It should be emphasized that at this time only two School Boards, London and Bradford, employed full-time medical officers, although a number of Boards, Birmingham among them, did have the part-time services, in a consultative capacity, of a doctor.

Both the Birmingham special class teachers came from infants' schools. Both of them had been pupil teachers. Neither of them was certificated. Both of them, however, because they taught in special classes, were paid as if they were certificated. Before opening the first class, one of the teachers had spent some weeks attached to the London special schools. On her return, she helped to train the other teacher who, in her turn, opened the second class. Birmingham thus embraced all that was best in the London schools.

There was, however, one novel feature. Since it was not possible to classify the children under different teachers, classification had to be within the class itself. Each class, therefore, had two divisions. In the lower division were the newly admitted children. Although they were all over seven years of age many had not previously been to school. Consequently, some were unable to speak, their senses had been little cultivated, they were unaccustomed to discipline, and unused to correct social behaviour. The work in this division of the class was aimed at rectifying these deficiencies, and only when the children moved to the upper division could any kind of formal work be started. Even then very little was attempted. Indeed, with the necessity of also teaching the children in the lower division, very little could be attempted. Reading and writing took second place to singing, drill, knitting and sewing, and occupations, but, nevertheless, after two years, a number of children were working at Standard II level and two had been returned to the ordinary school.[2]

[1] *C.D.E.C.*, Vol. 2, p. 199, Evidence of W. J. Abel, Clerk to the School Board, 15.4.1897.
[2] *Ibid.*, Vol. 2, Evidence of Miss G. Dale, 19.2.1897.

In 1893 the Independent Labour Party was founded in Bradford. Partly because of this, and partly because of the intimate connection with its School Board of two remarkable persons, Margaret McMillan and James Kerr, Bradford, in the last decade of the nineteenth century, became one of the most progressive school authorities. Sir George Kekewich is reputed to have said that Bradford so beset the Board of Education with new problems and instances of doubtful expenditure that 'during the whole of the last eight years it had been in bad odour with the Board of Education'.[1] Margaret McMillan's presence in Bradford was due entirely to the formation of the Independent Labour Party. At that time a militant socialist and agitator, she had travelled North from London in order to give succour to the newly-founded movement. There were few opportunities for women to serve a political party in a representative capacity, but membership of a School Board was one form of public service which they could undertake. Accordingly, Margaret McMillan was elected to the Bradford School Board. At the same time, 1893, the Board appointed James Kerr as its medical officer.[2] The London School Board had, three years earlier, made a similar appointment. But Dr. W. R. Smith at London had only the duty to advise on new and existing school buildings in relation to ventilation, sanitation and light. Kerr, on the other hand, was responsible for the health of the school children.[3]

In 1894 Kerr carried out the first recorded medical inspection of school-children at Usher Street school, Bradford,[4] and in the same year he examined children put forward by teachers as likely to be in need of special education, and selected 117 who, he felt, should not be in the ordinary school. There were probably twice as many as this, Kerr estimated, in addition to children who were defective in speech or hearing, or were, what he termed, half-blind.

The 117 children were used as material for the first special class of twenty which was opened in November 1874. As at Birmingham, Bradford preferred to have a number of special classes rather than a school. Four others were established in the succeeding two years, and Kerr was responsible for the selection of the children to all of them. His judgement was based on the report of the teacher in the ordinary school, and on the physical characteristics which he himself observed.

[1] Cited by Mansbridge, *Margaret McMillan* (1932), p. 52.
[2] Kerr was subsequently to play an important part in the foundation of the School Medical Service and the establishment of schools for partially sighted children.
[3] *Report of the Inter-Departmental Committee on the Medical Inspection and Feeding of Children* (1905), Vol. 2, Appx. 5, p. 235, and *Annual Report for 1908 of the Chief Medical Officer of the Board of Education*, p. 4.
[4] Warner's earlier examination of London school-children was more in the nature of research than medical inspection.

II. School Board Classes for the Mentally Handicapped

He gave the children no educational test, and when questioned by the Committee on Defective and Epileptic Children found it difficult to analyse what he was looking for. He summed it up by saying: 'There is a tout ensemble about a child that is defective that you cannot describe.'[1] Nevertheless, whether the symptoms for which he searched were describable or not, he was convinced that it was a doctor's place to select the children, otherwise teachers would try to get rid of all their dull children to the special class.

Kerr's opinion of teachers was not very high. He was dissatisfied with the way they conducted the special classes. He had tried to get them to work rationally in developing the intellect, 'but unfortunately they are all bound up in the idea of standards and codes, and what not, and they have the inspector after them, and superintendents over them with the same ideas, and it is very difficult to get them to use rational means. . . . They are too anxious to get the children to do Standard I mental rather than to draw a straight line.'[2] Of course, he was quite right; and perhaps he realized, what he half implied, that the teachers were not entirely to blame. Certainly, the realization appeared to be there when, referring to visits to the special classes by inspectors of the School Board, he stated: 'They are my chief trouble.'[3]

Although many of Kerr's views were tinged with idealism, he was in fact a stern realist who did not suffer fools gladly. Efficient and conscientious himself, he expected others to be the same. But where handicapped children were concerned, his outward harshness concealed a wealth of compassion. For their sake he made himself unpopular in London and Bradford. Of him, as of Stevenson's Lord Hermiston, it could be written: 'On he went up the great, bare staircase of his duty, uncheered and undepressed.'

Warner, it will be remembered, had claimed a share in the founding of Leicester's special school. He also played a part in opening the first class for feeble-minded children at Brighton. The School Board had appointed a Sub-Committee to consider the education of defective children. Warner was invited to Brighton by the Committee. There, he examined the dullest of the 800 children at Brighton's largest school—Elm Grove. In his report he recommended that ten of the children, who were feeble-minded, should receive special education, and these formed the nucleus of the special class.[4] By the end of 1895 the number of children had increased to thirty-eight, and the class was being called the school for afflicted children. Apart from the difference in name, the school showed one other change

---

[1] *C.D.E.C.*, Vol. 2, p. 18, Evidence of Kerr, 11.2.1897.   [2] *Ibid.*, Vol. 2, p. 19.
[3] *Ibid.*, Vol. 2, p. 23.   [4] *Ibid.*, Vol. 2, Evidence of Warner.

from the practice of the time. Whereas the teachers in other special schools and classes, all of whom were women, had previously had considerable experience with infants, the mistress in charge of the Brighton school had done very little teaching of any description. Her father was a country clergyman, and she had taken her teaching certificate in order to be able to help out in the parish school when necessary. She was a friend of Miss Verrall, Chairman of the Sub-Committee on special education, who had recruited her for the work. Before the school opened she spent six weeks visiting the London special schools, and the attachment appears to have compensated for her lack of experience. She had little assistance with the thirty-eight children, only one sixteen-year-old girl who was not even a pupil teacher, but merely called a helper. Yet the school was a success, and within two years of its opening it was moving into new buildings, specially erected, with accommodation for eighty children.[1]

Bristol was the last of the School Boards which made special provision for feeble-minded children during this period. Following the now established tradition, the teachers of its two special classes spent a period of attachment at the London schools of special instruction under the supervision of Mrs. Burgwin. Like other teachers in special schools, they received additions to their salaries, and although both of them were certificated, they, like the teacher at Brighton, lacked the usual experience. They were aged twenty and twenty-one respectively, and were chosen for the work because of their brightness, originality and patience. Unlike some special schools which were loth to accept crippled children unless they were of sub-normal intelligence, the Bristol classes would admit even bright physically handicapped children, if it meant that this was the only way in which they could be educated. At the classes, therefore, were a number of children who had hitherto remained at home, since it was considered that they were too badly disabled to attend school. One such child was carried daily into the school by the caretaker. Though this was not the ideal solution, the children were at least being educated, and the School Board was to be commended on its initiative. Yet the Chairman of the Committee for special classes, the Rev. J. J. Martin, complained that the Board was by no means wholly in favour of the classes. There had been great difficulty in getting them started, as some members had been, and still were, opposed to them on the grounds of expense. As for the general public, he continued, 'there is great opposition to all educational progress'.[2]

[1] *C.D.E.C.*, Vol. 2, Evidence of Miss A. Verrall, 19.2.1897.
[2] *Ibid.*, Vol. 2, p. 143, Evidence of Martin, 12.3.1897.

II. School Board Classes for the Mentally Handicapped

The opposition, however, came not only from members of the public or of School Boards. It came too from educationists. One of H.M. Inspectors gave his views to the Committee on Defective and Epileptic Children. He had been an Inspector for twenty-five years, and he believed it to be disastrous to separate the feeble-minded from ordinary children. If they were not separated they would be 'driven through, and the result was that there never was any accumulation of them'.[1] But to allow them to accumulate together would only bring disaster. He recalled with approval a girl 'without any brains at all' who was kept among young children year after year and became dirty and spiteful. But when she was moved into Standard IV with her contemporaries she became 'good and orderly'—although equally as ignorant. He was not dismayed that she remained equally as ignorant, since, he maintained, 'she could never learn anything'. Therefore, he felt it was better to push the children through the school, even if they learnt nothing, than to send them to a special class where they would still learn nothing. Moreover, there existed the danger that if they were sent to a special class, the teacher in the ordinary school would become discouraged from doing his best with them. Aldis had no doubt that it would be better for feeble-minded children to be in a class of seventy ordinary children, where they could be assisted by the brighter ones, than in a special class of twenty where they would receive, according to him, but little individual attention from the teacher.

It is in the light of opinions such as these that the work of Moberly, Shuttleworth, Warner, Major, Kerr and the teachers themselves in the special schools has to be assessed. Their actual achievement may seem small—some 1,300 children in thirty-one special schools by the beginning of 1897—but they had vindicated their theories, and when at length the Government established an enquiry into the education of defective children, the evidence was there to be seen.

[1] *Ibid.*, Vol. 2, p. 89, Evidence of T. Aldis, 28.2.1897.

11

THE PERIOD OF STATE INTERVENTION: III. THE DEPARTMENTAL COMMITTEE ON DEFECTIVE AND EPILEPTIC CHILDREN[1]

IN January 1897 a letter from the Treasury to the Education Department, in reply to a query as to what expenses might be claimed in connection with the Departmental Committee on Defective and Epileptic Children, stated 'My Lords will raise no objection to an allowance being made for luncheon in the Office on those days when the hours of meeting require it, at the rate of 2/- a head.'[2] These luncheon expenses and other incidentals cost £228 4s. 2d. It was money well spent, for in 1898 the Committee published a most enlightened *Report*.

The appointment of the Committee had been due to a number of influences. The Royal Commission on the Blind and Deaf had, of course, recommended in 1889 that feeble-minded children should receive special instruction. It should have been the duty of the Education Department to implement this recommendation by suggesting to School Boards the action they might take. No suggestions were forthcoming. However, as has been seen, the London School Board sought and obtained approval of plans to educate its feeble-minded children in special schools. Subsequently other School Boards established special schools and classes, but there was lacking that which

---

[1] Material in this chapter is taken from the *Report of the Committee*, Vol. 1, unless otherwise stated.   [2] Public Record Office, Education Class 23, Piece 5.

was so dear to the administrators at Whitehall—uniformity of procedure.

A second influence was the research work carried out by Dr. Francis Warner. The results of his examination of 50,000 London school-children had been published in 1893.[1] He was encouraged by the Congress of Hygiene and Demography held in London in 1892 to continue with his investigation,[2] and by 1894 100,000 children had been examined. His *Report*[3] showed that one per cent of these were defective, and in his opinion required special education. Warner had looked for four classes of defect: imperfections in bodily development and physiognomy, abnormal neurological responses, poor physical condition due to lack of adequate nutrition or chronic illness, and mental dullness. The one per cent which he estimated should receive special education were not only all mentally dull, but also suffered from the first three classes of defect. Thus, if Warner's thesis was to be accepted, there were in London alone over 6,000 feeble-minded children who were also physically handicapped.

Thirdly, the passing of the Elementary Education (Blind and Deaf Children) Act, and the publication by the Charity Organization Society in 1893 of *The Feeble-minded Child and Adult* and *The Epileptic and Crippled Child and Adult*, in which the duty of School Boards to provide for handicapped children was stressed, gave further emphasis to the need for action by the Education Department. Nor did the Charity Organization Society confine its agitation to its publications. Its members brought pressure to bear upon Members of Parliament and even upon the Vice-President of the Education Department,[4] and in 1896 the Society sponsored the formation of the National Association for Promoting the Welfare of the Feeble-Minded, one of whose aims was the implementation of the Society's recommendation that the State should be responsible for educating feeble-minded children. In the same year, a Committee under the Chairmanship of Lord Egerton of Tatton submitted to the Lord President of the Council an extensively signed memorial calling for the extension of the 1893 Blind and Deaf Children Act to include physically and mentally handicapped children.

Fourthly, the London School Board once again entered the lists. Since the special schools worked shorter hours, the grants they received were only the same as for infant schools. But their expenses in fact were considerably in excess of those of ordinary schools, and

[1] Charity Organization Society, *The Feeble-minded Child and Adult*.
[2] *C.D.E.C.*, Vol. 2, Evidence of Warner, 12.2.1897.
[3] Warner, *Report on the Scientific Study of the Mental and Physical Conditions of Childhood with particular reference to Children of Defective Constitution* (1895).
[4] Public Record Office, Education Class 14, Piece 43.

so in 1894 the Board requested the Department of Education to pay increased grants. At the same time it urged that legislation should be enacted to allow school authorities to provide for defective children on the lines of the 1893 Act. As a result of this appeal, the Department in March 1895 asked H.M. Inspectors and some of the larger School Boards for their views on the desirability of extending the 1893 Act to include defective children. The replies received, stated the Department, 'while they showed that attention was being directed towards the subject, did not afford a sufficiently clear basis for further action on the part of the Department'.[1] It is difficult to understand what basis for action the Department demanded. Unwilling to admit defeat, the London School Board determined to give it one. On June 12th, 1896 a deputation from the Board waited upon Sir John Gorst, Vice-President of the Department. They requested a bigger grant for special schools and urged that the compulsory age for attendance should be raised to sixteen. They stressed the desirability of school authorities being empowered to provide institutions for the education and maintenance of defective and epileptic children. They also repeated the recommendation of the Egerton Commission that the powers of school authorities should be extended so as to include the education of imbeciles.[2]

Finally, when the *Report of the Poor Law Schools Committee* was laid before Parliament in 1896, it was found to contain a recommendation that separate provision should be made for feeble-minded children in Poor Law schools.[3] Under the mounting pressure the Department eventually bowed, and in December 1896 the Duke of Devonshire, Lord President of the Council, appointed the Committee on Defective and Epileptic Children. Its Chairman was the Rev. T. W. Sharpe, H.M. Chief Inspector of schools, who in 1891 had amicably agreed with the London School Board the conditions for the establishment of special schools. He was supported by another Inspector, A. W. Newton, the Senior Examiner of the Education Department, H. F. Pooley, and four persons unconnected with the Department—Shuttleworth, W. R. Smith, Medical Officer of the London School Board, Mrs. Burgwin, Superintendent of London's special schools, and Miss Townsend, a member of the Council of the Association for Promoting the Welfare of the Feeble-Minded. The Committee examined its first witness at the beginning of February 1897, and within four months had completed the taking of evidence. In that time it asked nearly 8,000 questions of doctors, inspectors, administrators, teachers and representatives of welfare organizations. Its

[1] *C.D.E.C.*, Vol. 1, p. 4.
[2] Public Record Office, Education Class 14, Piece 43.　　　[3] *Op. cit.*, p. 88.

members visited every special school for feeble-minded children in the country. They also inspected Darenth and the epileptic colony at Chalfont St. Peter's.

The Committee's terms of reference were to enquire into, and advise upon any changes to, the existing system of education of 'feeble-minded and defective children not under charge of Guardians and not idiots or imbeciles'; to report upon the means of discriminating between educable and non-educable children, and between those who could be taught in the ordinary school and those in special classes; and to enquire into the provision of elementary education for children suffering from epilepsy. One of the first tasks of the Committee was a definition of terms. There was very little past legislation to assist in formulating concepts of feeble-mindedness, idiocy and imbecility. The distinction between an idiot and a lunatic had been first made in the reign of Edward I. The former was the born fool, *fatuus naturalis*, and the term was applicable to all mentally deficient persons. The latter was someone who had lost the use of his reason. A similar distinction was made in the Statute of Prerogatives under Edward II when the person of unsound mind, but with lucid intervals, *non compos mentis, sicut quidam suut per lucida intervalla*, was contrasted with the idiot. The difference was of practical importance, since if a man was found by the Inquisition to be a lunatic the Crown sequestered his property only during the period of his lunacy, whereas in the case of an idiot the Crown entered into permanent possession of the property.

Gradually the distinction became blurred, until in the early nineteenth century it disappeared altogether, and lunacy was taken to include idiocy. All the main lunacy legislation of the nineteenth century (the Acts of 1845, 1853, 1890 and 1891) dealt with the powers of the lunacy authorities to provide for mental defectives. Not until the Idiots Act of 1886 was a differentiation made between idiot and lunatic. Then for the first time, the sub-division of imbecile was mentioned, and it was suggested that both idiots and imbeciles were capable of being trained. This was a departure from the earlier concept of an idiot as one who was legally held to be completely incapable mentally. Under the Act the few existing voluntary idiot asylums were permitted to admit patients with less formality than hitherto, but there was no authority for local or central public bodies to establish institutions.

It was left to the Lunacy Act of 1890 to grant such powers. In addition, sanction to cater for pauper idiots had been given by the Metropolitan Poor Act 1867, under which Darenth had been established, so that when the Departmental Committee met, there existed, in addition to Darenth, the voluntary asylums and the power vested in the local authorities to provide further asylums. None, however, had been provided. Consequently the provision for idiots and imbeciles was completely inadequate. Moreover, in all the legislation there was nowhere a definition of the degree of mental deficiency which would count as imbecility. Of feeble-mindedness there was not even mention, much less definition.

The members of the Committee, Shuttleworth and Smith, suggested that the term imbecile should be applied to all children who, by reason of mental defect, were incapable of being educated so as to become self-supporting. While this was by no means a technical definition, it did at least provide a criterion, albeit a social rather than an educational criterion. With regard to the term feeble-minded, the two doctors believed it should refer to children who were too mentally defective to be properly taught in the ordinary elementary schools, but not so defective as to be imbecile in the sense mentioned. The Committee gratefully accepted these two definitions, enlarging slightly upon the second. Feeble-minded children, they decided, were those not being imbecile 'who cannot properly be taught in ordinary elementary schools by ordinary methods'. However, they disliked the term feeble-minded, and recommended that it should not be used when dealing with the children referred to in the enquiry. Rather, such children should be known as defective children. But the terms of reference of the Committee had included both feeble-minded and defective children, and the latter term was taken to mean mentally normal children who by reason of physical defect could not properly be educated in the ordinary school. By this decision, the Committee accepted that all those children who by reason of mental or physical disability could not properly be taught in the ordinary school should be known as defective. Thus, the Committee made no distinction in nomenclature between physically and mentally handicapped children, and the term defective continued until 1944 to be applied to the children now known as delicate, physically handicapped and educationally sub-normal.

When the Committee came to consider what criterion should be applied for admission to a special school, they encountered a difficulty. Although they had recommended that imbeciles should not be admitted to special schools, they found that no child could be certified as an imbecile until legal provision, in the form of admission to an asylum, was made for him. Since there was an extreme shortage of accommodation in the existing asylums, a large number of imbecile children remained uncertified. Because of this shortage of accommodation, and the fact that no adequate definition of imbecility existed, it was difficult for the special schools to refuse entry to children who were obviously imbecile yet uncertified. Thus there were some imbeciles in the existing special schools as, equally, because of the lack of suitable provision for them, there were some feeble-minded children certified as imbeciles in the asylums. Before special schools were established, imbecile children were even to be found in the board schools. General Moberly described how all that the teachers could do was to keep them occupied, though sometimes they were 'taught to fetch and carry as a dog might be'.[1] It was only a slight consolation to know that they were 'exceedingly kindly treated by the other children'.[2]

The question therefore arose as to how far down the scale the duties of school authorities extended. If there had been complete provision for imbeciles, then the answer could have been all non-imbeciles. In practice, however, because of the lack of asylum provision, such a solution would have entailed the admission of uncertified imbeciles to the schools. Therefore the school authorities must lay down their own boundary of imbecility, and the test must be 'incapacity to receive proper benefit from instruction in the special classes'.

This recommendation was made before Binet and Simon produced their first intelligence test. Nevertheless, the doctors who gave evidence before the Committee believed that they could detect imbecility by physical signs. Moreover, they declared that the same signs, in a less marked degree, would indicate that the children concerned were feeble-minded and could not be taught in the ordinary schools by the ordinary methods. Thus, educational judgements were being based upon physical manifestations. Warner had already reduced to a system the means of detecting weak-minded children by nervous signs,[3] and he would only admit to a special class those children who had visible defects.[4] Fletcher Beach, who had been Medical Superintendent of Darenth, had also devised a test of feeble-mindedness. Among other things, he looked for malformation of the head, a V-shaped palate, large, coarse, outstanding ears, a fixed stare, a curved little finger, and distractability noticeable by a constant movement of the eyes. Beach felt that his test was more efficient than Warner's for detecting feeble-mindedness, but agreed with Warner that only a medical man was capable of diagnosing mental weakness. However, he cast some doubt on the practicability of his system when he stated that there were not more than six doctors in England capable of discriminating between imbeciles and feeble-minded children.[5]

[1] *R.C.B.D.*, Vol. 3, p. 868, Evidence of Moberly. [2] *Ibid.*, Vol. 3, p. 869.
[3] Warner, 'A Method of Examining Children in Schools as to their Development and Brain Condition', *British Medical Journal*, 22.9.1888, pp. 659–60.
[4] *C.D.E.C.*, Vol. 2, Evidence of Warner.
[5] *Ibid.*, Vol. 2, Evidence of Beach, 10.2.1897.

Shuttleworth, too, was of the opinion that medical knowledge was necessary to determine feeble-mindedness, 'because the conditions of feeble-mindedness are so mixed up with physical conditions that it is important that a person who has been trained to discriminate between various abnormal physical conditions should have the decision as to the state of the child'.[1] He was in no doubt that the opinion of a doctor with experience of the work was more important than that of a teacher, although he would be glad to know the opinion of the teacher. Asked whether, if no views from a teacher were available, a doctor could still reach a conclusion, he replied that in such a case the doctor would have to carry out the same processes as a teacher would. He himself, when testing children, did not confine himself to a physical examination:

'I proceed to talk to the child, noticing the degree of intelligence he displays in answering my questions, and whether he is quick or slow in his answers and so on, and then, of course, I attempt to find out for myself what degree of education he has attained to and compare that with the ordinary standard for the child's age, in forming an opinion as to whether the child is mentally defective. I mean I would ask a child to read out of a book and ask him to write his name, and above all to apply some tests of power of calculation; but these are matters that a teacher could do better than myself, and I should be glad to take the report of a skilled teacher thereon.'[2]

At least Shuttleworth realized that the teacher could play an important part in assessing mental weakness. In fact, he conceded, there were occasions when the teacher's view might be of the greatest importance. The work of diagnosing mental deficiency was that of a specialist not a general practitioner, 'consequently very often the ordinary country practitioner would from want of experience be in no better position for forming a complete opinion than the teacher, if as good'.[3] In cases such as these, he was asked, could teachers be trained to detect a child's mental state by certain tests? To a certain degree they could, but without physiological training he felt that their conclusions would not be as valid as a doctor's. However, when it came to leaving the special school for the ordinary school, the teacher's opinion was the more important.

F. D. Harris, one of the medical officers of the London School Board, was also a strong advocate of a doctor having the ultimate decision regarding admission to a special school. He based his

[1] *C.D.E.C.*, Vol. 2, p. 3, Evidence of Shuttleworth, 10.2.1897.

[2] *Ibid.*, Vol. 2, p. 5, Evidence of Shuttleworth.

[3] *Ibid.*, Vol. 2, p. 6. See also: Shuttleworth, 'The Differentiation of Mentally Deficient Children', *Transactions of the International Congress on School Hygiene* (1908), p. 742.

conviction on the fact that only those children should be admitted who had defects that could be diagnosed by a doctor. Like Shuttleworth, he was ready to accept advice on the question of the educational attainments of a child. When he conducted an examination he invited an inspector to be present who would advise as to what could be expected of an ordinary child of similar age. He would not, however, seek the opinion of the child's teacher since the teacher would wish to get rid of the child, and would, therefore, be biased. Mrs. Burgwin, as the only teacher on the Committee, appears to have objected to this statement, and she closely questioned Harris on the value of a teacher's opinion. Eventually, he was asked if he would admit to a special school, even if there was no obvious defect, a child who was dull and had attended regularly, but who at the age of ten could not do Standard I work. Harris admitted that he would, and in reply to the question as to how he would conclude that the child was defective, he stated that he would conduct the usual examination and ask the teacher. 'Then,' said Mrs. Burgwin, triumphantly one presumes, 'it would be the teacher's judgement that would cause you to form an opinion.'[1]

In view of the extent of this evidence, the prestige of the witnesses, and the fact that no non-medical witness suggested any other method, the Committee concluded that selection of children for a special school should be undertaken by a doctor. Of course, the question was a difficult one, since the judgements to be made were of two kinds. In the first place, it was necessary to differentiate between feeble-minded children and imbeciles; in the second place between those who could be educated in the ordinary and those in the special school. As far as the first case was concerned, the practice of the time was for children who were not attending school because of doubts as to their educability to be excused officially by a school attendance officer. Alternatively, children could be permanently excused from attending school on a certificate from the family doctor. Both methods were open to criticism. Since it was felt that a teacher was not in a position to judge whether a child could receive benefit from the education given in a special school, how much less would a school attendance officer be in a position to do so. As for the family doctor, there would be neither the necessary knowledge nor an uniform standard. Therefore, the Committee recommended that a child absent from school because of mental or physical defect should be examined by a medical officer appointed by the school authority, who would determine whether the child should be educated in the ordinary school, in the special school, or not at all.

[1] *C.D.E.C.*, Vol. 2, p. 44, Evidence of Harris, 17.2.1897.

With regard to children who were already attending school, the procedure would be different. Preliminary selection for special schools would be carried out by teachers in the ordinary schools. No selection, however, would be attempted before the age of seven, since it was felt that below that age the children should be able to manage adequately in the infant schools. Moreover, selection under the age of seven presented difficulties in that what might be taken for a defect could in fact be a natural delay in development. It was therefore recommended that head teachers of infant schools should report any children still in their schools who after the age of seven had failed to gain promotion. Head teachers of other schools should report any child who had been at the school for more than six months, and concerning whom there was any doubt. Finally, should one of Her Majesty's Inspectors find a child obviously in need of special education, he should notify the Education Department.

All children so reported should be examined by the medical officer of the school authority. Three other persons, recommended the Committee, should be present at the examination. First, the teacher who had suggested that the child should be given special education should attend to give an account of the attainments and behaviour of the child. Secondly, the head teacher of the special school should be present both to receive information from the medical officer and the teacher who brought the child, and to express an opinion as to the suitability of the child for a special school. Thirdly, H.M. Inspector for the area should be in attendance in order that he might be familiar with the details of the case. Finally, the parent of the child should be given the opportunity of attending the examination. Whether or not the parent attended, it was desirable that a personal explanation should be given in addition to the official notification of the examination. The Committee realized that prejudice existed against what were frequently termed the silly schools, 'and this prejudice, though it tends to disappear, must still be reckoned with'.[1] Hence the best way to allay the fears of the parent was for the child's teacher in the ordinary school to explain the advantages of the special school.

Despite the presence of others at the examination, the duty of recommending what educational provision would be the best for the child lay with the medical officer. Admittedly it was suggested that he should confer with others present, and especially should he pay regard to the opinion of the teacher, but nevertheless the Committee strongly urged that an examination, conducted by a medical officer, of all children to be admitted should be a necessary condition of recog-

[1] *C.D.E.C.*, Vol. 1, p. 12.

nition of a special school by the Education Department. Thus, since psychology was in its infancy, and no means of mental measurement existed, the decision was made which has led to the present day position whereby the recommendation concerning a child's ability is made by a doctor, and not by a psychologist or a teacher.

As for the number of children who came within the scope of the enquiry, it was estimated that some one per cent of all children of school age were feeble-minded. This figure was based partly upon the experience of the German *hilfs-schulen*, and partly on the result of enquiries by H.M. Inspectors, doctors and teachers in a number of the larger English towns. Despite the fact, however, that there were considerable discrepancies in the returns of the enquirers, and that even the Committee's estimate was no more than a rough guess, there was no support for a suggestion that the Education Department should conduct a scientific and statistical investigation. The diagnosis of feeble-mindedness was a medical matter, and therefore the Department could only accept expert advice. However, the Committee did suggest that consideration should be given to the appointment of a full-time medical officer to advise the Department on questions pertaining to the education of defective children. Coupled with this was the strong recommendation that school authorities should appoint, usually on a part-time basis, medical officers to examine children suitable for special schools.

In the year that this suggestion was made, a doctor was in fact appointed to the staff of the Education Department, but it is highly doubtful whether the Committee's views had any bearing on the matter. The Department's Code of Regulations for 1890 had recognized for the first time that the State had a duty to care for the physical welfare of its children. To this end, physical training was made an integral part of school life. George Kekewich, Secretary to the Department, who was partly responsible for this addition to the Code, felt that expert guidance should be available on the question of physical training. The Secretary had a poor opinion of his superior, the Lord President. 'He never initiated any change, and was quite content to accept the present position and to avoid the more laborious work of providing for the future.'[1] Nevertheless, Kekewich eventually broached the question of an adviser. 'I did, however, dare to suggest to the Duke of Devonshire that, as a beginning, at least one Medical Inspector might be obtained, and that his services might be utilized in special cases, but the Duke, as was customary with him, threw a douche of cold water upon the proposal. But, with some difficulty, I managed to secure one fully qualified medical man, Dr.

[1] Kekewich, *The Education Department and After* (1920), p. 93.

Eichholz, as a member of the ordinary inspecting staff, and I found his services most valuable.'[1]

Whatever the reasons for his appointment, Alfred Eichholz rendered valuable service not only to Kekewich, but also to special schools of all kinds. Since his appointment coincided with the publication of the Committee's *Report*, he was not, of course, called upon to give evidence. However, his extremely far-sighted views on the special schools of the period are known. They are contained in a memorandum on London's special schools written by him in January 1899 while he was H.M. Inspector for West Lambeth.[2] Eichholz commented that the sites for special schools had been selected purely on geographical grounds with the result that each school contained children 'affected very diversely as regards physical health, moral perception, and intelligence, the only condition common to all being utter failure in the matter of attainments. In each school there are many species of backwardness each in reality demanding special treatment.' Since defective children of all descriptions were sent to the same school without classification, it became very difficult to apply suitable methods to the different kinds of cases. Moreover, such a system imposed an unnecessary strain upon the teachers, 'which I have known to contribute largely to absolute breakdown in the case of one very capable headmistress'.

Eichholz, therefore, suggested that, since the existing system was largely experimental, a second guiding principle supplementary to the geographical one might be introduced. This principle would involve the classification of children with a view to dealing with each class separately. There would be three main groups. The first would consist of 'children of pronounced mental deficiency, bordering on imbecility, exhibiting depravity of morals or conduct, with no idea of responsibility, and a minimum of intelligent response'. The second group would be composed of physically defective and epileptic children. In the last group would be children who were 'physically and morally healthy—but backward. These children are a very numerous class and many of them become fit to return to the ordinary school.' They might well be taught in the existing day special schools. There they would be near their homes, and could return to the ordinary schools when ready. Thus, the existing special schools would approximate more to the German *hilfs-schulen*, and would truly be an aid to the ordinary schools. Further, much of the stigma attaching to the special schools would disappear, and parents and teachers would have no qualms regarding sending a merely backward child to such a

---

[1] Kekewich, *The Education Department and After* (1920), p. 56.
[2] The memorandum is in Education Class 14, Piece 43 at the Public Record Office.

school. However, it was understandable that as matters stood there should be hesitation at the 'prospect of associating such a child with depraved or sore or epileptic schoolfellows'.

For the physically defective group, Eichholz considered that the selection of the sites of the schools was of great importance. Ideally new buildings should be erected in semi-rural districts around London. There the children would all have to be resident, and their accommodation should be based on the cottage homes system. There, too, they would have the advantages of fresh air, dietary supervision and periodical medical inspection. Eichholz felt that the first of the three groups was the most difficult for which to make provision. Certainly, the children in this group should not attend the day special schools. What was required for them were schools in the country, 'where the lowest forms of outdoor agriculture or garden or farm work might be employed as a means of gaining their best efforts'. Any attempt at ordinary school work would impose an unnecessary strain on both staff and children. 'Teaching through the hands,' he concluded, 'and not through the brain is essentially the method—outdoor labour away from the town and therefore away from the possibility of doing harm.'

Eichholz's ideas, as expressed in his memorandum, were in advance of contemporary educational thought on special education. His concept of the special school as a place of remedial education foreshadowed current practice in this respect. His advocacy of fresh air in semi-rural surroundings for physically handicapped children, among whom he included the delicate and the undernourished, was made almost ten years before the establishment of the first open-air school. Finally, his views on the treatment of lower grade feeble-minded children contrasted sharply with the justifiable optimism of Shuttleworth and Beach, and anticipated the dark pessimism of the early twentieth century. While some of his ideas were less valuable than others, it is unfortunate that they were not made available to the Committee on Defective and Epileptic Children.

Despite the lack of any assistance from Eichholz, the Committee in its comments on the time-tables and curricula of special schools showed itself to be remarkably enlightened. The school day should not exceed four and a half hours teaching time. Lessons should be short. Save for manual work they should never be longer than thirty minutes. Brainwork should alternate with handwork, and the most difficult brainwork should be tackled in the mornings. Physical exercises between all lessons were strongly advocated. However, the time-table should never be inflexible. It should be possible for the teacher to vary it especially 'in cases of atmospheric disturbances which appear to have peculiar effect on feeble-minded children.'[1] Here was a case of a sound recommendation based on a false premise.

Each child should receive six hours of manual work every week. For younger children, macramé work, clay modelling, painting, paper pattern work, knitting, bead threading and building with wooden cubes were recommended, with the qualifications that the work should be specially suited to the feeble-minded, that frequent changes of media were desirable and that there should be a freedom of choice of the best form for each child having regard to his particular defect. All this implied a liberal provision of materials, and consequently a liberal grant. With older children, one of the direct objects of manual work was to be the provision of vocational training. Boys were to receive instruction in some of the following traditional trades for the handicapped: woodwork, basket weaving, chair caning, book binding, shoe making, mat and mattress making, gardening and farm work. Girls were to be given instruction which was applicable to their work in the home—needlework, cookery, laundry work and housewifery. Despite this emphasis on manual subjects, the basic skills of reading, writing and arithmetic were not to be neglected. Teachers were exhorted to recognize 'the importance of concrete teaching of arithmetic and of adopting various methods of teaching children to read in a manner calculated to excite their interest'.[2]

With regard to the age of attendance at a special school, the Committee heard conflicting evidence. There was little doubt concerning the lower age limit. Children should not be admitted before the age of seven. As to the age at which they could leave, the practice in the schools varied, but despite the fact that some witnesses advocated raising the school leaving age to sixteen, the Committee would go no further than to recommend that all should stay until fourteen and some until sixteen. The decision as to whether the children would remain the extra two years was to rest with the school authorities. They should be given discretionary powers to compel attendance until sixteen if they had suitable facilities available. However, whether they stayed until fourteen or sixteen, it should be the duty of every school authority to make special provision for all defective children in its area, and to this end the authorities should be given special powers to compel the attendance of a child at a special school.

Attempts to compel children to attend special schools had already been made. In the majority of cases no opposition was encountered. Occasionally, however, a parent would evade the necessity of sending a child to a special school by exercising the option contained in the

[1] *C.D.E.C.*, Vol. 1, p. 17.   [2] *Ibid.*, Vol. 1, p. 18.

III. Committee on Defective and Epileptic Children

Act of 1870. Under this, parents could choose which school their child could attend, and by choosing a voluntary school the parents would place the child beyond the control of the School Board.[1] This anomaly was to disappear when, by the Education Act of 1902, voluntary schools came under the control of local education authorities. In the meantime, there were more defective children in the voluntary than in the board schools. Not only was this because the endowed schools provided sanctuary from the School Board, but also because, in the words of Dr. Warner, 'they had a less hard cast-iron system and could do more what they liked'.[2] They were therefore prepared to accept children who would be rejected by the board schools. Warner knew of the headmaster of an elementary endowed school in London who made a point of never refusing admission to any child in his district. Naturally, his examination results were poor, but one can only agree with Warner when he says, 'I think all honour to him.'[3]

Such a policy naturally had its disadvantages. Miss Blackmore, Headmistress of St. Michael and All Angels, Woolwich, described the position in her school. Standards I and II were educated in the same class room. The former was under the charge of a girl pupil teacher aged fifteen. It contained fifty-one children. The Standard II teacher who had over-all responsibility for both classes was qualified under Article 68 of the Code, whereby women over eighteen years of age approved by the Inspectors were allowed to teach.[4] Among the fifty-one children in the lower of the two standards were four low-grade feeble-minded children. One, a girl of thirteen, could barely speak, was in a nervous condition, and had to be assisted upstairs. Another aged ten could say only a few words and was very vicious, while the other two were also extremely badly behaved and could not learn anything. Had a special school existed in the neighbourhood, Miss Blackmore would have been pleased for the children to attend it. As it was if they did not attend her school they would be on the streets, for no board school would admit them.[5]

Evidence such as Miss Blackmore's convinced the Committee that classes in special schools should be small and the teachers well qualified. Generally there should not be more than twenty children to a class, although it would be permissible for the senior classes to have

[1] *Ibid.*, Vol. 2, Evidence of Kerr, 10.2.1897, W. B. Chard, 17.2.1897 and Miss Dale, 19.2.1897.
[2] *Ibid.*, Vol. 2, p. 35.   [3] *Ibid.*, Vol. 2, p. 35.
[4] Augustine Birrell, President of the Board of Education under the Liberal Administration of 1906, stated that the only qualifications of Article 68 teachers were that they had been successfully vaccinated: Smith, *A History of English Elementary Education* (1931), p. 339.
[5] *C.D.E.C.*, Vol. 2, Evidence of Miss M. M. Blackmore, 17.2.1897.

thirty. All head teachers should be certificated, and so should the majority of the assistants. No teacher aged under twenty-one should be appointed to a special school. Moreover, ordinary teaching qualifications were not considered to be sufficient. It was recommended that after having had experience of work in the ordinary school, certificated teachers desiring to teach in a special school should be given special training. The duration of the course was not specified, but the curriculum should include lectures on kindergarten methods, the observation of children, physiology and school hygiene. The teachers should also be trained in gymnastics, articulation and voice production, Sloyd (the Swedish system of manual training through woodwork) and other creative activities. In addition there would be two months practical work in special schools. The progressive views of the Committee were evident in these recommendations. At a time when classes in the ordinary schools contained as many as seventy children, twenty was a very small number to suggest. Equally, the insistence on well qualified teachers must be seen against the lack of qualifications among teachers generally. Of the 140,000 teachers in the elementary schools in 1899, only 62,000 were certificated, and of these 26,000 had received no training.[1] Finally, the advocated period of extended special training was still fifty years distant. When it did come, it contained many of the features suggested by the Committee.

In cases where children could not attend a special school, either because of the severity of their disability or because they lived in an area where there were insufficient children to warrant the establishment of a school, three possible courses of action were recommended. First, school authorities should be empowered to provide 'guides or conveyances' to take children to school. Secondly, children might be boarded out in private houses near special schools. Although this would entail leaving home, the children would still be in touch with normal life, and so would not suffer the disadvantages of those who were dealt with under the third solution of attendance at institutions. The Committee did not anticipate that the power to send children into residence would be widely used, for they foresaw the danger that when school authorities established residential schools, the dividing line between feeble-minded and imbecile children might be drawn too low. In any case, the power to send a child to a residential school was limited by the necessity of having to obtain the parents' consent. On the other hand, since the Committee suggested that one of the reasons for sending a child into residence would be the poorness of the home conditions, it was also pointed out that under the Prevention of

[1] Tropp, *The School Teachers: the Growth of the Teaching Profession . . . from 1800 to the Present Day* (1957), pp. 117–18.

III. Committee on Defective and Epileptic Children

Cruelty to Children Act 1889[1] it was possible to remove a child from the care of its parents if there was any question of ill-treatment.

In a section devoted to physically defective children, the *Report* stated that, as most feeble-minded children were physically defective, a large number of them would be found in the special schools for mentally defective children. This statement was based upon the evidence of the doctors, in particular that of Warner. It served, however, to confuse the issue. The slight physical manifestations which were said to accompany feeble-mindedness were very different from the crippling defects which could affect locomotion and manual dexterity. Yet children suffering from either type of defect were termed physically defective, although only those who were also feeble-minded were considered to need education of a special kind. Handicapped children of normal intelligence, the Committee felt, should attend the ordinary school, and school authorities should be empowered to provide transport or guides to assist the children to school. Where this would not be possible, they might be boarded out near the ordinary school or else sent to a special residential school in which, the Committee insisted, the instruction should be that of the ordinary school. Thus, although provision was made for the accommodation of the severely handicapped child, no account was taken of the educational difficulties which might arise from the psychological disturbance associated with the disability, the deprivation of experience, or the backwardness which would result from the frequent absence from school. In fact, it was specifically stated that if the handicap was so severe that the child could not stand the regular instruction that would satisfy the conditions of the public elementary school, the relaxation of teaching conditions with a view to giving a certain amount of instruction under special arrangements was not recommended. 'These children will in most cases,' concluded the Committee, 'be capable of occasional attendance at a public elementary school, and we do not think that instruction in the home or at the bedside, or in the hospital, can be undertaken by school authorities.'[2]

However, this was considered to be a 'fair field for voluntary effort', and it is thanks to the efforts of voluntary bodies that many of our badly physically handicapped children do receive, at the present time, education in their homes, in special schools for spastics, and in hospital schools.

Much of the evidence which the Committee heard on epileptic children was given by Fletcher Beach.[3] While he was at Darenth, almost one-third of the children there had suffered from epilepsy, and

[1] 52 and 53 Victoria, c. 44.   [2] *C.D.E.C.*, Vol. 1, p. 29.
[3] *Ibid.*, Vol. 2, Evidence of Beach, 10.2.1897.

his subsequent appointment as physician to the epileptic colony at Chalfont St. Peter's and the West End Hospital for Epilepsy and Paralysis had extended his experience. He felt, and the Committee adopted his view, that if children were of normal intelligence and their epileptic attacks occurred at no less than monthly intervals they were capable of attending the ordinary school. Moreover, he had found that other children were not alarmed by epileptic fits. On the contrary, they were most helpful and affectionate towards the epileptic children. Optimistically, the Committee recommended that teachers in the ordinary schools should be instructed how to deal with the attacks, and school authorities should be empowered to provide the usual transport or guides to take the children to the ordinary school, or, if they were feeble-minded, to the special school.

There would, however, be some children whose attacks were so frequent and severe that it would be dangerous for them to travel to school. Moreover, their presence in the school would cause serious disturbance, and there existed the possibility that they might cause injury to other children. Nevertheless, it was essential that they should be educated, since if they remained at home their condition would rapidly deteriorate. It was therefore suggested that school authorities should be given the power to provide residential schools, or to contribute towards the education and maintenance of the children in voluntary institutions. In any case, it should be incumbent upon school authorities to educate epileptic children, and in this connection they were to have the right of compelling attendance at a residential school even without the consent of the parents.

In January 1898, a little over twelve months after its appointment, the Committee, with commendable promptitude, completed its deliberations. The following month its *Report* was laid before Parliament. By November the draft of a Bill giving effect to the recommendations of the Committee was in Devonshire's hands.[1] As usual, and understandably, the Treasury took an interest in the Bill. The interest on this occasion took an unusual form. On January 14th, 1899 the Lord President received a letter from Hicks Beach, Chancellor of the Exchequer, in which the following appeared:

'The definition of "defective" children—which must be in the Bill —will have to be very carefully settled. Whatever the amount of the grants may be, they must, I suppose, be a good deal larger than those made to ordinary children: and there would be a great temptation to

---

[1] The original framework of the Bill was the work of H. W. Orange, a permanent official at the Education Department, who had acted as Secretary to the Departmental Committee: Ministry of Education Archives, Education Class 31, Piece 16.

school authorities, especially in Ireland, to include in the term "defective" a good many children who ought not to be included.'[1]

Hicks Beach had been Irish Secretary in Salisbury's Second Ministry, and it is probable that his experience in that office was responsible for the thrust at Ireland. Be that as it may, when the Bill was introduced to the Lords in June 1899, it contained a comprehensive definition. Children coming within the scope of the measure were those who 'not being imbecile, and not being merely dull or backward, are defective, that is to say, those children who by reason of mental or physical defect are incapable of receiving proper benefit from the instruction in the ordinary public elementary schools, but are not incapable by reason of such defect of receiving benefit from instruction in special classes or schools'.[2] During the Second Reading, Devonshire enlarged upon this. Defective children, he said, 'are those who are feeble-minded and by that term is meant not those who are merely dull and difficult to teach, nor, on the other hand, those who are incapable of receiving any instruction in school and who are absolutely imbecile, but a class that is somewhat between these two extremes'.[3] This was a perfectly adequate definition of feeble-mindedness, but it was not, as it purported to be, a correct interpretation of the term defective. Whereas it was stated specifically in the Bill that a defective child could be one suffering from mental or physical defect, Devonshire confined the meaning to feeble-minded children. The error could be partly attributed to the Departmental Committee who by no means made it clear that physically defective children of normal intelligence would require special education. Since Devonshire's comment produced no change in the Bill, of greater importance was his statement that although the Departmental Committee had thought that authorities should be compelled to educate their defective children, the Education Department felt 'that there would be great difficulty in applying such compulsion, and in some cases the expenses would be too great'.[4] Consequently, the Bill was enabling, not compulsory.

This was unfortunate. It vitiated to a considerable extent the good effects of the measure. But again the Departmental Committee was not immune from blame. Unlike the Egerton Commission, which had recommended that every school authority should have the duty of educating its blind and deaf children, the Committee had only suggested that the Education Department should 'require provision of special schools in all districts where they think special provision is

---

[1] Ministry of Education Archives, Education Class 31, Piece 16.
[2] 62 and 63 Victoria, c. 32, s. 1.   [3] *Hansard*, 23.6.1899, col. 395.
[4] *Ibid.*, 23.6.1899, col. 397.

necessary'.[1] The Government seized the loophole, and the Elementary Education (Defective and Epileptic Children) Act 1899 merely permitted school authorities to make provision for the education of mentally and physically defective and epileptic children, with the result that ten years later only 133 out of 328 local education authorities had exercised their powers.[2] Nevertheless, a start had been made, and a class of children who had hitherto been neglected received official recognition.

Tributes were paid in both Houses of Parliament to the work of the Departmental Committee; but Egerton in the Lords and Trevelyan in the Commons had praise for others. The former thought that the part played by private and philanthropic bodies over the previous ten years should be recognized;[3] the latter felt that the London School Board should be regarded as the promoter of the legislation.[4] No one mentioned the small Rhineland town of Elberfeld which had provided the original inspiration.

[1] *C.D.E.C.*, Vol. 1, p. 22.

[2] *Annual Report for 1909 of the Chief Medical Officer of the Board of Education*, p. 152.

[3] *Hansard*, 23.6.1899, col. 398.   [4] *Ibid.*, 31.7.1899, col. 936.

12

THE PERIOD OF GROWTH:
I. ADVANCES IN THE EDUCATION
OF THE PHYSICALLY HANDICAPPED

'IT is not the evils that are new', wrote Macaulay, 'it is the recognition of them.' Towards the close of the nineteenth century came the recognition of some of the evils which produced crippling defect. With it came a desire to mitigate the effects of the evils. Of assistance to both recognition and desire was the development of modern orthopædic surgery, the rise of voluntary organizations and the foundation of schools for the physically handicapped.

In the years between the establishment of the industrial schools for cripples at Marylebone and Kensington[1] and 1890, very little was done for physically handicapped children. Shortly before 1870 a cripples' nursery had been opened in Old Quebec Street, London. A charitable institution, it accepted children between the ages of three and eight. The number of children attending was always small, and in 1890 there were only forty-six at it and the branch nursery at Margate.[2] Of hardly greater educational significance was the Moore Street Home for Crippled Orphan Boys, London. Opened by the Committee of the National Industrial Home for Crippled Boys, Kensington, its professed aim was the teaching of a trade to children aged eight to thirteen, by means of which they would be enabled to earn a livelihood. Jewellery and boot making were the two trades taught, and no boy was admitted unless he was both ambulant with the aid of crutches and likely to become self-supporting.[3] Apart

---

[1] See Chapter 5, p. 63.
[2] Bartley, *The Schools for the People* (1871), p. 362, and Charity Organization Society, *The Epileptic and Crippled Child and Adult* (1893), p. 118.
[3] Charity Organization Society, *The Epileptic and Crippled Child and Adult*, pp. 119–20.

from these two establishments, there were five other small residential homes at Abingdon, Tiverton, Berkhamsted, Newcastle-upon-Tyne, and Clifton. Very little education was given in any of them.[1]

Isolated and often unsuccessful attempts had been made to educate crippled children in the ordinary schools. In 1881 the London School Board resolved that cripples, even though they were aged over seven, might be admitted to, and retained at, infants' schools, and the Education Department gave its approval to the scheme.[2] But few badly handicapped children were admitted to the board schools. 'Parents,' reported the Charity Organization Society, 'demur to the loss of time and money in accompanying their children, and the cost of carrying those who cannot walk; and magistrates will not compel attendance.'[3] Even when parents and school co-operated to admit a child, other factors intervened. One enlightened school agreed to accept a boy with a hip disease who was confined to a perambulator bed. After his third attendance the boy wearied of attempting to learn lessons while lying helplessly in bed and he was withdrawn.[4] Consequently, almost all the severely handicapped children were permanently exempted from attending school.

To assist such children the Invalid Children's Aid Association was founded in 1888. Its declared object was 'to help seriously invalided and crippled children, chiefly by visitors each of whom takes charge of one or more children'.[5] Although it was primarily a society for care in the home, since it was often impossible to give adequate assistance in the home, the sending of children to convalescent hospitals became part of the Association's work. Equally difficult was the provision of education and training, and so the Association paid for children to be admitted to the few institutions which were available. Four years after its foundation, 2,200 were being visited and assisted at home, while a further 143 were in various hospitals and institutions at the Association's expense. The Charity Organization Society encouraged both the formation and the work of the Association, and itself played an active part in caring for handicapped children. In 1893 it suggested that there was an urgent need for the establishment of special facilities for the elementary education of crippled children. It further recommended the extension of the provision of industrial homes in which handicapped children could receive preliminary education and industrial training.

[1] Charity Organization Society, *The Epileptic and Crippled Child and Adult*, p. 121.
[2] Public Record Office, Education Class 14, Piece 19, and *School Board Chronicle*, Vol. XXVI, No. 565, 10.12.1881.
[3] Charity Organization Society, *The Epileptic and Crippled Child and Adult*, p. 113.
[4] *Ibid.*, p. 111.
[5] *Ibid.*, pp. 117–18.

I. Advances in the Education of the Physically Handicapped

With regard to what it felt were the hopeless, home-bound cases, little more could be done in the way of education than was being attempted by the Invalid Children's Aid Association, although there was a need for more hospitals and homes for the care of such children.[1]

Allied to the efforts of these two voluntary organizations was the work carried on by some of the London Settlements which were established for general social work at this time. The Women's University Settlement at Southwark first took an interest in physically handicapped children when some of its ladies started teaching crippled children at their homes.[2] It was found that almost all the children were illiterate and unable to amuse themselves. Under home teaching conditions the children, at best, could be visited only twice a week. However, if the children could attend a small day class they would receive much more tuition. Moreover, they would have the stimulus of each other's company. Hence, in 1894 the Settlement opened a class in a room at the London School Board's centre for deaf children at Southwark. From the outset there were difficulties. Some of the children visited by the Settlement workers were so severely handicapped that they could not be expected to attend a day school, and could, therefore, only be taught at home. But travel, even to those who could attend, presented problems. The obvious solution was to supply transport, and a fund was opened for the purchase of a carriage. For the first few years, however, the children had to make their own way to the school, with the result that the attendance fluctuated between six and twenty.

A second difficulty was to obtain sufficient voluntary assistance. All the teaching at the school was carried out by the ladies of the Settlement, and few of them had the necessary training or knowledge. One of them, Miss Sparks, became so enthusiastic about the work that she voluntarily took a course in kindergarten work, and returned to take charge of the school. The continuance of the school under adverse circumstances was later to be due almost entirely to the initiative of Miss Sparks. Despite Miss Sparks' example, there was a constant shortage of volunteers, and since it was felt desirable to have two teachers always present, the school was able to open only on four mornings and two afternoons a week. Finally, there was the problem of accommodation. As the number of children attending the deaf school at Southwark increased, the School Board required the room which had been lent to the Settlement. So the tiny

[1] *Ibid.*, p. 131.
[2] *C.D.E.C.*, Vol. 2, Evidence of C. S. Loch, 19.3.1897. Loch was Secretary of the Charity Organization Society.

school moved from one hired room to another, each with its own particular disadvantages.[1]

At the same time as Miss Sparks was engaged in her work at Southwark, Mr. and Mrs. G. T. Pilcher, in collaboration with the Invalid Children's Aid Association, opened a similar school in Old Church Road, Stepney. They were fortunate to have a wagonette in which to collect their children, but otherwise they experienced many of the difficulties of the Southwark school. The Bermondsey Settlement, too, interested itself in physically handicapped children. Several of its workers assisted in the work of the Bermondsey and Rotherhithe branch of the Invalid Children's Aid Association, and, as at Southwark, they determined to gather some children together. The Rev. J. Scott Lidgett, Warden of the Settlement, was the moving spirit in the scheme to provide occasional classes for crippled children. The classes were largely recreational in purpose, although the children were given a little drawing and allied subjects, but even these were treated in a recreative way.[2]

Nor was Settlement work for physical handicapped children confined to London. In June 1897, the Union of Women Workers established the Victoria Settlement in the Everton district of Liverpool. Before the year's end, a small number of handicapped children, who previously had been receiving some home instruction from the Invalid Children's Aid Association, were brought together to form a school. They met for the first time in the Mission room of St. Matthew's Church, which was to house the school for the first twelve months. The Vicar of St. Matthew's, the Rev. G. G. Monck, described the early days. 'The Cripples' School, as we call it, meets every Tuesday and Friday morning, from 10 to 1 p.m. Children who are crippled, or blind, or too delicate for school, are gladly welcomed, made warm and comfortable, have a little teaching, a good deal of play, and the loving care of the ladies who have taken up this work.'[3] Despite the fact that the school met at first on only two mornings in the week, the usual transport difficulties were encountered. Miss Edith Eskrigge, who was in charge of the school, reported that although there were forty children on the register, there were never more than fourteen present at any one time. This was because the school had 'not yet attained to the convenience of having the children brought to the class in a governess cart. There are, therefore, cases where, but for the negligence and indifference of the parents, the

[1] *C.D.E.C.*, Vol. 2, Evidence of Miss Sewell, Warden of the Southwark Settlement, 26.3.1897.
[2] *Ibid.*, Vol. 2, Evidence of Scott Lidgett, 5.3.1897.
[3] *Parish Magazine for January 1898, St. Matthew's, Scotland Road.*

I. Advances in the Education of the Physically Handicapped

children could be brought to us, but against these are one or two in which the mothers, at a great sacrifice of time and strength, bring their children most regularly.'[1]

By the end of 1898, the class was meeting on three mornings and one afternoon each week, a governess cart was hired at a cost of three shillings weekly, and the average attendance had almost doubled.[2] All the children were taught to read and write, and in some cases simple arithmetic was attempted. The remainder of the time was devoted to simple object lessons and hand work. As far as the latter was concerned, with great wisdom each child was allowed to concentrate 'on that which it does best'.[3] Some of the children who attended the school were extremely deprived. A girl pushed in at the door one morning during class was in a deplorable condition, neglected in body and mind, and almost blind. A call at her home showed her to be utterly uncared for, and her blindness was attributed to rats having entered her cot when she was a baby. Similarly, a boy was brought to the school who was paralysed in all four limbs and who suffered from frequent epileptic fits yet had never received any medical attention. In both these cases the Settlement was able to give more than educational assistance. The girl was removed from her home and subsequently entered a school for the blind; the boy was operated upon and, in much better health, continued to attend the school.[4]

Early in 1900 the Industrial and Special Schools Committee of the Liverpool School Board recommended that two ladies from the Victoria Settlement should be invited to assist in organizing the establishment of schools for defective children. Four such schools were planned, three for mentally and one for physically handicapped children. With the children from the Settlement class as its nucleus, the physically handicapped school opened in Shaw Street at Easter 1900.[5] This was but the second of its kind in the country to be established by a School Board.

The first had been in London, and its foundation had also been due to the work at a Settlement. Especially had it been due to the influence of one person at a Settlement. The name of Mrs. Humphry Ward, novelist and social worker, is closely connected with the welfare of handicapped children. A granddaughter of Arnold of Rugby, she was born in Tasmania where her father, also named Thomas Arnold, was an inspector of schools. After her marriage,

---

[1] *First Report of the Victoria Women's Settlement, 1898*, p. 12.
[2] *Second Annual Report, 1899*, pp. 7–8.
[3] *First Report, 1898*, p. 13.   [4] *Ibid.*, p. 14.
[5] *Third Annual Report, 1900*, pp. 4–5.

and the family's return to England, Mary Ward felt that the decline of Christianity could be halted if its social mission were to be emphasized at the expense of its miraculous element. Her views were embodied in her best known novel, *Robert Elsmere*, which brought her into touch with others who wished to work among London's poor. In 1890 with the assistance of her associates, she founded a Settlement at University Hall, Gordon Square, for popular Bible teaching, simplified Christianity and social work. Seven years later this developed into the Passmore Edwards Settlement, Tavistock Place. There she established children's play hours, a system of organized recreation designed to keep the children off the streets after school hours. These were immediately successful. Soon there were 1,200 children on the roll, and the foundations of the future play centres had been laid.[1]

Since most of the Settlement's activities took place in the evenings, Mary Ward felt that some use should be made of the premises which lay empty by day. Children who could benefit were those who were physically handicapped and confined to their homes both by day and in the evenings. Enquiries in the Autumn of 1898 showed that there were more than sufficient children in the area of the Settlement to warrant the establishment of a school. The enquiries also showed, as did the experience of the Pilchers and Miss Sparks, that to be successful the school must have a nurse and an ambulance in addition to full-time salaried teachers. While it appeared out of the question for the Settlement to provide everything that was required, Mary Ward was convinced that sufficient money to pay for the ambulance and nurse could be raised, but the salaries of the teachers would have to come from a different source. Accordingly, in December she wrote to the London School Board. Her letter proposed that a school should be opened, with the Settlement providing accommodation, transport and medical care, and the Board being responsible for the teaching staff, equipment and stationery. The children attending, she suggested, should come from among those scheduled by the Board as exempt from ordinary school, those recommended by out-patient departments of hospitals, especially the nearby Alexandra Hip Hospital, and those visited by the Invalid Children's Aid Association. The Settlement had already made a preliminary selection of twenty-five children. Of these only nine were officially exempted by the Board, but some of the remainder were not attending schools, others but very irregularly, and then only at great personal risk. Within the month the Board accepted the proposal. Formal permission to open the school was requested and received from the Education

[1] *The Times*, 25.3.1920, and Trevelyan, *The Life of Mrs. Humphry Ward* (1923).

I. Advances in the Education of the Physically Handicapped

Department, and on the last day of February 1899 the school opened under the superintendence of Miss Milligan.[1]

In the few brief references which exist to the history of the development of schools for the physically handicapped in England, the school at the Passmore Edwards Settlement, Tavistock Place, is credited with being the first of its kind.[2] Certainly it was the first to be opened by a School Board, the first to be recognized, and later certified, by the Education Department under the Act of 1899, the first to employ full-time teachers, and the first to be open on every morning and afternoon of the week. It was not, however, the first attempt at giving education to physically handicapped children in a day school, and less than justice is done to the work of Miss Sparks, Mr. and Mrs. Pilcher and Miss Eskrigge by George Newman's statement, in his first *Annual Report* as Chief Medical Officer to the Board of Education, that the school at the Passmore Edwards Settlement 'was the beginning of the cripple school movement in this country'.[3]

Another feature of the Tavistock Place school was its success.[4] Within a year forty-five children were being taught by two teachers. Many of them had never been to school previously, some had attended for a short period before becoming handicapped, all were 'backward, languid, and ill-prepared, incapable of working the same hours and in the same way as healthy children'.[5] Nevertheless, at the end of the school's second year, Mrs. Burgwin was able to report: 'The improvement in the pupils—physically and intellectually—demonstrates the value of the classes to these afflicted children, who in spite of pain and disease, seem generally bright and happy.'[6] Part of the happiness was undoubtedly due to the dinners which the children were given. At first, children were not admitted to the ambulance which collected them in the mornings unless they had with them their own dinner or $1\frac{1}{2}d$. to pay for the meal at school. Gradually the number of children bringing their own dinners decreased until all were taking the school dinner.

The feeding of the children was the responsibility of Mary Ward and the Settlement workers. They brought and cooked the food, waited on the children and superintended their playtime afterwards.

[1] Public Record Office, Education Class 14, Piece 43, and letter to *The Times*, 26.9.1901. In her three-column letter to *The Times* Mrs. Humphry Ward gave a comprehensive account of the opening of the school and subsequent developments.

[2] Leff, *The School Health Service* (1959), p. 281, and *Annual Report for 1908 of the Chief Medical Officer of the Board of Education*, p. 118.

[3] *Op. cit.*, p. 118. Mrs. Ward knew of the existence of the Southwark and Stepney schools before she approached the London School Board with the idea of a school at Tavistock Place, and she subsequently paid tribute to their pioneer work: *The Times*, 26.9.1901.

[4] It exists today as the Mary Ward School.   [5] *The Times*, 26.9.1901.   [6] *Ibid.*

157

From the beginning the meals were good, but Mrs. Ward felt that they were not always tempting to sickly appetites, nor, on the other hand, was there always enough. This was understandable since the cost of the food did not exceed the contributions paid by the children. It was seen that if the children were to receive more and better food, the meals would have to be provided at a loss. This Mrs. Ward decided to do, and from May 1901 the children were given eggs, milk, cream and fruit as part of their meals.[1] The improvement in health more than justified the additional expenditure, and the success of the venture led in 1902 to the establishment of the Cripple Children's Training and Dinner Society. With the approval of the London County Council, the Society provided dinners for all children attending London's schools for physically defective children. By 1905 1,100 at sixteen schools were being fed. The children paid 2*d.* per day, the L.E.A. provided cooking equipment and half the salaries of the cooks, and the Society provided everything else. Children of very poor parents received their meals free of charge, while others had to pay only a penny.[2]

Mary Ward's work for physically handicapped children did not end with the foundation of the Tavistock Place school and the Dinner Society. For the remainder of her life she continued to advocate better provision for them. Her husband was on the staff of *The Times*, and her views were frequently to be found in its pages, so much so that *The Times* itself joined in her campaign. Its leader of September 26th, 1901 praised the work being done at the school for physically handicapped children under the Bristol School Board. The children were so happy, it continued, 'that when a general holiday was given to celebrate the relief of Mafeking, there was an unanimous petition from the cripples that they might be exempted from it'.

However, her greatest achievement was still to come. In 1914 a statutory duty was laid upon L.E.A.s to educate feeble-minded children.[3] Mary Ward determined that a similar duty should extend to physically handicapped children. As the war neared its end, she sought the views of ninety-five of the largest L.E.A.s, and sent a summary of their replies, which were favourable to her cause, to every Member of Parliament. As a result, a clause was added to the Education Bill of 1918, and the 1899 Act ceased to be permissive in any respect. On her death two years later, Sir Robert Jones wrote to her daughter: 'One of the last pieces of work accomplished by Mrs.

[1] *The Times*, 26.9.1901.

[2] *Report of the Inter-Departmental Committee on the Medical Inspection and Feeding of Children attending Public Elementary Schools*, 1905, Vol. 2, Evidence of Mrs. W. Phipps, 19.5.1905.

[3] See Chapter 14, p. 188.

I. Advances in the Education of the Physically Handicapped

Ward for cripples was the insertion of the P.D. clause in the Fisher Education Act, and the reports obtained for that purpose are largely the groundwork and origin of this Committee, in whose work she took a great interest.'[1]

The Committee to which Robert Jones referred was the Central Committee for the Care of Cripples, of which he was Chairman. Its formation in 1919, as he implied in his letter, had owed a great deal to the initiative of Mrs. Humphry Ward. While her earlier work had been mainly confined to the social and educational advancement of cripples, she realized that the future lay with the provision of definite orthopædic treatment combined with education for severely handicapped children. She therefore joined with Robert Jones, Agnes Hunt, G. R. Girdlestone and members of the Invalid Children's Aid Association and the British Red Cross Society in establishing the Central Committee, whose aim it was to promote a national scheme for the complete provision of treatment and education for physically defective children throughout the country.[2]

Sir Robert Jones and Dame Agnes Hunt both started their work for crippled children at the turn of the century. The former, in practice at Liverpool, realized that orthopædics, as an emerging branch of surgery, had more than an operative function. Hitherto, the surgical treatment of crippled children had been generally limited to excisions of joints aimed at avoiding subsequent suppuration and destruction. In such cases obvious deformities resulted, and it was left to Robert Jones to see the problem as a curable and preventable one. He realized that the solution lay in treatment in special hospitals. These should be situated in the country, so that if operations were necessary the children would have the benefit of fresh air after being operated upon. On the other hand, they should not be regarded as convalescent homes, since the children should be under constant medical treatment. At the instigation of Robert Jones, a public meeting was held in Liverpool in 1898 at which it was agreed to promote the foundation of such a hospital. As a result of the subsequent publicity, the West Kirby Convalescent Home for Children offered to provide a ward until a suitable hospital was established.[3] There in 1901 a special school was established for the long-stay orthopædic cases. This was the first hospital school, although it was for long known as a school for physically defective children by both

---

[1] Cited by Trevelyan, *The Life of Mrs. Humphry Ward*, p. 294. Janet Ward, who wrote her mother's *Life*, married Professor G. M. Trevelyan.

[2] Girdlestone, *The Care and Cure of Cripple Children* (1924), p. 10, and Watson, *The Life of Sir Robert Jones* (1934), p. 244.

[3] Its establishment was not long delayed. In April 1900 the foundation stone of the Royal County Hospital for Children, overlooking the Dee at Heswall, was laid.

the Liverpool Education Committee, which maintained it, and the Board of Education, which certified it.[1]

Both Robert Jones and Agnes Hunt contributed more to the welfare of disabled children than came directly within their respective spheres of surgery and nursing. Dame Agnes, a member of a well known Shropshire family, had herself been crippled by osteomyelitis at the age of ten, but her indomitable spirit and the spartan attitude of her family enabled her to overcome her disability to a considerable extent. On the death of her father, Agnes was taken by her rather eccentric mother to Australia. The intention was to purchase an island and raise Angora goats. Fortunately for the cripples of this country, neither island nor goats materialized. On her return to England she trained as a nurse, and in 1900 established at Baschurch, in Shropshire, a small convalescent home for children. The home, in an old country house, was, because of its many stairs, unsuitable for cripples. Nevertheless a number, whom doctors considered needed fresh air and sunshine by day, were admitted. However, the laborious work of carrying children up and down stairs persuaded Agnes Hunt to attempt the experiment of giving the children fresh air at night also. Accordingly, three-sided sheds were constructed in the grounds, 'most of the timber and corrugated iron of which they were composed being stolen from Boreaton Park, in the merciful absence of my brother at the South African War'.[2]

The character of the venture now changed. No more convalescent children were admitted; an operating theatre was constructed, and Robert Jones became consulting orthopædic surgeon; and the name was changed to the Shropshire Surgical Home. So was founded the first open-air hospital for cripples in the world, which in 1921 became the Robert Jones and Agnes Hunt Orthopædic Hospital at Oswestry. At first the children at Baschurch received neither education nor training, but in 1904 the Home started making its own splints, and a blacksmith's shop was opened. Soon, some of the girls in the Home were padding the splints, and the boys were assisting the blacksmith. Here was to be found the germ of the Derwen Cripples' Training College which in 1927, through the initiative of Agnes Hunt, was opened near the Oswestry Hospital. Its purpose was to provide vocational training for children leaving schools for physically handicapped children at the age of sixteen.[3]

---

[1] *Annual Report for 1910 of the Chief Medical Officer of the Board of Education,* Girdlestone, *op. cit.,* p. 81, and Watson, *op. cit.,* pp. 108–11.

[2] Agnes Hunt in a contribution to Girdlestone, *The Care and Cure of Cripple Children,* p. 74.

[3] Girdlestone, *op. cit.,* pp. 8–9 and 73–4, Watson, *op. cit.,* pp. 114–23, and Hunt, *This is My Life* (1938), pp. 122–63 and 181–7.

I. Advances in the Education of the Physically Handicapped

In 1903 at Chailey, Sussex, another experiment was initiated. It developed into the first residential school for physically handicapped children which combined hospital treatment with education and training. Its origins were to be found in the previous century, when in 1894 Mrs., later Dame, Grace Kimmins established the Guild of the Brave Poor Things in London. For its headquarters, the Guild used the Bermondsey University Settlement where Scott Lidgett was Warden. There, cripples of all ages and sexes met weekly to be entertained by the voluntary workers of the Guild. Gradually the activities of the Guild increased. The cripples were given outings, holidays and surgical appliances. Still Mrs. Kimmins was not satisfied. Philanthropic assistance was a mere palliative. What the handicapped required were the means to become independent, the means to be freed mentally and socially from the old traditions of deformity. With these aims in mind she took seven badly handicapped boys from the Guild and housed them in the green heart of Sussex. The buildings they occupied were originally rented, and subsequently purchased, from the local Parish Council. They had once formed a workhouse and an industrial school, and were in an extremely poor state of repair. With the aid of the boys and the donations which came in response to appeals,[1] the buildings were renovated, and others added, to form the Heritage Craft Schools and Hospital.[2] There was, as the name implied, considerable emphasis on the teaching of crafts for vocational purposes. But the educational side was not neglected. Much of its development was due to Mrs. Kimmins' husband, Dr. C. W. Kimmins, Chief Inspector of Schools under the L.C.C. However the three R's, even in the case of the younger children, were confined to the mornings. The afternoons were devoted to handicrafts, and, as the children grew older, the handicrafts became vocational training which sometimes encroached upon the morning lessons, for the aim of the Heritage was to make the children self-supporting.

There was another aim, too. Over the main door of the boys' craft school was inscribed: 'Men are made here'. Certainly, twenty-eight boys who had passed through the hospital and craft school were sufficiently well made to fight and fall in the First World War.

The early success of the Heritage was undoubtedly due to Mrs. Kimmins. Sir Cyril Burt has written that the schools were 'one of the most remarkable voluntary institutions in this country, and are due

---

[1] A letter to *The Times* from Princess Louise, Duchess of Argyll, who was a Patron, brought in £5,000.

[2] Girls were admitted from 1908, and a separate craft school was founded for them.

entirely to her wonderful insight, imagination and energy'.[1] At the same time there were others who should not be forgotten: the first Chairman of the Governors, Scott Lidgett; the first Headmaster, Percy Sykes; and the founder and first Chairman of the Medical Board, Robert Jones, whose opinion of Chailey is worth recording.

'The spirit of Chailey is not spartan, but there is no maudlin sentimentality encouraged. The child's deformities and disabilities are rarely alluded to. He is filled with emulation and a desire to excel. If he has lost an arm or a leg, he still has one or the other so trained as to minimize his disability. . . . Every boy and every girl fully realize that they are to be of service in the world. . . . They are taught the joy and morality of work.'[2]

William Purdie Treloar, carpet manufacturer and philanthropist, became Lord Mayor of London in 1906. Inspired by the same ideas as Dame Grace Kimmins, in a year free of national disaster he launched an appeal for the foundation of a hospital and college for cripples. The former was to provide combined treatment and education for children up to the age of twelve, the latter a three year course in trade training for boys aged fourteen to eighteen. Royal approval and support were given to the appeal, and by the end of Treloar's term of office £60,000 had been subscribed. The Princess Louise Military Hospital at Alton, Hampshire, built during the South African War, was acquired, and the Lord Mayor Treloar Cripples' Hospital and College was opened in 1908. At the hospital, up to 230 children, all surgical T.B. cases, stayed for an average of eighteen months. On admission, the children were tested in their educational attainments, and put in wards according to their ability. There they were taught until they were well enough to attend school in a large thatched shed in the grounds. The College, which was separate from the Hospital, although under the same management, provided courses in leatherwork, tailoring or boot making for fifty boys. Treloar, who died in 1923, devoted much of the remainder of his life to the interest of the children at Alton, and with Dame Grace Kimmins he showed that the rehabilitation of crippled children was a practical possibility.[3]

The third of the trio, who were created Dames of the British Empire in recognition of their work on behalf of the physically unfit,

---

[1] Kimmins, *Heritage Craft Schools and Hospitals, Chailey, 1903–1948* (1948), in Preface, p. 7.
[2] Cited by Watson, *The Life of Sir Robert Jones*, p. 123.
[3] *Annual Report for 1910 of the Chief Medical Officer of the Board of Education*, p. 114, *Annual Report for 1926*, p. 142, Girdlestone, *op. cit.*, pp. 59–60, and Lawrence, *William Purdie Treloar* (1925).

I. Advances in the Education of the Physically Handicapped

showed the same thing. Dame Georgiana Buller was the only child of General Sir Redvers Buller, who won renown and the Victoria Cross in the Boer War. Before the outbreak of the Great War of 1914–18 she had become prominent in the British Red Cross Society, and when the War came she established the Exeter V.A.D. Hospital. Soon the hospital had forty-five auxiliary hospitals attached to it, with Dame Georgiana in charge of the whole complex organization. Shortly before August 1914 she had injured her spine in a hunting accident. Her tireless work on behalf of the wounded aggravated her old injury, and at the War's end she collapsed and herself became a semi-invalid. With great will power and the assistance of her doctor she rehabilitated herself, and determined to assist others to do likewise. She served on, and became Vice-Chairman of, the Central Council for the Care of Cripples, and in 1933 started her fund raising activities for the foundation of two colleges for the training of the disabled. The first of these, called originally the Cripples' Training College, and now the Queen Elizabeth's Training College for the Disabled, Leatherhead, opened in 1934; the second, St. Loyes College, Exeter, in 1937. Both owe their existence primarily to the vision of Dame Georgiana. Both accept children leaving schools for physically handicapped children. Both provide for a continuation of their general education alongside their trade training.[1]

Many of the early lines of development of schools for physically handicapped children, the day special school, the orthopædic hospital school, the trade school, were the results of the efforts of individual philanthropists, but the residential school of rest and recovery had as its model a school established by a local education authority. The improvement in medical facilities in general, and in orthopædic surgery in particular, allied to the discovery of X-rays by Röntgen in 1895, brought, in the first decade of the twentieth century, an optimistic assessment of the needs of physically handicapped children. Day special schools, it was felt, would soon become unnecessary as the number of crippled children decreased, and those remaining would have recovered sufficiently to attend the ordinary school. In support of this view, Manchester L.E.A. established in 1905 the Swinton House School of Recovery. There, children would be taken in the early stages of disease, and treated and taught, at first in bed, until fit to return to the ordinary school. The school was sited near the Manchester Hospital for Sick Children in order that those requiring surgical treatment could be easily moved to the hospital, and subsequently returned to the school. Situated in a large house in

[1] From notes supplied by Mr. W. King, Principal of St. Loyes College, and *Annual Report Queen Elizabeth's Training College for the Disabled, 1957.*

eight acres of grounds, the school contained six wards each of ten beds. Most of the teaching took place in the wards, though in summer some of the children were given their lessons on the lawn. The teaching staff of five was augmented by a matron and six nurses, and the whole emphasis of the school was on invalid care over a period of some two years. It was an immediate success, and soon there was a long waiting list, despite the fact that the L.E.A. had acquired a nearby house, thus doubling the accommodation.[1]

By 1908 five other authorities had followed Manchester's lead, and the Board of Education welcomed the development. 'If it were possible to deal with all cases in this way,' wrote its Chief Medical Officer, 'the method would be preferable to the special day school; but at present it is not possible to hope that Education Authorities will follow the Manchester scheme so extensively as to make day schools for cripples unnecessary.'[2]

This was only partly correct. Certainly day schools did not, and have not, become unnecessary. Equally, residential schools would be required for some physically handicapped children. But they would not be schools which aimed at keeping their children for a mere two years. Rather, they would cater for those in rural areas for whom a day school was impracticable. More especially would they cater for the very severely handicapped for whom residential care was essential. Both these groups of children were largely ignored; the former because until 1918 there was no compulsion upon education authorities to provide for physically handicapped children, the latter because it was believed that their handicap was too severe to warrant education at school. Nevertheless, although the schools of recovery in their original form and intention were short-lived, they did show the way for the future residential schools.

Other valuable experiments in the education of physically handicapped children were made during this period. A residential school in Kensington for girls suffering from infective inflammatory diseases of the eye was opened by the Dominican Sisters. Their request that the school should be officially recognized by the Board of Education presented a problem to the administrators in Whitehall. Such a school had not been envisaged by the framers of the 1899 Act. Yet the girls were suffering from a physical defect, contagious ophthalmia, and they could not receive proper benefit from the instruction in the ordinary school, because they could not be admitted to such a school for fear of infecting others. This argument, advanced by

---

[1] *Annual Report for 1908 of the Chief Medical Officer of the Board of Education*, pp. 118–19, and *Annual Report for 1909*, p. 142.

[2] *Annual Report for 1908*, p. 119.

I. Advances in the Education of the Physically Handicapped

Eichholz, carried the day, and in 1905 the Board certified the school.[1] A similar ophthalmic school for boys at Chigwell, Essex, was certified three years later.[2] The previous year the L.C.C. had opened a day school at Whitechapel for children suffering from favus, a fungal skin disease, and the school had been granted recognition on the same grounds as the ophthalmic schools.[3]

The extension of the provisions of the 1899 Act to defects other than crippling ones was carried a stage further with the establishment of schools in hospitals for children suffering from pulmonary tuberculosis. At first the children were taught by voluntary teachers, but soon the Board of Education was being asked to approve schools with full-time teachers. There existed, considered the Board, three categories of consumptive children. First, there were those who had a consumptive tendency, or the disease in a mild and non-communicable form, who could be educated in the ordinary school. Secondly, children who had the disease in a sub-acute or chronic form could attend a special school, since their debility would prevent them attending the ordinary school. Lastly, there was a group of children who, with the disease in an acute or rapidly advancing form, required hospital treatment, 'and are practically incapable of receiving benefit from any instruction whatever'.[4] The Board, having regard to the wording of the 1899 Act, felt that education authorities had the power to provide special education only for the children in the second category. Consequently, it was not prepared to approve schools in hospitals. Fortunately, this decision was soon reversed. In 1911 the Chief Medical Officer could comment: 'It is most desirable that every residential institution for tuberculous children should provide systematic and suitably organized school teaching.'[5] As a result of the change of policy, the first sanatorium school for children suffering from pulmonary tuberculosis was certified in 1912, and seven years later nineteen had been established.

Hence, when in 1919 the compulsory clause, concerning physically handicapped children, contained in the Fisher Act became operative, the provision for their education was already varied. There existed, in addition to the open-air schools for delicate children described in Chapter 13, day and residential schools for cripples, schools of rest and recovery, schools in convalescent homes, trade schools, orthopædic and T.B. hospital schools, ophthalmic schools and a favus school. But though the variety of schools was great their

[1] Ministry of Education Archives, Education Class 32, Piece 109.
[2] *Ibid.*, Education Class 32, Piece 18.
[3] *Annual Report for 1908 of the Chief Medical Officer*, p. 118.
[4] *Annual Report for 1909 of the Chief Medical Officer*, p. 149.
[5] *Annual Report for 1911 of the Chief Medical Officer*, p. 81.

number was insufficient. Of the 328 education authorities only twenty-eight had provided day special schools, and many of the residential schools were maintained by voluntary organizations.[1] Gradually, however, the children in the rural areas were catered for, and by 1939 satisfactory provision had been made for the majority of physically handicapped children. One group only remained without education. The very badly handicapped children, some of them bedridden, many of them incontinent, all of them desperately in need of help, for whom it was still thought to be out of the question to provide education, stagnated at home. It was to be left to the Education Act of 1944 to allow some of them to be given home teaching, and to the voluntary spastic organizations of the post-war years to cater for others. Some, even today, remain without education.

[1] *Annual Report for 1918 of the Chief Medical Officer*, p. 113.

13

THE PERIOD OF GROWTH: II. ADVANCES IN THE HEALTH SERVICES

ONLY in the second half of the nineteenth century did the health of school-children receive any systematic attention. It is true that as far back as 1812 James Ware published a report on the eyesight of school-children in Chelsea, but in England the next seventy years were barren. What advance there was during this period occurred in Germany, where in 1866 Hermann Cohn started his research into the eyesight of 10,000 school-children in Breslau. The extent of his work and the theories he formulated, as distinct from the statistics he produced, mark Cohn as the originator of the systematic study of the health of school-children. When at length in 1883 he published his findings, he recommended, both on general grounds and as an oculist, the appointment of school doctors. In the same year the first school medical officer was appointed in Germany, at Frankfurt-am-Main.

Meanwhile, in England Clement Dukes, medical officer to Rugby School, published his *Health at School* in 1882. Two years later Dr. Crichton Browne reported to the Education Department his findings that a great deal of 'mental over-pressure' existed in the elementary schools of London.[1] The research work of Francis Warner has already been mentioned, as has the appointment in 1890 of Dr. W. R. Smith as medical officer to the London School Board, and in 1893 of James Kerr to Bradford.[2] Kerr in 1902 succeeded Smith, and in the same year Margaret McMillan also left

[1] *Annual Report for 1908 of the Chief Medical Officer of the Board of Education*, pp. 2–4.   [2] See Chapter 10, p. 128.

Bradford for London. The partnership which had been so successful in Bradford now turned its attention to the national scene. Together the doctor and the social worker agitated for nation-wide medical inspection of school-children.[1]

The time was propitious. The Acts of 1893 and 1899, regarding the education of handicapped children, had contributed to a rising public opinion that action should be taken concerning children suffering from other forms of physical impairment. In addition, the implementation of the 1899 Act necessitated the employment of a doctor in the work of ascertainment. Indeed, this aspect of the Act gave, for the first time, statutory powers regarding school administration to a medical officer. Moreover, in 1903 the Royal Commission on Physical Training (Scotland) revealed the extent and degree of physical defect in Scotland. The Commissioners pointed out that they had experienced considerable difficulty in obtaining data, and this difficulty, added to the large number of defective children they had found, impelled them to recommend both the medical inspection and feeding of school-children. Finally, opinion, both public and parliamentary, was aroused by the revelations of the lack of physical fitness among potential recruits for the South African War. Of the volunteers who came forward, only one in every three was fit enough to become a soldier.[2]

More than any other factor, this was the one that counted with the Government. Slowly the realization was coming that upon the health of the school child depended the fighting strength of the nation. An investigation was called for, and the Duke of Devonshire, Lord President of the Council, appointed the Committee on Physical Deterioration. Its *Report*, published in 1904, was described by Sir George Newman as 'an exceptionally human document which carried great weight not only with the legislature but in the formation of public opinion'.[3] Kerr and Eichholz gave evidence before the Committee. Both advocated the establishment of a system of special schools for semi-invalid children who were in the ordinary schools. These required education in the country, where fresh air and regular meals would re-establish their enfeebled constitutions. Although neither witness used the term open-air school, this undoubtedly was what they both had in mind.[4] In addition, Eichholz considered that

---

[1] See Leese, *Personalities and Power in English Education* (1950), p. 249.

[2] See Leff, *The School Health Service*, p. 21, and Lowndes, *The Silent Social Revolution* (1937), p. 227.

[3] Newman, 'The Evolution and Policy of the School Medical Service', *The Year Book of Education, 1933*, p. 399.

[4] *Report of the Inter-Departmental Committee on Physical Deterioration*, Vol. 1, p. 63.

II. Advances in the Health Services

medical inspection was the greatest single need in the existing school organization. He pointed out that, despite the fact that the London School Board employed a team of medical officers, they confined themselves to examining defective eyesight, feeble-minded children and teachers.[1]

Of the fifty-three recommendations which the Committee made, three were directly concerned with school-children. Consideration should be given to the possibility of establishing schools for the temporary treatment of children who, because of ill health, were not up to normal school standards. Secondly, it was recommended that the medical inspection of children should be laid as a duty upon every school authority. Thirdly, authorities should be compelled to assist underfed children by providing school meals. In spite of these definite recommendations and Newman's comment that the *Report* carried weight with the legislature, the Government procrastinated, and yet another investigation was ordered. The Committee on the Medical Inspection and Feeding of Children was appointed, met and reported in 1905. Its terms of reference were confining. It was required merely to enquire into the existing arrangements for medical inspection and the provision of meals. This it did. Forty-eight areas, it found, had established some degree of medical inspection. School meals, in the few places where they were given, were provided by voluntary bodies. Although recommendations were not asked of it, the Committee could not forbear to point out that there was much room for improvement in the matter of medical inspection. Moreover, it stressed that where medical inspection existed, nothing was done regarding treatment, although it clearly implied that something should be done.[2]

In December 1905 Balfour, hopeful of a Liberal split over Home Rule, resigned. At the General Election of the following month the Liberals were returned with an overwhelming majority over Balfour's Conservatives. In addition, the emerging Labour Party had fifty-three representatives. One of their first actions was to sponsor a Private Member's Bill to give L.E.A.s the power to provide school meals up to the cost of a halfpenny rate. Campbell-Bannerman's Government offered no resistance, and in 1906 the Education (Provision of Meals) Act was passed. During the same year the Government itself attempted to legislate on medical inspection. Birrell, President of the Board of Education, added to a Bill with much wider implications a clause which would give power to education authorities 'to make arrangements . . . for attending to the health

[1] *Ibid.*, Vol. 1, p. 64.
[2] *Report of the Committee*, Vol. 1, pp. 31–2.

and physical condition of the children educated in public elementary schools'.[1] Although the clause met with no opposition, the Bill as a whole, which was the first of three attempts made by the Liberals to overthrow the 1902 Act, was drastically amended by the Lords, and the measure was dropped.

A further stimulus to action was provided by the International Congress on School Hygiene which was held in London in 1907. At it, attention was drawn to the need for medical care of children in school. When, therefore, in the same year the Government introduced its Education (Administrative Provisions) Bill, it included a clause which compelled, not empowered as the abortive 1906 Bill had done, L.E.A.s to provide for the medical inspection of children. The Bill was passed without difficulty, and as a result the School Medical Service, later to be called the School Health Service, came into being. At the same time the Board of Education established its Medical Branch with George Newman as its first head.

Since the 1907 Act dealt only with medical inspection, not treatment, it had been the intention of the legislators at Westminster that when a parent was informed by a school doctor of a child's ailment treatment would be sought from the family doctor. This did not prove to be the case. Instead, Newman encouraged authorities to establish their own clinics, as Bradford had done in 1908, where children could be treated by the school doctors. The growth of clinics was slow, but by the time of Newman's retirement in 1935 nearly 2,000 had been established. Much of the early success of the new service was due to Sir George Newman. Of him G. A. N. Lowndes has written: 'He was a public servant who by his work saved more lives than were ever lost in our national wars.'[2]

Apart from its function of supervising the medical inspection and treatment of children, the Medical Branch of the Board of Education was given the task of inspecting special schools. Until 1903 special schools came under the District Inspectors of the Elementary Branch of the Board. In that year Dr. Eichholz, who, as has been seen, was appointed in the first instance in an ordinary inspecting capacity, became responsible for the supervision of schools for the blind, deaf, defective and epileptic in England and Wales. Some special schools, however, continued to be inspected under the old system. On the establishment of the Medical Branch, Eichholz was attached to it, and was soon joined by other medical officers. Some of these shared with Eichholz his duties in connection with special schools, and in 1920 came the definite ruling that all special schools

[1] Education (England and Wales) Bill, c. 35.
[2] Lowndes, *The Silent Social Revolution*, p. 231.

should be inspected and reported upon by the Board's medical officers.[1]

To many, such a system seemed completely wrong. Writing in 1930, J. M. Ritchie commented on the transfer of the responsibility for special schools to the Medical Branch:

'As far as schools for the blind were concerned, this transfer did violence to educational considerations. Such institutions do not require more medical inspection than ordinary schools, while the curriculum and methods of instruction are closely akin. The Staffs are ordinary teachers and their work is entirely pedagogical. To decree that the work shall be inspected by members of another profession is indefensible.'[2] Ritchie's complaint was on behalf of schools for the blind, but his comment was applicable to other types of special schools. In response to continual protests, the Board in 1931 appointed to the Inspectorate of the Medical Branch an educational psychologist with special responsibility for schools for handicapped children, and with this token of goodwill the special schools had, for the moment, to be satisfied.[3]

The foundation of the School Medical Service gave added impetus to a movement which was already gathering momentum. Kerr and Eichholz had advocated schools for delicate children in their evidence before the Committee on Physical Deterioration, and the Committee had repeated their advocacy in its recommendations. This had been in 1904, the year which saw the foundation of the first open-air school in the world. It was opened in the woods of Charlottenburg outside Berlin. It was attended by physically debilitated children. It was successful. The children, though they attended for only half-day sessions, improved in health and educational attainment. Soon other German towns took up the experiment, and similar schools were opened at Mülhausen, München-Gladbach, Dresden and the progressive little town of Elberfeld.[4] Across the Atlantic in the United States a school for delicate children was established at Providence, Rhode Island, and in Canada on Toronto Island.

Meanwhile in 1907 at Bostall Wood, Plumstead, the L.C.C. opened the first English open-air school. In the following year it moved to the grounds of Shrewsbury House, Woolwich; the L.C.C. opened two other schools; and Bradford, Norwich and Halifax one each. Two of the London schools were conducted partly in large

---

[1] *Report of the Joint Committee of the College of Teachers of the Blind and the National Institute for the Blind* (1936), p. 5.

[2] Ritchie, *Concerning the Blind*, p. 107.

[3] In September 1934 the educational inspection of day schools for physically and mentally defective children became the responsibility of District Inspectors.

[4] *Annual Report for 1908 of the Chief Medical Officer*, p. 120.

houses and partly in sheds in the grounds. In the third case, where the house was not available, two buildings were erected in the grounds. Each building consisted of a light framework set on a wooden base and covered with a heat-proof canvas material. In fine weather all four canvas walls were rolled up. The Chief Medical Officer in his first *Annual Report* praised this kind of building,[1] and many of the open-air schools which were subsequently founded copied its bandstand type of structure. By 1912 a voluntary organization, the Marylebone Dispensary for T.B., had opened a school in a bandstand off the Broad Walk, Regent's Park. Forty-eight children, all delicate with a family history of consumption, attended. They brought their own food which they ate at noon and at 4 p.m. They could not bring sufficient clothing to keep them warm. Therefore, in cold or wet weather they were supplied with clogs, rugs, shawls and foot and hand warmers, consisting of slow combustion briquettes.[2]

Not all the schools were of such flimsy construction. Bradford provided the first permanent school. The premises consisted of iron buildings with additions in brick and woodwork. There were two classrooms, a verandah, kitchen, and slipper and shower baths.[3] But whether the schools were housed in permanent or temporary buildings the emphasis everywhere was on fresh air. Whenever the weather allowed it, lessons were given in the open, and when the children were compelled to move indoors the work continued 'under some simple shelter sufficient to afford protection from the sun or rain'.[4] The children who attended the schools, the nervous, debilitated, undernourished and anæmic, and those suffering from bronchial catarrh or incipient T.B., or recovering from tonsil or adenoid operations, were better off than had they remained in their own dark, overcrowded and poorly ventilated schools. They were also often very cold, for the British climate is not ideally suited to open-air education. But in the heyday of the open-air movement this was a minor consideration. The important thing, it was felt, was that delicate children should be given the opportunity of rebuilding their strength under conditions far removed from those obtaining in their homes. Therefore, in addition to the benefit of fresh air the children received wholesome and regular meals, adequate rest, and, occasionally, the care of a trained nurse. Almost all the schools provided breakfast, dinner and tea. Some went further. Halifax, for instance, also gave the children supper and a mid-morning snack. Parents were invited to contribute towards the cost of the meals; where they

---

[1] *Annual Report for 1908 of the Chief Medical Officer*, p. 121.
[2] Ministry of Education Archives, Education Class 32, Piece 164.
[3] *Annual Report for 1908*, p. 122.   [4] *Ibid.*, p. 121.

were unable to do so the education authority bore the cost. In some areas voluntary organizations supplied the schools with footwear and clothing. London was assisted in this way by the Ragged School Union, Bradford by its Cinderella Club.[1]

The time table in London was typical of most of the schools.[2]

Breakfast	9 a.m.
School	9.30–10.45 a.m.
Playtime	10.45–11 a.m.
School	11–12.20 p.m.
Preparing for dinner . . .	12.20–12.45 p.m.
Dinner	12.45–1.30 p.m.
Rest and sleep	1.30–3.30 p.m.
School	3.30–5 p.m.
Tea	5 p.m.
School-recreation . . .	5.30–7 p.m.
Home	7 p.m.

It was a long day. For a great part of the year the children arrived home in the dark. However, they had been given two hours rest. Undoubtedly they needed it. Its value was more open to doubt. 'At first,' reported George Newman, 'many of the children were restless and disinclined to sleep.'[3] In an attempt to counteract this, regimentation crept in. All were made to close their eyes, all to lie on their right side. The effect of two hours of such unnatural constraint on a nervous child may be imagined.

All the earlier schools catered for day pupils only. But in 1911 Halifax, which had been among the first authorities to open a day school, purchased a mansion which was adapted to form the first residential open-air school in Britain. The open-air element was confined to the children's day-time activities. At night they slept in dormitories in the mansion.[4] It was left to Margaret McMillan to experiment with open-air sleeping arrangements. In the year that the School Medical Service was founded, she opened a clinic for minor ailments at Bow, followed two years later by another at Deptford. The condition of the children attending the clinics convinced her that their greatest need was for fresh air and adequate food. Accordingly, on waste ground lent by the L.C.C., near the Deptford clinic, were erected a number of sheds. One of them housed a nursery school by day, and after school hours became a night camp for girls who attended from six in the evening until six in the morning. Soon the sixteen

[1] *Ibid.*, p. 126, and Ministry of Education Archives, Education Class 32, Piece 69.
[2] *Annual Report for 1908*, p. 127.   [3] *Ibid.*, p. 127.
[4] *Annual Report for 1911*, pp. 222–3.

older girls were joined at night by the twenty-four children from the day nursery school. They all slept in the large, three-sided shed constructed of wood and corrugated iron, which by day became the school-room for the younger children. Nearby, a camp school for boys operated on the same lines. Forty boys aged seven to fourteen were taught and slept in a sixty-foot-long shed open at the front. Adjoining was an open shed with a concrete floor, two showers and three zinc tubs. Hot water from a copper provided each boy with a daily bath followed by a cold shower. In addition, the boys were expected to take a shower when they rose at six in the morning.[1]

Margaret McMillan's enterprises at Deptford suffered from a shortage of money. For this she was inclined to blame officialdom. In fact, both the Board of Education and the L.C.C. offered financial assistance. Acceptance would have entailed inspection. This her independent nature would not allow.[2] Margaret McMillan's pioneering work on behalf of nursery schools has been fully recognized. But because of the financial difficulties, her contribution to the development of open-air schools is less well known. Nevertheless, she had considerable success. 'I have had results with boys who were 2 years at the school that are quite remarkable,' she wrote to George Newman, 'I have seen them grow suddenly after 18 months or a year at Camp into tall strong lads, and remain in splendid health henceforward.'[3]

Margaret McMillan's enthusiasm, George Newman's encouragement[4] and the example of London, Bradford, Halifax and Norwich did not dispel all the difficulties. The *Western Morning News* of November 7th, 1913 contained an account of the proceedings of the Devon Education Committee:

'On the recommendation that it was desirable that an open air residential school should be established, Col. Moore-Stevens expressed strong opposition. The time had come when they must stop the frightful expenditure. They could not meet it.

'The Chairman: It is only a pious opinion. There is no intention of acting upon it at present. . . . The clause was withdrawn.'

Opposition was encountered, too, for reasons other than financial.

---

[1] Ministry of Education Archives, Education Class 32, Piece 87, and McMillan, *The Camp School* (1915).

[2] This is clearly shown in the correspondence which passed between her and the President of the Board of Education during the period January 1913 to January 1915. The correspondence is in Ministry of Education Archives, Education Class 32, Piece 87.

[3] Letter to Newman, 28.11.1914, in Ministry of Education Archives, Education Class 32, Piece 87.

[4] Every *Annual Report* from 1908 to 1916 contained a chapter extolling the virtues of open-air schools.

II. Advances in the Health Services

In 1918 the Board of Education received a petition from certain Plymouth residents regarding a school for delicate children which the education authority proposed to open near their homes. Healthy people, the petition complained, would not come near the school, and therefore 'owners find it difficult to let their houses or apartments, and hotels and boarding houses suffer, and property depreciates in value'.[1]

Occasionally, children prone to epileptic attacks were sent to open-air schools. The Committee on Defective and Epileptic Children, however, had recommended that children whose attacks were mild and infrequent should remain in the ordinary school. On the other hand, those with severe epilepsy would require residential schooling, but in an establishment devoted entirely to the care of epileptics. The first institution solely for epileptics was established at Laforce in France by Jean Bost in 1862. Bost was a dedicated man who devoted his life to the epileptics in his care. On one occasion he is reputed to have pointed to two imbecile epileptic girls, whom he accommodated in his own house, and said, 'There is my theology.'[2] However, it was not at Laforce but in the institution at Bielefeld, Westphalia, that the pioneering work for epileptics really started. Founded in 1867 by Pastor Bodelschwingh, it became the model for English colonies.

It was first copied in 1888 at Maghull, near Liverpool. Prior to this, the only provision for those suffering from severe epilepsy was in the asylums. At one time a third of all the children at Darenth were epileptics.[3] Nor were they all imbeciles. According to the Medical Superintendent some of them were 'very bright, intelligent, and exceedingly sharp',[4] though with the recurrence of attacks their mental powers declined. They may well have declined for another reason, since no child subject to diurnal attacks, however bright, was admitted to the school. Even at Maghull, at first, their lot was little better. There was no schooling and the few children who were admitted were mixed with the adults. All the patients worked in the fields or the gardens, and they were drilled by a retired army sergeant. Discipline was strict. 'One spoilt and irascible epileptic boy, who had learned the lesson of yielding to law and order, was heard to tell a new-comer, "You'll find, like me, that a good lot of your impertinence is knocked out of you." '[5]

But soon education came to Maghull. Even before the 1899 Act

[1] Ministry of Education Archives, Education Class 32, Piece 10.
[2] Charity Organization Society, *The Epileptic and Crippled Child and Adult*, pp. 11–12.
[3] *C.D.E.C.*, Vol. 2, Evidence of F. Beach, 10.2.1897.
[4] *Ibid.*, Vol. 2, p. 116, Evidence of F. M. Walmsley, 5.3.1897.
[5] Charity Organization Society, *The Epileptic and Crippled Child and Adult*, p. 85.

there was some class teaching, and grants had been earned for evening school work. However, the first institution to undertake definite educational work was the Roman Catholic colony at Much Hadham, Hertfordshire. Its school was approved by the Board of Education in 1903, and two years later two residential schools established by the Christian Social Service Union at Lingfield, Surrey, and Starnthwaite, Westmorland, also received approval.[1] In 1910 Manchester opened a school for epileptics at Soss Moss in Cheshire. This was the first, and for long the only, school to be opened by a local education authority. By the end of the First World War there were six schools, all of them residential, with accommodation for 500 children.

Almost from the outset a difficulty appeared which has troubled the schools ever since. It was found that each school contained a proportion of children who, because of low intelligence or temperamental difficulties or a combination of both, could not be educated even by the special methods appropriate to a school for feeble-minded children. The Board of Education set the proportion of these children as between one-tenth and one-eighth. In addition, a further third of the children would, on the grounds of intelligence, qualify for admission to a school for mentally defective children.[2] With so many low grade children in the schools, teaching became extremely difficult. Moreover, it was felt that they were occupying accommodation which could be better used by children of good mental calibre. Therefore, it was recommended that teachers and medical officers should not hesitate to exclude those children who could not benefit from the education provided. Unfortunately such children could not be provided for elsewhere, and consequently there was a natural reluctance to recommend exclusion. Newman's comment was that consideration should be given to 'the wider advantages to the school and of the brighter epileptic child who cannot be admitted for want of accommodation. A kind heart is not always the best guide in this matter.'[3]

[1] Ministry of Education Archives, Education Class 32, Piece 204. In the *Annual Report for 1908 of the Chief Medical Officer*, p. 115, it is erroneously stated that the first school was established at Lingfield in 1905. The 1919 *Report*, p. 133, gives Much Hadham as the first school, and this is repeated in Ministry of Education, *Pamphlet No. 30* (1956), p. 14.
[2] *Annual Report for 1932 of the Chief Medical Officer*, p. 73.
[3] *Ibid.*, p. 75.

14

THE PERIOD OF GROWTH:
III. ADVANCES IN THE EDUCATION
OF THE MENTALLY HANDICAPPED

FOR the greater part of the nineteenth century, educational work with mentally defective children was based upon the precepts formulated by Itard and Séguin. Their sensationalist theories had inspired both the foundation of idiot asylums and the teaching therein. Mental deficiency, it was felt, was partly curable, and the idiot asylums based their early regulations, that children should remain for only four to seven years, upon this concept. Shuttleworth and Fletcher Beach, while realizing that some defectives would require institutional care, strongly supported the view that the higher grade defectives, particularly the feeble-minded, were capable of being educated to take their place in society. Their well-founded optimism communicated itself to the Committee on Defective and Epileptic Children, with the result that day special schools controlled by education authorities came to be the main provision for feeble-minded children. Hence, the movement founded upon sensationalism, and dedicated to the integration of the feeble-minded in society, reached its climax at the turn of the century. At this time it received further encouragement from Decroly and Alice Descoeudres in Belgium, and more especially from Maria Montessori in Italy.

In 1897 Montessori, as an assistant doctor at the psychiatric clinic of the University of Rome, visited asylums for the insane, and there found a number of mentally defective children. Feeling that they were wrongly placed, she applied herself to their study, and concluded that they 'presented chiefly a pedagogical, rather than mainly a medical, problem'.[1] Her ideas commended themselves to Baccelli, the Minister of Education, and in 1898 was founded an observational school for feeble-minded children with Montessori as its Director. There she not only taught the children, but trained other teachers in the special methods she considered applicable to the mentally defective. The basis of her method was derived almost entirely from the works of Itard and Séguin. This she fully admitted.

'I did a thing which I had not done before, and which perhaps few students have been willing to do,—I translated into Italian and copied out with my own hand, the writings of these men [Itard and Séguin] from beginning to end, making for myself books as the old Benedictines used to do before the diffusion of printing. I chose to do this by hand, in order that I might have time to weigh the sense of each word, and to read, in truth, the spirit of the author.'[2]

But she went beyond her mentors. To the didactic materials for sense training which she derived from Séguin, she added others of her own. Moreover, encouraged by her success with handicapped children, she applied her methods to ordinary children. To the House of Childhood, which she established in Rome, came children of normal intelligence aged three to seven. This was the beginning of the Montessori school movement, which stressed not only the sensationalism of Itard and Séguin but also the individualism of Rousseau and Froebel. The Montessori method has been frequently criticized. Its over-emphasis on didactic materials has made the transfer of learning to real life situations more difficult, while the need for uniformity in the use of the materials has tended to inhibit the development of individuality which Maria Montessori was at such pains to emphasize. However, her contribution to educational practice has been a real one. Especially has it shown the need for sense training in the education of the handicapped. Moreover, through her the sensationalism of Itard and Séguin has found a place in the ordinary school, and this represents one of the first examples of reform in general educational practice arising out of work for the handicapped.

But Montessori's triumphs with the mentally defective were not sufficient to stem the rising tide of opinion which ran completely against the earlier optimism. It came in three waves. First, the work of Sir Francis Galton in England, and of Goddard and Dugdale in the United States, tended to show that mental defectives were a danger to society. Galton, related to Darwin, associated himself with the latter's evolutionary theories. In his *Hereditary Genius* and *Natural Inheritance* he claimed that Mendel's Law was applicable to humans, and that mental ability as well as physical characteristics were trans-

---

[1] Montessori, *The Montessori Method* (1912), p. 31. [2] *Ibid.*, p. 41.

mitted to the offspring. His views led to the systematic study of eugenics, and were apparently supported by the findings of the American geneticists. Dugdale traced the descendants of five mentally defective sisters named Juke. Of the 700 he discovered, he found that over 400 of them were criminals, prostitutes or paupers.[1] Goddard's investigation of another family at the beginning of the twentieth century produced similar results.[2] Such findings contributed to fears of degeneration of the race, and led to demands for the segregation and sterilization of defectives.[3]

Secondly, developments in the testing of intelligence contributed to the belief that a child shown by an intelligence test to be of low intellectual ability would never increase that ability. There was little realization of the fact that an intelligence test did not reveal a child's possible reaction to his environment. Binet, who at the beginning of the twentieth century perfected the earlier work on testing of Galton and Cattell, made the realization no easier. His book, written jointly with Simon,[4] severely criticized both the optimism and methods of Séguin, and suggested that attempts at educating feeble-minded children were often quite fruitless. Nevertheless, Binet advocated that despite the difficulties they should be taught the social skills of reading and writing:

'It has been remarked, and justly, that reading is the triumph of abstraction, and that a defective may require two years to learn to read by syllables, and very poorly even then. No matter: if the thing is possible, even with considerable effort, such a defective ought to learn to read. This is demanded, not by the state of the child's intelligence, but by the society in which he lives, where illiteracy would bring shame upon him.'[5]

This, however, the geneticists conveniently overlooked, with the result that there developed a notion that the feeble-minded could not benefit from education in the usual sense of the word.

Thirdly, difficulties in obtaining employment encountered by leavers from special schools led to a movement which advocated the permanent care of the feeble-minded. Such advocacy necessarily implied segregation, though it was sought not as an end in itself but merely as part of the care which was essential if the feeble-minded were not to be exploited and led astray by society. It was based more on the interests of the feeble-minded than the interests of society,

---

[1] Dugdale, *The Jukes: A Study in Crime, Pauperism, Disease and Heredity* (1877).
[2] Goddard, *The Kallikak Family* (1912).
[3] See Tredgold, *Mental Deficiency* (1914).
[4] Binet and Simon, *Mentally Defective Children* (1914).
[5] *Ibid.*, p. 34. See also O'Connor and Tizard, *The Social Problem of Mental Deficiency* (1956), p. 4.

although the geneticists as a matter of policy supported the movement.

Attempts to provide for the welfare of the feeble-minded were first made in the closing years of the nineteenth century. The National Vigilance Association and the Metropolitan Association for Befriending Young Servants were both appalled at the defenceless condition of feeble-minded women and girls whom they found to fail and fall under the pressure of life.[1] Their agitation, coupled with that of the Charity Organization Society, resulted in the foundation of a number of homes for the care of feeble-minded girls of over school age. The first of these, established in 1887, was the Aubert Park Home, Highgate. The girls for whom it catered came from workhouse schools. They were taught general housework and to become self supporting.[2] By 1896 there were ten similar homes with a total accommodation for some two hundred girls.

In that year was founded the National Association for Promoting the Welfare of the Feeble-Minded. One of its first actions was to co-ordinate the work of the existing homes, and to encourage and initiate the formation of others.[3] All the homes had the joint aim of protecting and training adolescent girls. Consequently, although no formal education was given, the girls were given instruction in such things as mat and rug making. In the main, however, they assisted in the domestic work of the home. Since no girl was allowed to remain for more than six years, all left before they reached the age of twenty. This was considered by some to be still too early, and gradually there grew up a school of thought that believed that any age would be too early. Among the leaders of this school of thought were Mary Dendy and Dame Ellen Pinsent. Both played a prominent part in the formation of the National Association for Promoting the Welfare of the Feeble-Minded. Both were to figure largely in the later success of the Association.

Miss Dendy became a member of the Manchester School Board in 1894. Taking her work seriously she was a frequent visitor to the board schools where she was astounded by the number of feeble-minded children for whom no adequate provision was made. Her protest to the Board resulted in a deputation visiting London's special schools. On its return a resolution to take action was passed. None was taken—save by Mary Dendy. She personally inspected 40,000 children in the Manchester schools, and selected 525 whom she considered to be severely sub-normal.

[1] Charity Organization Society, *The Epileptic and Crippled Child and Adult* (1893), pp. 3–4.　　[2] *C.D.E.C.*, Vol. 2, Evidence of E. Tait, 10.3.1897.
[3] *Ibid.*, Vol. 2, Evidence of Miss F. A. Cooper, 3.3.1897.

III. Advances in the Education of the Mentally Handicapped

'I took the report on these children . . . to our own School Board,' she later stated. 'The School Board then said I did not know anything about it, which was perfectly true in a sense, and they said that if the matter were referred to a medical man we should probably weed out a great number of these cases.'[1]

A medical man, Dr. Henry Ashby, did examine the children during the winter of 1897, with the result that two years later Manchester opened its first day special schools. But by now Mary Dendy had seen not only the children but many of their parents, and had become convinced that the provision of day special schools was not the answer to the problem. Accordingly, in 1898, she formed the Lancashire and Cheshire Society for the Permanent Care of the Feeble-Minded, 'with the intention of getting hold of a certain number of children, and trying to prove that those children in proper conditions could be kept happily throughout their lives without hardship or forcible detention; though we should be very glad indeed to have powers of forcible detention'.[2]

In August 1902 a school and two houses, containing respectively fifteen boys and fifteen girls, were opened at Sandlebridge in Cheshire, on land given to the Society by the David Lewis Fund. The children all came from Manchester board schools, and the intention was that they should remain on in the adult industrial colony after attaining the age of sixteen.[3] The school was immediately recognized by the Board of Education, and became the first residential school for feeble-minded children to be certified under the 1899 Act.[4] Within ten years there were 150 children at Sandlebridge with an equal number of adults in the industrial colony.

Miss Dendy has left an account of the work in the school.[5] Much of the teaching was based on the Montessori method and its apparatus. Extensive use was also made of apparatus devised by Walter Fernald, Superintendent of the Massachusetts school where Séguin had taught. There was therefore considerable emphasis on the development of hand and eye co-ordination and sense training. Each classroom contained sense cupboards. One would contain objects which a blindfolded child would smell and identify: pepper, mustard, onions, lavender—all in bottles with wide necks. Equally, there were taste, hearing and touch cupboards. On reading and writing there was

---

[1] *Report of the Royal Commission on the Care and Control of the Feeble-Minded*, Vol. 1, p. 39, Evidence of Miss M. Dendy, 5.12.1904.
[2] *Ibid.*, Vol. 1, p. 41.
[3] *Annual Report for 1911 of the Chief Medical Officer of the Board of Education*, pp. 201–3, and Lapage, *Feeble-Mindedness in Children of School Age* (1920), pp. 7–8.
[4] *Annual Report for 1908 of the Chief Medical Officer*, p. 114.
[5] In Appendix to Lapage, *op. cit.*, pp. 215–32.

little concentration. 'As to writing,' Mary Dendy wrote, 'I confess to being sceptical as to its value. In at least one great institution, the knowledge of how to write has led to great difficulties in managing high-grade cases, the men and women communicating with each other by means of notes.'[1]

In addition to their work in school the children were expected to assist in keeping their living quarters clean. These were extremely spartan. Apart from beds, the dormitories were devoid of furniture. Even the beds were without mattresses. The children slept on two thicknesses of felt placed over the wire mattresses. The floors were covered with linoleum which the children polished. 'Polishing this is one of the earliest forms of work that children can be put to. A line of little boys or girls can quickly polish a large floor-space and will enjoy doing it.'[2] Whether in or out of school the education of the children was regulated by Mary Dendy's pre-occupation with the idea of permanent care. She assumed that all children on reaching sixteen would remain in, and work at, the colony. Hence her concentration on getting children used to work from the beginning. Hence, also, her views on the teaching of writing. She was convinced that it would hold no value for the children. For the same reason she had little enthusiasm for the teaching of reading. Social skills would not be required by those who would not form part of society.

Nevertheless, Miss Dendy was enlightened and well-meaning, and always had the best interests of the children at heart. Her seemingly proud description of the spartan atmosphere at Sandlebridge was merely in keeping with the ideas of the time, for she constantly emphasized that despite the lack of amenities the rooms should be bright and attractive. Well did Sir George Newman write of her: 'Miss Mary Dendy's untiring and successful efforts on behalf of the feeble-minded are widely recognized not merely throughout the country but almost equally abroad.'[3]

While Mary Dendy was working on behalf of the feeble-minded children of Manchester, Ellen Pinsent was performing a similar service in Birmingham. A member of the School Board Committee which supervised special schools, she was surprised at the small number of children attending them. Like Miss Dendy, she visited all the ordinary schools, and personally selected 250 children who would be suitable for the special schools. As a result of her work the Board appointed a medical officer to examine the children, and within a few years the number of children at the special schools had increased six-

---

[1] Lapage, *Feeble-Mindedness in Children of School Age*, Appendix, p. 231.
[2] *Ibid.*, Appendix, p. 217.
[3] *Annual Report for 1911 of the Chief Medical Officer*, p. 201.

fold. This did not entirely satisfy Ellen Pinsent, for she suspected that many of the children required more assistance than a day school could give. Therefore, in 1901 she induced the Board to establish an After-Care Committee of which she became Chairman. Its function was both to assist the children leaving the special schools in finding employment, and to investigate the value of the schools. The aim of the investigation was the provision of evidence which would reveal the need for boarding schools, supplemented by permanent industrial colonies or custodial homes, for those unfit to face life on their own.[1]

Thus by the beginning of the twentieth century there had developed a strong movement in favour of the segregation of the feeble-minded. It was supported both by geneticists and disinterested social workers. It also came to be supported on financial grounds. It was felt that heavy expenditure on the education of the feeble-minded could only be justified if it was seen as preparatory training for a more permanent type of care than could be given under the existing laws. The strength of the movement impressed the Government,[2] and in 1904 the Royal Commission on the Care and Control of the Feeble-Minded was appointed. The Commission sat for four years. During that time it heard evidence concerning the relationship between mental defect and crime, drunkenness, poverty, prostitution and illegitimacy. It also heard evidence on the rôle to be played by the special school. On this topic there was considerable unanimity among the witnesses. Three main points emerged. First, a large proportion of the children in the special schools would never be able to become self-supporting, and would therefore require some form of residential care. Secondly, the existing day special schools were of little value for those who would eventually require residential treatment. Therefore the schools should be used merely as observational and classifying centres. Thirdly, whether feeble-minded children were to be educated in day or residential schools, the bulk of the instruction should be of a manual nature.

Evidence on the first point was heard from James Kerr: 'A considerable proportion [of special school children] show little moral restraint, some are almost without speech, some incapable of work, others work without progress or intelligence; very frequently too they are addicted to staying out or even wandering at night, and many of this last class come into the hands of the police. Some have bad

[1] Pinsent, 'On the Permanent Care of the Feeble-Minded', *Lancet*, 21.2.1903, pp. 513–15.

[2] A petition signed by 140 influential persons calling for a Royal Commission was presented to the Home Secretary in April 1903. Lapage, *op. cit.*, p. 8.

habits, and immoral tendencies are common.'[1] Fewer than one-third of the children, Kerr considered, would be capable of materially contributing to their own livelihood,[2] a third could make a partial contribution, but only with the assistance of an after-care association, while the remainder 'should not be allowed to mix with the rest of the community, but should receive some kind of custodial treatment'.[3]

A number of witnesses supported the second point. W. A. Potts, a member of the Birmingham Special Schools Committee, felt that the schools should be used solely for observing doubtful cases.[4] A London medical officer testified: 'I would regard the special schools as largely sorting places where those that are going to improve are recognized, and those that are not going to improve are also recognized.'[5] Damer Harrison, medical officer for special schools in Liverpool, found it 'extremely difficult—in fact I think it is impossible—to decide by 2 or 3 examinations of a child as to how far it is amenable to ordinary elementary education'.[6] Therefore, like Potts he wanted to use the schools for diagnostic purposes.

On the last point the Commission heard the views of Mary Dendy and Ellen Pinsent. 'I would myself very much prefer to make the training of older children, when it is proved that they are feeble-minded, with few exceptions, entirely manual,' said the former.[7] Mrs. Pinsent supported this: 'The education should be manual with classes in the three R's for those capable of benefiting by such classes.'[8] Some went further. Headmistresses of special schools in London and Liverpool would have been content to make all the work, without exception, manual.[9]

In the face of such testimony it was not surprising that the Royal Commission was not enamoured of the day special school system with its emphasis on academic achievement. The intelligence of feeble-minded children, the Commission felt, was roused 'through the hands and eyes working together in making or doing some actual thing rather than by the secondary and more abstract accomplish-

---

[1] *Report of the Royal Commission on the Care and Control of the Feeble-Minded,* Vol. 1, p. 435, Evidence of Kerr, 23.6.1905.

[2] Yet of 279 children who left the London special schools during 1908, 212 found employment. *Annual Report for 1908 of the Chief Medical Officer of the Board of Education,* p. 115.

[3] *Report of the Royal Commission on the Care and Control of the Feeble-Minded,* Vol. 1, p. 436.

[4] *Ibid.,* Vol. 2, Evidence of Potts, 2.2.1906.

[5] *Ibid.,* Vol. 2, p. 10, Evidence of R. Hutchinson, 13.10.1905.

[6] *Ibid.,* Vol. 1, p. 621, Evidence of Harrison, 4.8.1905.

[7] *Ibid.,* Vol. 1, p. 41, Evidence of Miss Dendy, 5.12.1904.

[8] *Ibid.,* Vol. 2, p. 457, Evidence of Mrs. Hume Pinsent, 2.2.1906.

[9] *Ibid.,* Vol. 2, Evidence of Miss H. Gavin, 3.11.1905 and Evidence of Miss T. M. James, 17.11.1905.

ment of reading, writing and arithmetic'. It was therefore of the opinion that 'the simple occupations of the earliest years of schooling should develop into systematic industrial training, while the scholastic teaching should become entirely subordinate, and indeed, in some cases, should be discontinued'. Further, experience had shown that the special school by itself was 'largely unserviceable, from the point of view of the after-life of the child. The feeble-minded child can, in the main, become only a feeble-minded adult educated into a rather better routine of thought and habit. If special education is required on his behalf in his school days, special care will probably be necessary for him when he has left school; and, moreover, later on in life.'[1] From this standpoint it was logical for the Commission to suggest that the childhood and schooling of the feeble-minded could not be treated apart from later life, and that no age could be selected as separating school life from supervision and after-care.[2] It therefore concluded that an institutional system, coupled with admission to the institution at an early age, was superior to the day special school system.[3] Since there would be difficulties in transferring the children, when they left school, from one authority to another, it would be best if the local mental deficiency committees controlled all special schools. In this way there would be a single and continuous control over each child. Moreover, it was not only a case of administrative convenience, since 'the educational system of the country, established for the teaching of the normal child is, in our opinion, unsuitable for the child, who, unlike the blind and deaf, can never reach the mental level of the normal'.[4] This was a highly dangerous philosophy which, had it been extended to its logical conclusion, would have removed large numbers of children from the purview of the education authorities. As it was, the Commission recommended that the 1899 Act should be amended to exclude mentally defective children, and that, instead, local mental deficiency committees should be under a statutory obligation to provide for the manual, industrial and other training of feeble-minded children. Existing special schools should cease to be the responsibility of the Board of Education, and should be inspected by officers of the new central authority for mental defect and illness—the Board of Control. Finally, local education authorities which had established special schools should be compelled either to transfer the schools to the mental deficiency committees or to continue to educate the children in the schools under the direction of, and with payment from, the mental deficiency committees.[5]

[1] *Ibid.*, Vol. 8, p. 103. [2] *Ibid.*, Vol. 8, p. 9. [3] *Ibid.*, Vol. 8, p. 105.
[4] *Ibid.*, Vol. 8, p. 116. [5] *Ibid.*, Vol. 8, pp. 354–7.

The Period of Growth

The Commission's *Report* was laid before Parliament in 1908. It aroused considerable controversy. It also bred uncertainty, for not until 1913 was it finally known what action was to be taken on the Commission's recommendations. It is not therefore surprising that the provision of special education by L.E.A.s proceeded only slowly. Indeed, it is surprising that it did not proceed even more slowly. The 1899 Act had been permissive. The larger towns, some of whom had already established special schools, took advantage of the power it conferred. But not until 1902 were the county councils given any educational responsibility. Hardly had they assessed the extent of their commitments than the Royal Commission was appointed. Although the Board of Education hopefully suggested that the wider educational areas created by the 1902 Act should facilitate the making of provision for defective children,[1] its Assistant Secretary recognized that 'the county authorities are waiting, seeing how things develop, and attending, in the first instance, to the ordinary children'.[2] When the Commission's *Report* was published there was even greater reason to wait. If special schools were to be taken over by the mental deficiency committees, it seemed rather pointless for L.E.A.s to establish them. Nevertheless, by 1913 there were 177 schools catering for over 12,000 children, and 175 L.E.A.s had used their powers to provide education for feeble-minded children, although under one third of these had actually established schools.[3]

Moreover, many of the schools were showing that the Royal Commission had painted too black a picture. In 1904 the L.C.C. had opened a senior day school for feeble-minded boys aged twelve to sixteen. With the separation of the sexes it was possible to provide higher manual work and trade training. The boys received instruction in gardening, carpentry, metal work, tailoring and boot and shoe making. Soon Birmingham and Liverpool had also established such schools for both boys and girls.[4] In addition it was found that a high proportion of children leaving the special schools were successfully adapting themselves to life, and in 1908 the Chief Medical Officer of the Board of Education was able to report that the schools were only admitting children 'of a higher mental grade from whom some tangible result may be expected in after-life whether as semi-skilled or unskilled wage-earners'.[5] Therefore, when the time came for the im-

---

[1] Board of Education, *Circular 432*, 1904.

[2] *Report of the Royal Commission on the Care and Control of the Feeble-Minded*, Vol. 1, p. 243, Evidence of H. F. Pooley, 21.11.1904.

[3] *Annual Report for 1912 of the Chief Medical Officer of the Board of Education*, p. 239.

[4] *Annual Report for 1908*, pp. 115–16, and *Annual Report for 1909*, pp. 160–1.

[5] *Annual Report for 1908*, p. 115.

plementation of some of the recommendations of the Royal Commission, there existed a body of opinion which adopted an entirely different view from the Commissioners on the value of the day special schools.

The delay in the introduction of legislation which had given this opinion time to develop had been due to two main factors. In the first place the *Report* of the Commission had been a compromise, and its reception therefore was only lukewarm. Its refusal to advocate sterilization displeased the supporters of the eugenics school. Its support of compulsory segregation perturbed the champions of liberty. It was obvious that any measure dealing with such a subject would have to be very carefully drafted. It was equally obvious that it must have the support of public opinion. Hence the public must be given the time and opportunity to become articulate.

The second reason was less altruistic. In 1909 the Conservative Lords had taken up the gage thrown down by the Liberal Commons. They rejected out of hand Lloyd George's challenging budget, and reversed a tradition of over two centuries standing. The Cabinet was faced with a serious constitutional crisis involving the future of parliamentary democracy. Two general elections during 1910 failed to resolve the deadlock, and it required a pledge from the new King, George V, that he would allow the creation of peers in large numbers, before the Parliament Act, restricting the power of the Lords, was passed in 1911. During these two discordant years the Government had little time for controversial social legislation. It was not, therefore, until 1912 that a Bill was introduced. Even then the measure provoked so much discussion that it was talked out. Re-introduced the following year, it again met with opposition, but eventually received the Royal Assent in August.[1]

As far as the education of feeble-minded children was concerned, the Mental Deficiency Act 1913 bore little resemblance to the recommendations of the Royal Commission. Even the definition of the children was different. In the Act, the feeble-minded were those who 'require care, supervision, and control for their own protection or for the protection of others, or, in the case of children, that they by reason of such defectiveness appear to be permanently incapable of receiving proper benefit from the instruction in the ordinary schools'.[2] This, in so far as it related to children, was an educational criterion, whereas the recommended definition, even for children, had been based solely on the lack of

---

[1] For an account of the proceedings in the Commons, see Jones, *Mental Health and Social Policy 1845–1959* (1960), pp. 63–6.
[2] 3 and 4 George V, c. 28, s. 1.

social competence: 'Persons who ... are incapable ... of competing on equal terms with their normal fellows; or of managing themselves and their affairs with ordinary prudence.'[1] This was among the least of the differences. The major difference was to be found in the fact that the education of feeble-minded children still remained the responsibility of the L.E.A. Education authorities were now given the specific duty of ascertaining which children aged seven to sixteen were defective. Of those so ascertained, they had to decide which were incapable of being educated in special schools. These, and these alone, they would pass on to the mental deficiency committees.

The Act, since it was not an educational measure, said nothing regarding the duties of L.E.A.s towards the feeble-minded children who fell within their competence. However, as education authorities were obliged to ascertain them, they must obviously be called upon to make suitable provision for their education. Hence in 1913 the President of the Board of Education, J. A. Pease, introduced a Bill which would have the effect of making the 1899 Act obligatory, and not permissive, as far as mentally defective children were concerned. The Bill encountered a certain amount of opposition, due mainly to the fact that it was erroneously thought to be duplicating the Mental Deficiency Act, and lapsed at the end of the Session. However, in the following year it was passed without difficulty. On the day that Germany declared war upon Russia, and sent an ultimatum to France, it was placed upon the statute book.[2] Three days later Britain herself was at war. This prevented the Act having an immediate impact, and the number of children in special schools increased but slowly.

The end of hostilities made little difference. In 1914 there were 13,563 children in the mentally defective schools.[3] By the outbreak of the Second World War, the number was a little under 17,000, although as early as 1924 twice this number had been shown as feeble-minded in returns by L.E.A.s.[4] The lack of expansion in the 'twenties was partly due to the appointment of the Wood Committee which, between 1924 and 1929, examined the educational provision for feeble-minded children. Since its recommendations might well affect the structure of special education, L.E.A.s were unwilling to take any action. Indeed, the Board of Education encouraged them in their passiveness. In a Circular in 1927 it advised that 'save in exceptional circumstances, it would not seem prudent to incur heavy expenditure at the present moment on new schools for feeble-minded children or

[1] *Report of the Royal Commission on the Care and Control of the Feeble-Minded*, Vol. 8, p. 324.
[2] *Elementary Education (Defective and Epileptic Children) Act, 1914.*
[3] *Annual Report for 1914 of the Chief Medical Officer of the Board of Education*, p. 13.
[4] *Annual Report for 1925*, p. 79.

III. Advances in the Education of the Mentally Handicapped

on enlargement of existing schools'.[1] Hardly had the Wood Committee reported than the country found itself in the grip of the economic depression of the early 'thirties, and building projects had once again to be shelved.

The Wood Committee was appointed by George Newman. Its Chairman, A. H. Wood, had recently retired from the Assistant Secretaryship of the Medical Branch, and among its members were Professor Cyril Burt, Ellen Pinsent and A. F. Tredgold. It was very much an informal Committee, and was given no specific terms of reference. Newman had, however, suggested that two questions should be answered. The first concerned the incidence of feeble-mindedness. The returns submitted by L.E.A.s to the Board of Education of the number of feeble-minded children in their areas showed considerable variation. In one case it was as high as 16 per thousand school-children, in another as low as 0·7 per thousand, with a complete range of intermediate figures in the remaining areas. Obviously, no sound administration could be built up on such returns, and it was hoped that the Committee would provide an accurate figure. As its second task the Committee should examine the existing system of educating feeble-minded children, and suggest any changes that might be necessary in the light of the experience gained since 1899. For the satisfactory completion of its investigations the Committee found that it would be necessary to extend its deliberations to include all mentally defective persons, be they children or adults. Hence the Board of Control joined the Board of Education in financing the enquiry, and the Committee's findings were published under the title of the *Report of the Mental Deficiency Committee.*

To assist the Committee in its task of assessing the number of feeble-minded children, Dr. E. O. Lewis was seconded to it by the Board of Control. Lewis was well qualified for the work. He had taught in elementary and secondary schools, and lectured in teaching method at training colleges and in educational psychology at universities. In addition, he had been a medical officer under the L.C.C., and a medical inspector of the Board of Control. Lewis spent three years over his enquiries which were based on a study of mental defectives in six areas, each with a population of 100,000. His findings, which ran to 70,000 words, were included in Volume 3 of the Committee's *Report.* He made no claims to infallibility:

'Many of our experiences in the course of this investigation reminded us of the anomalies of some of the earliest censuses made of the general population, such as those in China, where it is said that a census was made in 1711 in connection with the poll tax and military

[1] Board of Education, *Circular 1388*, February 1927.

service, and the population was estimated to be only 28 millions; but when some years later another census was taken with a view to certain measures for the relief of distress, the total arrived at was 103 millions.'[1]

On the other hand, he was confident that the data was sufficiently complete as far as children were concerned for the Committee 'to estimate with a considerable degree of accuracy the real magnitude of the problem'.[2]

Lewis's results showed that there were 105,000 school-children who were mentally defective within the meaning of the 1914 Education Act.[3] Of these, only one-third had been formally ascertained by L.E.A.s, and 16,000, but a sixth of the total, were actually in attendance at special schools.[4] The figure of 105,000 obtained by Lewis was confirmed to a large extent by the returns from those authorities who had made adequate provision for their feeble-minded children. The Committee therefore accepted this figure, and so answered the first of its two questions.

In considering the second question, the Committee was influenced by its answer to the first. Save in the larger towns, the expansion of the existing special school system was felt to be impossible. Yet something must be done for the 90,000 feeble-minded children still in the ordinary schools. Therefore the system and the legal basis upon which it rested would have to be changed. Moreover, in addition to the large number of feeble-minded children for whom no adequate provision had been made, there existed an even larger group of children who, although not feeble-minded, were below average in ability and were failing at school for a variety of reasons. These severely retarded children, whom the Committee estimated represented some ten per cent of the school population, could not be admitted to special schools, since they were not mentally defective. Nor had L.E.A.s a duty to provide special education for them. In fact, the statutory requirements regarding the feeble-minded had tended to distract attention from them.

The solution which the Committee suggested was that the feeble-minded and the retarded should be dealt with in one comprehensive scheme, which would cater for 'all children who though educable in a true sense are unable to profit from the instruction in the ordinary

---

[1] *Report of the Mental Deficiency Committee*, Vol. 3, p. iii.

[2] *Ibid.*

[3] In 1921 the provisions of the 1893 Blind and Deaf Children Act, the 1899 and 1914 Defective and Epileptic Children Acts, and that part of the 1918 Education Act which referred to physically handicapped children were covered by sections 51 to 69 of a consolidating Education Act.

[4] *Report of the Mental Deficiency Committee*, Vol. 1, pp. 44 and 84.

schools'.[1] To achieve this it would be necessary to abolish the need for certification, since hitherto the special schools had been reserved for children certified as feeble-minded within the meaning of the Mental Deficiency Act 1913. The need for certification had in the past contributed towards the uneven provision of special schools. Teachers had frequently been reluctant to put children forward for possible certification. Medical officers had been equally reluctant to certify save in the clearest possible cases. Hence children had been deprived of special education which they badly needed, because it was thought that the deprivation was a lesser hardship than certification. Nor would the end of certification entail the end of special schools. Rather, if all the children requiring special education were classified in a single educational unit, the substance of the special schools would remain intact while their numbers and scope would materially increase.

'We do however contemplate,' continued the *Report*, 'that these schools would exist with a different legal sanction, under a different system of nomenclature and under different administrative provisions. If the majority of children for whom these schools for retarded children[2] are intended are, *ex hypothesi*, to lead the lives of ordinary citizens, with no shadow of a "certificate" and all that it implies to handicap their careers, the schools must be brought into closer relation with the Public Elementary School system and presented to parents not as something both distinct and humiliating, but as a helpful variation of the ordinary school.'[3]

This was a far cry from the recommendations of the Royal Commission twenty years earlier. Then it had been suggested that the special school should be the responsibility of the mental deficiency committee. Now it was advocated that the special school, with its specialized methods of individual approach, its elastic and varied curriculum, and its freedom from examinations, would continue under a new name as a particular type of elementary school. Previous objections to the mixing of the retarded with the formally certified and officially labelled feeble-minded should therefore disappear. Especially should they disappear when it was realized that the only special aspect of the new schools was that they would employ special methods of education, and that entry to them would be based not only on ability but also on attainment. The Committee envisaged that the new schools would be supplemented by a system of special classes.

[1] *Ibid.*, Vol. 1, p. 93.
[2] The Committee included within this term both children of below average ability who were failing at school work and feeble-minded children.
[3] *Report of the Mental Deficiency Committee*, Vol. 1, p. 117.

Thus in rural areas and small towns most of the retarded children would be educated in the special classes, although the increase in the number of children who could be admitted to the new schools should allow some authorities to provide schools where previously there had been insufficient feeble-minded children to warrant a school. Even in the large towns there would be a need for special classes and special departments in the ordinary schools for the less severely retarded.[1] Therefore the essence of the Committee's recommendations was that within the ordinary school system various types of specialized provision should be made; the existing special schools, under another name, would be merely one of the types of provision; and the provision, when made, would be for a much larger group than the feeble-minded.

Of the views of the Wood Committee, George Newman wrote: 'One of the greatest values of this Report is its attitude and constructive spirit of reform. It is true that it expresses its proposals in a series of Recommendations, some of which concern matters not immediately referred to it, and involving somewhat far-reaching legislative and financial proposals. . . . Obviously it is not suggested that they can all be carried out immediately.'[2] Whether or not it was so suggested, they were not carried out immediately. Not until 1944 did certification disappear. Not until 1944 did the concept of one comprehensive group of backward children appear. Not until 1944 were the Wood Committee's views vindicated.

While the Wood Committee was deliberating, another aspect of mental handicap was receiving attention; the first child guidance clinic was established in England. It was opened in London in 1926 by the Jewish Health Organization. Important though the pioneering work of this first clinic was, it had been preceded thirty years earlier by the psychological laboratory opened by Professor Sully at University College, London, to which teachers had been invited to take their more difficult pupils for examination.[3] Sully's inspiration had come from the earlier work of Francis Galton, and the efforts of these two were largely responsible for the foundation of the British Child Study Association in 1893. As the Association grew, so there developed the realization of the need for psychologists to work within the education service. The first step towards fulfilling the need was taken by the L.C.C. when in 1913 it appointed Cyril Burt as its psychologist. Among his manifold duties was the investigation of

---

[1] *Report of the Mental Deficiency Committee*, Vol. 1, pp. 157–61.
[2] *Annual Report for 1928 of the Chief Medical Officer of the Board of Education*, p. 100.
[3] *C.D.E.C.*, Vol. 2, Evidence of Sir D. Galton, 24.3.1897.

'cases of individual children, who present problems of special difficulty and who might be referred for examination by teachers, school medical officers, or care committee workers, magistrates or parents'.[1]

Meanwhile in the United States, William Healey was studying and treating delinquent children at the Institute of Juvenile Research in Chicago. He soon realized that psychiatry alone would not solve the problem. What was required was a team approach, and each team must contain a psychologist and a social worker in addition to a psychiatrist.[2] On this foundation was built the American conception of child guidance—a team of workers based on a clinic—and it was upon this model that the Jewish Health Organization drew when it opened the East London Clinic in 1926. In the following year the Child Guidance Council was formed. Its foundation was largely the work of the National Council for Mental Hygiene and the Central Association for Mental Welfare.[3] Its aim was 'to encourage the provision of skilled treatment of children showing behaviour disturbances'.[4] As a result of its efforts more clinics were established by voluntary bodies and hospitals, but not until 1932 did a local education authority enter the field.

In that year the City of Oxford, with the approval of the Board of Education, opened an educational clinic for the purpose of examining children for, among other things, mental deficiency. However, despite the fact that it was organized on the lines of a child guidance clinic, the Board refused to allow it to rank as a precedent for approving child guidance clinics as part of the school medical service.[5] In the same year Birmingham Education Committee established a child guidance clinic. For the first three years all the costs were met from voluntary sources. When this financial source ceased in 1935 the L.E.A. decided that the success of the clinic justified its continuance out of public funds. Accordingly, the Board of Education was requested to recognize it for grant purposes. Recognition was given, and so child guidance clinics became an official part of the school medical service.[6]

[1] *Report of the Committee on Maladjusted Children* (1955), p. 8.
[2] *Report of the Chief Medical Officer of the Ministry of Education 1939–1945*, p. 63.
[3] The Central Association for Mental Welfare was a direct descendant of the National Association for Promoting the Welfare of the Feeble-Minded, which in 1914, since its own aims had been achieved with the Mental Deficiency Act 1913, became part of the larger body. In 1946 the Child Guidance Council amalgamated with the National Council and the Central Association to form the National Association for Mental Health.
[4] *Report of the Chief Medical Officer 1939–1945*, p. 63.
[5] Pinsent, *The Mental Health Services in Oxford City, Oxfordshire and Berkshire* (1937), p. 14, and *Annual Report for 1934 of the Chief Medical Officer of the Board of Education*, p. 115.
[6] *Annual Report for 1934 of the Chief Medical Officer*, pp. 115–16.

By 1939 twenty-two clinics were wholly or partly maintained by L.E.A.s but progress in other forms of provision for maladjusted children was slower. In 1932 Leicester, which had led the way with schools for the feeble-minded, opened an experimental day school for disturbed children. The example was not followed by other authorities. Rather, advantage was taken of the Board of Education's agreement to sanction the payment of fees for the boarding out of maladjusted children in homes maintained by voluntary organizations. Since maladjusted children were not officially recognized as a category of handicapped children,[1] the boarding out arrangements were approved under Section 80 of the Education Act 1921, which allowed authorities to attend to the health and physical education of children. Hence L.E.A.s had no power to provide residential schools for the maladjusted. It took a world war to show how necessary such schools were.

[1] Five categories were recognized: blind, deaf, mentally defective, physically defective and epileptic.

15

THE PERIOD OF GROWTH:
IV. ADVANCES IN THE EDUCATION
OF THE BLIND AND DEAF

BY the end of the Victorian era, when provision for the education of
the epileptic and mentally and physically handicapped was still in its
infancy, the elementary education of the blind and deaf was well
advanced. There was still, however, much room for improvement.
There was room, too, for growth. The early education of both blind
and deaf was still largely neglected. The lower age of compulsory
education for the deaf was seven, and although the blind had to
attend school from five, there was a marked reluctance on the part
of the voluntary boarding schools to accept them at this age. In fact,
the headmasters of the schools resolved in 1894 that the Government
should be asked to amend the 1893 Act so as not to make it incumbent upon boarding schools to accept children under seven.[1] Yet it
was essential that both blind and deaf children should commence
their training at as early an age as possible, and there was therefore
a need for nursery education for them. Secondly, there was a need
for an expansion of the facilities for grammar school education.
There was no provision at all for girls, and no public provision for
boys. Thirdly, partially sighted and, to a lesser degree, partially deaf
children were frequently not receiving education appropriate to their
disability. Many of them remained in the ordinary schools. Others
were in special schools for the blind and deaf but were being taught
by methods devised for the completely blind or the totally deaf.

Apart from the problems concerning the education of children, the
question of the education of teachers also presented difficulties. The

[1] *Report of the Conference on the Education of the Blind at Birmingham, 1894.*

colleges for teachers of the deaf at Ealing and Fitzroy Square still existed. So did the antipathy between them. Neither was recognized by the Board of Education. Both granted certificates to successful students. These, too, the Board refused to recognize. Certificates of competence to teach the deaf were bestowed by a third body. This was the College of Teachers of the Deaf and Dumb. It had been established in 1885 purely as an examining body. Its founders, Elliott, Stainer, Howard, Schöntheil and Sleight,[1] had two aims in view. First, they wished to raise the status of teachers of the deaf by forming them into an organized body.[2] Secondly, they desired to counter the monopoly of Fitzroy Square and Ealing, whose certificates, naturally, would be given only to their own students. Yet there were many in the deaf schools who considered that they, too, should have a qualification. Therefore, to those who, at the date of the foundation of the College of Teachers, had taught the deaf for ten years, a certificate was given without examination. Teachers with shorter service and new entrants to the schools could obtain the certificate by passing the annual examination of the College.[3]

In 1894 the position was further complicated when Van Praagh founded the Union of Teachers on the Pure Oral System in direct opposition to the College of Teachers. With three examining bodies, none officially recognized, and two professional associations, it appeared as if teachers of the deaf were never to be united. In an attempt to heal the breach Richard Elliott, in the following year, launched yet another body which all teachers of the deaf were invited to join. Not, however, until Van Praagh's death in 1907 did the National Association of Teachers of the Deaf achieve success. In that year it assisted in establishing a joint examining body of the College of Teachers and the colleges at Fitzroy Square and Ealing. In 1909 the Board of Education officially approved the examination of the joint examining board, and recognized the diploma that it awarded.[4]

At the same time teachers of the blind had become concerned about their lack of status and professional qualifications. In July 1907 a meeting was held at the offices of the British and Foreign Blind Association. Echoes of the pioneers of the previous century were to be found in the presence of Francis Campbell, now seventy-three years old, and the daughters of Moon and Armitage.[5] It was

[1] *R.C.B.D.*, Vol. 3, Evidence of R. Elliott, 5.3.1886.
[2] *Report of the College of Teachers of the Deaf and Dumb, 1898.*
[3] *R.C.B.D.*, Vol. 3, Evidence of W. Stainer, 5.3.1886.
[4] *Annual Report for 1909 of the Chief Medical Officer of the Board of Education,* p. 136.
[5] Getliff, 'The College of Teachers of the Blind', *Teacher of the Blind*, Vol. 43, No. 5, June 1955, pp. 190–201.

decided to establish an examining body, the College of Teachers of the Blind, which would grant diplomas to successful candidates. The College and the qualification it awarded were recognized by the Board of Education, which, now that facilities existed for the examination of teachers of the blind and the deaf, ruled that, in the future, teachers in schools for the blind and the deaf must obtain within two years of their appointment an approved qualification.[1]

Meanwhile, the colleges at Fitzroy Square and Ealing continued to train their student teachers. They continued, also, to compete against and weaken each other. The number of students attending declined;[2] the annual deficit increased. In 1915 St. John Ackers died. The way to amalgamation now lay open, and in the same year the Association for the Oral Instruction of the Deaf and Dumb and the Society for the Training of Teachers of the Deaf combined to form the National Association for the Oral Instruction of the Deaf.[3] It continued to maintain the college at Fitzroy Square. It was short-lived. In 1919 it was absorbed into the Faculty of Education of Manchester University.[4]

The foundation of what was later to become the Department of Education of the Deaf at Manchester was due to the benevolence of a Lancashire cotton merchant, Sir James Jones.[5] His son, Ellis, born deaf, was so well educated by private teachers that he was able to follow a course of study at Oxford, and later, during the First World War, to work in a canteen for the troops in France. The son's untimely death in 1917 induced the father to donate £16,000, land and a building to the University for the establishment of a hall of residence for women students of the deaf, and facilities for their instruction. When the hall of residence and department opened in 1919 both were named after Ellis Jones. Eight students, some of whom had come from Fitzroy Square, attended during the first session. Their lecturer was Miss Irene Goldsack who had come from the Royal Schools for the Deaf, Manchester, where Sir James was Chairman of the Governors. Irene Goldsack made the Department. Of her, her husband, Sir Alexander Ewing, has written:

'It would be true but entirely inadequate to say that Irene Ewing

[1] Board of Education, Regulations for the Training of Teachers for Elementary Schools, 1908, Chapter VII and *Annual Report for 1908 of the Chief Medical Officer*, p. 119.

[2] In 1912 there were only five at Fitzroy Square. *Annual Report of the Association for the Oral Instruction of the Deaf and Dumb, 1912.*

[3] *Final Report of the Society for the Training of Teachers of the Deaf, 1915.*

[4] Eichholz, *A Study of the Deaf in England and Wales, 1930–1932, being a Report to the Minister of Health and the President of the Board of Education* (1932), p. 30.

[5] See Whitton, 'Sir James E. Jones: Benefactor to the Deaf', *Teacher of the Deaf*, Vol. 54, No. 321, June 1956, pp. 66–70.

gave inspiration to her students. . . . Her own teaching of deaf children and their response to it were a revelation, even to students who . . . had previous experience of schools and had watched the work of some of those who were at that time rated very good teachers of the deaf.'[1]

Apart from its work in raising the standard of teaching, the Department, which in 1934 was given full status within the Faculty of Education, initiated valuable experimental work in electroacoustics. A pure-tone audiometer, the first electronic audiometer in the United Kingdom, was obtained in 1928. By its aid it was discovered that few children were totally deaf. Therefore it was possible by means of hearing aids to enable children previously suspected of being stone deaf to hear some sounds, and so the problem of teaching them was considerably eased.[2]

Irene Goldsack's contribution to the education of the deaf was not confined to her work at the University. In 1912 she had become the teacher in charge of the first residential school for young deaf children. The school, Worrall House, was part of the Royal Residential Schools for the Deaf, Manchester, where fifty years earlier the infant deaf had first been taught in a day school.[3] Children were admitted at the age of five, and were taught lip-reading and speech from the beginning.[4] This was admirable. But it was still not good enough.

Steps in the right direction, as far as the blind were concerned, were taken in 1918 when the National Institute for the Blind[5] opened the first of its Sunshine Homes at Chorleywood, Hertfordshire. A residential nursery school, it accommodated twenty-five children aged two to five whose home conditions were poor. According to the Chief Medical Officer of the Board of Education, it fulfilled 'the ideal of a Nursery Special School. . . . The provision includes decorative kindergarten room with small tables, dining-room with all the appearance of a miniature first-class restaurant, dormitories in white enamel and tasteful equipment, in fact the whole aim of the founder, Sir Arthur Pearson,[6] has been to establish an institution which shall be

---

[1] Ewing, 'The Education of the Deaf: History of the Department of Education of the Deaf, University of Manchester', *British Journal of Educational Studies*, Vol. 4, No. 2, May 1956, p. 112.

[2] *Ibid.*, pp. 103–28.

[3] See Chapter 3, p. 28.

[4] Nelson and Lunt, *Royal Residential Schools for the Deaf, Manchester, Historical Survey* (1923).

[5] In 1914 the British and Foreign Blind Association changed its name to the National Institute for the Blind. By command of Her Majesty the prefix Royal was added in 1953.

[6] President of the National Institute for the Blind.

perfect to the eye in order that the pleasure derived by sighted persons shall be reflected upon the blind.'[1]

Some of the children at the school had been neglected and rejected by their parents, others over-protected. All of them were more backward than they need have been from their blindness alone. Therefore, one of the main purposes of the school was that 'the children should be taught to grow up as normal human beings, and to treat their blindness as a handicap to be overcome'.[2] This was the spirit that was to permeate all the Sunshine Homes, of which there are at present nine.

Chorleywood was also the scene of the next venture by the National Institute for the Blind. Chorleywood College, which it opened in 1921, was intended for the higher education of blind girls. As such it was the first in the world. It was run on public school lines, and the first headmistress, Miss Phyllis Monk, had taught at Roedean. Neither she nor any of her staff had previously taught the blind. However, before taking up the post she visited Worcester College, and learnt to read and write Braille. Her ability and enthusiasm more than compensated for her lack of experience, and it was mainly due to her drive and determination that the school remained open despite the financial difficulties that beset it during its early years.[3] Five girls were present for the first lessons in January 1921. Their ages ranged from nine to seventeen. Of one of them Miss Monk recorded that she 'could not go far intellectually'.[4] Here at the outset were the troubles which were to plague the school: too few pupils, too great an age range, and an uneven standard of attainment. There was also, of course, the perennial problem of finance. All the girls paid fees. In the first year these were £35 per term. Within two years, so great were the difficulties, they were raised to over £50. By then there were eighteen girls at the school. The youngest was six years old, the oldest over twenty. Gradually the early storms were weathered. The number of girls increased substantially, classification into age groups became easier, and the National Institute for the Blind subsidized the losses. When in 1944 Chorleywood College, still under the National Institute, became a selective grammar school, there were sixty girls, and one of its first pupils, who had entered at the age of six, had proceeded to Newnham

[1] *Annual Report for 1918 of the Chief Medical Officer*, p. 142.
[2] *Annual Report of Chorleywood Home*, cited by Thomas, *The Royal National Institute for the Blind, 1868–1956*, p. 77.
[3] Credit must also be given to Sir Beachcroft Towse, first Chairman of the Governors, and Chairman of the National Institute for the Blind. He was one of the few men to be awarded a bar to the Victoria Cross, and the deed which won him the bar cost him his sight.
[4] Monk, *Though Land be Out of Sight* (1952), p. 15.

where she had been the first woman to take a double First in Theology.[1]

In addition to the support that it gave to the higher education of blind girls, the National Institute for the Blind took an interest in Worcester College for blind boys. The College, no longer a private venture, but controlled by a Board of Governors under a Trust Deed, was nevertheless still in straitened circumstances. From 1917 onwards it received financial assistance from the National Institute for the Blind, and in 1922 the National Institute became the sole Trustee of the College, although control of expenditure remained in the hands of the Governors. However, this arrangement was satisfactory to neither side, and in 1936 the National Institute became responsible for the policy and finances of the College. Thus, by the outbreak of the Second World War the higher education of blind children was securely established, and in 1944 Worcester College, like Chorleywood, became a selective grammar school.[2]

During the inter-war years the Royal Normal College, Norwood, had supplemented to a certain extent the work of the other two colleges. In 1912 Guy Campbell had succeeded his father as Principal, and the work of training blind teachers continued until 1937. At that date the College contained two other departments: the technical, in which there were seventy young people aged between sixteen and twenty receiving tuition in music, piano tuning or shorthand and typing; and the school department which contained sixty children some of whom were following a grammar school course and sitting the School Certificate examination. After the general reorganization of 1944, the Normal College, evacuated from Norwood to Rowton Castle near Shrewsbury, ceased its grammar school work, and accepted children aged twelve to sixteen who were likely to be suitable for subsequent training in music or commercial subjects.[3]

Progress in the higher education of the deaf was slower. The school for boys at Northampton established by Thomas Arnold[4] was still in existence. There was also a school for girls at Burgess Hill, Sussex, conducted by Miss Mary Hare. Both were private schools. Neither was available to children under the administration of L.E.A.s. The need for better provision had long been felt. It was discussed at length at the International Conference on the Education of the Deaf held in London in 1925. As a result of a paper read by the

[1] Monk, *Though Land be Out of Sight* (1952), p. 75.
[2] Thomas, *The Royal National Institute for the Blind, 1868–1956*, pp. 81–3.
[3] Langdon, 'The Royal Normal College', *New Beacon*, Vol. 41, No. 485, July 1957, pp. 149–53.
[4] See Chapter 8, p. 89.

IV. Advances in the Education of the Blind and Deaf

President of the Gallaudet College for the Deaf, Washington, the National College of Teachers of the Deaf instituted an enquiry from which emerged the fact that some 100 children in schools for the deaf would be likely to derive benefit from a course of higher education. Therefore, in 1928, a Conference convened by the College of Teachers, and attended by representatives of local education authorities, agreed to form a committee to examine the question.[1] Although the desirability of establishing a grammar school for the deaf was recognized, no immediate action was taken. It was not until the death of Mary Hare in 1945 that the long-planned school came into being. Miss Hare had bequeathed her private school for the purpose of providing higher education for all who could benefit from it. With the trustees of her estate forming the first Board of Governors, the Mary Hare Grammar School for the Deaf was recognized in 1946 by the Ministry of Education, and admits boys and girls on payment by L.E.A.s.[2] As the Royal Normal College supplements the work of the blind grammar schools, so, from 1955, has Burwood Park School, Walton-on-Thames, completed the present provision for the higher education of the deaf. A technical school supported by private subscription, it caters for thirty-five boys aged twelve to nineteen.

Between 1930 and 1938 four enquiries relating to the education of either the blind or the deaf were conducted. One was by Dr. Eichholz at the request of Sir George Newman, two were by committees appointed by the Board of Education, and the fourth was by a joint committee of the College of Teachers of the Blind and the N.I.B. Teachers of the deaf had for many years suspected that the blind were receiving preferential treatment from the State. The suspicion had first arisen when the 1893 Act provided for compulsory education for the blind at an earlier age than for the deaf. It was accentuated by the appointment in 1914 of the Departmental Committee on the Welfare of the Blind, and by the subsequent Blind Persons Act 1920 which provided a comprehensive scheme for the training, employment and care of the blind. Therefore in the 1920's both the National Institute for the Deaf and the National College of Teachers of the Deaf agitated for an enquiry. In addition, the latter sought the lowering of the compulsory school age from seven to five, and at the same time its extension to twenty, with the period between fifteen and twenty being utilized for trade training. The National College

[1] *Annual Report for 1927 of the Chief Medical Officer of the Board of Education,* p. 158.

[2] Askew, 'The Mary Hare Grammar School for the Deaf', *National Institute for the Deaf Booklet No. 486* (1955), and *Times Educational Supplement,* No. 1964, December 19th, 1952, p. 1021.

also advocated that the totally deaf and the partially deaf should be classified and educated separately.

In 1930 Eichholz, who two years earlier had retired from the Board of Education, was asked to enquire into the education of the deaf, and to pay particular regard to the points raised by the National College.[1] He found oralism well established. In only one school were oral methods not in use, though all schools used manual methods with those children who could not benefit from oral teaching. Missionaries to the adult deaf, however, still used manual methods, and Eichholz reported that there was considerable estrangement between the schools and the missions.[2] With regard to the compulsory school age, while it was obviously advantageous for the deaf to be educated from the age of five, Eichholz felt that encouragement, not compulsion, was the answer, and only if encouragement failed should consideration be given to changing the statute.[3] Nor was the raising of the school leaving age recommended. There should however be more vocational courses for pupils both under and over sixteen, and, of course, there should be a grammar school for the deaf.[4] Eichholz considered that the question of the partially deaf warranted more attention than he could give it, and he therefore recommended that it be investigated by a special committee.[5]

Such a committee was appointed in 1934, and its *Report*[6] was published four years later. Thirty years earlier the first special class for partially deaf children had been established by the Bristol Education Committee.[7] This was quickly followed by a number of classes attached to L.C.C. schools. There the children were taught lip-reading, writing and spelling, and given speech training. For all other subjects they attended the adjoining elementary schools.[8] Such provision was not entirely satisfactory, but it was better than no provision at all. Many partially deaf children in schools for the deaf were taught as if they were wholly deaf. Others in the ordinary schools were given no special education.

The Committee of Inquiry suggested that children with defective hearing should be divided into three grades, the second of which was

---

[1] Eichholz, *A Study of the Deaf in England and Wales, 1930–1932, being a Report to the Minister of Health and the President of the Board of Education* (1932), pp. 1–5.

[2] *Ibid.*, p. 30.

[3] *Ibid.*, p. 84. In the event the Education (Deaf Children) Act 1937 did lower the age to five.

[4] *Ibid.*, pp. 176 and 185.   [5] *Ibid.*, p. 180.

[6] *Report of the Committee of Inquiry into the Problems relating to Children with Defective Hearing* (1938).

[7] *Annual Report for 1909 of the Chief Medical Officer of the Board of Education*, p. 141.

[8] Ministry of Education Archives, Education Class 32, Piece 88.

sub-divided. Children in the first grade could be educated in the ordinary school without special arrangements. Those in grade 2A could also be educated in the ordinary school but should be given hearing aids, and visited by a teacher of lip-reading. Grade 2B children would need to be taught in a special school. If they lived near enough, they should attend an existing school for the deaf, and be taught in separate classes. If, however, they were not within daily reach of such a school, they should go to a residential school for the partially deaf, one or more of which should be established. Since no residential schools for the partially deaf existed, it would be necessary at first for the children to be placed in residential schools for the deaf, which should be called upon to provide special classes for them. In the third grade would be those children whose hearing was so poor and their speech so little developed that they would require to be educated by methods appropriate to those without naturally acquired speech. Finally, the Committee recommended that teachers of grade 2B children should obtain the same qualification as teachers of the deaf.[1]

As a result of these recommendations residential schools for the partially deaf were opened, and in 1945 partially deaf children were listed as a separate category of handicapped children.[2]

In 1907, the year before Bristol opened its class for the partially deaf, London made the first special provision for partially sighted children. Prior to this the only specialized education available to the partially sighted was in blind schools, where their education did not differ from that given to the blind. As has been seen, James Kerr moved from Bradford to London in 1902,[3] and in the same year N. Bishop Harman was appointed as ophthalmologist to the L.C.C. While still at Bradford, Kerr had felt that special education was necessary for myopic children. A survey of the conditions in the elementary schools of London, and a personal examination of each child in the authority's blind schools, confirmed him in this view. Harman had come to the same conclusion, and Kerr in his *Annual Report* to the L.C.C. in 1905 advocated the formation of, what he termed, sight-saving classes.[4] Next, Bishop Harman, who had found that many children in schools for the blind were merely suffering from high myopia, brought the question of their education before the Second International Congress of School Hygiene held in London in 1907. As a result of the pressure by the two men, the L.C.C.

[1] *Report of the Committee of Inquiry*, pp. 130–2.
[2] The Handicapped Pupils and School Health Service Regulations, Statutory Rules and Orders No. 1076, 1945.
[3] See Chapter 13, p. 167.
[4] Kerr, *School Vision and the Myopic Scholar* (1925), pp. 13–14.

arranged for myopic children in their blind schools to be taught reading and writing from large types at a distance of a yard, instead of by Braille. At the same time the Nottingham Education Committee admitted highly myopic children to their school for the blind to be given similar instruction.[1]

In January of the following year, 1908, the first special class in the world for high myopic and other children with defective vision was opened by the L.C.C. in Boundary Lane School, Camberwell. Of the twenty children who were present at the opening fourteen were myopes. The class was not intended exclusively for myopes, but since they were in the majority, and as the class had come into being through agitation on their behalf, it was called the myope class, and the name was adopted by later classes and schools. 'This title', wrote Kerr, 'is to be regretted, but it has become fixed. "Sight-saving classes" would have been better in the way of expressing their work.'[2] The Committee of Inquiry into Problems relating to Partially Sighted Children had stronger comment to make: 'Special educational methods devised for myopes now dominate the curriculum and are applied to all children whether myopes or non-myopes.'[3]

The children in the Camberwell class joined the sighted children in the adjacent elementary school for their oral work. Manual work was taken by their own teachers. Of literary work there was very little. 'With the root ideas at the start,' Kerr commented, 'there might at first have been inscribed over the doors "Books, paper, pencils or pens cannot enter here", but experience has somewhat modified this veto.'[4] In fact the veto was soon removed, and the children read from large print, and wrote in large letters on blackboards or black linen rollers.[5]

The Camberwell class served as a model for both subsequent English schools and those abroad. It was visited in 1909 by Dr. Edward Allen, Director of the Perkins Institution for the Blind, Boston. On his return to the United States he recommended that similar provision should be made, and in 1913 the Boston Board of Education opened the first conservation of vision class on the

[1] *Report of the Committee of Inquiry into Problems relating to Partially Sighted Children* (1934), p. 10.
[2] Kerr, *School Vision*, p. 16.
[3] *Report of the Committee*, p. 11.
[4] Kerr, *School Vision*, p. 16. In *Education and Health of the Partially Seeing Child* (1954), p. 4, the American, W. Hathaway, states that a notice over the door stated 'Reading and Writing Shall Not Enter Here'. Kerr frequently visited the class and his account is therefore likely to be accurate. Hathaway's statement is probably a misinterpretation of Kerr's comment.
[5] *Annual Report for 1918 of the Chief Medical Officer of the Board of Education*, p. 144.

IV. Advances in the Education of the Blind and Deaf

American continent.[1] By the same year France and Germany had established special classes, and eight English L.E.A.s had made similar provision. Twenty years later there were thirty-seven schools in England with accommodation for 2,000 partially sighted children. In addition eighteen schools for the blind were giving them special education.[2]

Hence, when the third of the committees of the 1930's, the Committee of Inquiry into Problems relating to Partially Sighted Children, met in 1931, it found that the education of the partially sighted was well advanced. At least it was well advanced as far as provision was concerned, but there were still many partially sighted children in schools for the blind being educated by methods applicable only to the blind. The Committee emphatically condemned such a practice, which it regarded as 'a deplorable failure in educational administration, causing in many cases mal-adjustment and hardship'.[3] Moreover, the Committee felt that it was wrong for partially sighted children to attend even those blind schools which were making special provision for them. The whole tenor of the *Report* was that such children, both educationally and socially, belonged to the sighted world. They should be educated, where possible, in classes forming an integral part of the ordinary schools. They should join the ordinary children for those subjects which were taught by oral methods. They should, in short, have as much contact as possible with the social side of the ordinary school. As for their education, many of the existing restrictions should be relaxed. There should be more reading, more physical training,[4] in fact more education which approximated to that given in the ordinary school.

This emphasis on normality drew the following comment in the *Report of the Chief Medical Officer*: 'It may be thought by some Authorities that the Committee have gone too far in this respect and that in their desire to make the education of "partially sighted" children more "normal" they have made recommendations which exceed the bounds of safety.'[5] Be that as it may, many L.E.A.s did not separate their blind and partially sighted children until after the war. Indeed, the Committee realized that immediate separation was impracticable. Children living in rural areas would have to attend residential schools, and since no such schools existed for partially

[1] Frampton and Gall, *Special Education for the Exceptional,* Vol. 2, pp. 115–16.
[2] *Report of the Committee of Inquiry into Problems relating to Partially Sighted Children* (1934), p. 12.
[3] *Ibid.,* p. 49.
[4] Despite the prevalence of postural defects in partially sighted children, very little physical education was given, since there existed the danger of retina detachment in some myopes.
[5] *Annual Report for 1933,* p. 104.

sighted children it would be necessary, as a temporary measure, for the children to attend residential schools for the blind where special provision should be made for them. In the meantime the Board of Education should attempt a reorganization of blind schools in order that some of them should be set apart for partially sighted children from rural areas.[1]

The last of the four reports of this period[2] contained no startling or revolutionary recommendations. It contained an adequate account of the system of educating the blind, but otherwise it was little more than a hand-book of suggestions for teachers. Its theme was summed up in one sentence: 'The present educational provision for the blind in Great Britain is reasonably complete.'[3]

[1] *Report of the Committee of Inquiry*, p. 126.
[2] *Report of the Joint Committee of the College of Teachers of the Blind and the National Institute for the Blind* (1936).
[3] *Ibid.*, p. 6.

16

THE PERIOD OF CONSOLIDATION:
I. THE 1944 ACT

BY the summer of 1940 children who had been evacuated nine months earlier were streaming home. The air-raids of the following autumn and winter reversed the flow, and the second period of educational disorganization commenced. The first, at the outbreak of the war, had affected special as much as ordinary schools. Indeed, in many ways special schools were more severely affected. The handicapped children attending them could not easily be billeted as ordinary evacuees. Hence day special schools in the threatened areas were re-established as residential schools in the reception areas. But some of the children previously attending them remained behind, since their parents were unwilling that they should be evacuated. They could, therefore, attend only the ordinary schools which had remained open. Equally, as the threatened air attacks failed to materialize, children who had gone to the residential schools drifted back to the cities to attend the ordinary schools or to remain at home. To cater for these, some of the day special schools were re-opened, only to close again under the attacks that followed the Battle of Britain.

By the middle of 1941, with the attacks beaten off, the whole process started yet again. This time, however, the day special schools had lost many of their own buildings to other schools, the armed forces or Goering's Luftwaffe, and they had to open in unsuitable premises. In addition, the transport which had previously been used to take handicapped children to school was no longer available. It therefore became necessary to organize the children into small local groups which, because of the lack of classification, added to the difficulties of teaching. Nor were those day schools, which in 1939 had moved from the cities and re-opened as residential schools in the reception areas, without their problems. The German conquest of France and Belgium had made the reception areas in the south-east of England particularly vulnerable, and the bombing of other regions previously considered safe meant that a number of schools had to move for a second time. But this second move was made when most of the suitable mansions and hutted camps had already been taken over by other bodies. Hence the schools had either to occupy premises which were plainly inadequate in size, or move to remote areas where they would experience difficulties in obtaining and retaining staff.

Some of the schools which had always been residential also had their problems. Many of those in the larger cities moved to smaller premises in the country. A number of the smaller voluntary schools could not afford the expense of moving, and ceased to provide special education. Because of the reduction in boarding places available, there existed for the first time in many years a shortage of accommodation for all handicapped children, and consequently the number of children attending special schools fell sharply. In addition, the demand for labour induced some authorities to allow children to leave special schools at fourteen. At the same time, fewer children were being ascertained as in need of special education, partly because of the shortage of accommodation, partly because of the general disorganization of the education services, and partly because medical officers were pre-occupied with extra duties connected with evacuation and Civil Defence. It is therefore understandable that in 1941 the number of London mentally and physically handicapped children attending special schools had decreased by fifty per cent.[1] Other cities reported a similar decline, so that when, at the end of the war, the Butler Act introduced a new outlook on special education, there was a need not only to build afresh but to rebuild some of what had been lost.

Thirty years to the day after the outbreak of the First World War the Education Act, which was to build a brave new world after the Second, received the Royal Assent. This overhaul of the national system of education implemented some of the recommendations of the Bryce Commission of 1895, and drew heavily upon the *Hadow* and *Spens Reports*. In the same way the inspiration for the changes in special education was to be found in the recommendations of the Wood Committee and the *Reports of the Committees of Inquiry* on the partially sighted and partially deaf. All three committees had stressed the importance of bringing the special schools within the general

[1] *Report of the Chief Medical Officer of the Ministry of Education 1939-1945*, p. 84.

education framework. All three had deplored the tendency to look upon the handicapped as a class apart. All three had felt that the stigma attaching to special schools could be lessened.

The Act of 1944 not only gave expression to this change in outlook but itself helped to intensify the change. It was best exemplified by the fact that the provision of special educational treatment was merely made part of the general duty laid upon L.E.A.s to ensure that children were educated in accordance with their ages, aptitudes and abilities. Earlier legislation had dealt separately with the education of the handicapped. Even in the consolidating Act of 1921 they were excluded from the general provisions. Whereas Part III covered elementary education, and Part VI higher, blind, deaf, defective and epileptic children were treated as a distinct class in Part V. In 1944, however, the section which called upon education authorities to provide primary and secondary schools also required them to have regard 'to the need for securing that provision is made for pupils who suffer from any disability of mind or body by providing, either in special schools, or otherwise, special educational treatment'.[1]

Again it is worthy of note that reference is made to special education being given 'in special schools or otherwise'. The Act of 1921 provided only for education in special schools or certified special classes. But the 1944 Act instructed L.E.A.s to 'provide for the education of pupils in whose case the disability is serious in special schools appropriate for that category, but where that is impracticable, or where the disability is not serious, the arrangements may provide for the giving of such education in any school maintained or assisted by the local education authority'.[2] The reference to 'any school' meant that not only could special education be given in schools other than special schools, but it need not necessarily be given even in a special class.[3] The intention behind this was praiseworthy. It served, in the words of the Ministry, 'to emphasize that physical or mental handicap existed in all degrees, from the very slight to the serious, and that special educational treatment was not a matter of segregating the seriously handicapped from their fellows but of providing in each case the special help or modifications in regime or education suited to the needs of the individual child'.[4] One cannot quarrel with such a statement, but, unfortunately, the wording of the Act allows authorities to evade their responsibilities. The evasion, in

---

[1] 7 and 8 George VI, c. 31, s. 8.   [2] 7 and 8 George VI, c. 31, s. 33.
[3] This interpretation is confirmed by Ministry of Education, *Pamphlet No. 30, Education of the Handicapped Pupil 1945–1955* (1956), p. 1.
[4] *Ibid.*, p. 1.

so far as it exists, is not so much in the provision of special schools, as in the lack of provision of special educational facilities in the ordinary schools.

Section 34 of the 1944 Act stated that it was the duty of every L.E.A. 'to ascertain what children in their area require special education', but no mention was made of the categories of children who might need such education. In this respect the Act differed fundamentally from that of 1921, which not only stipulated which classes of children should attend special schools but also defined the classes. However, Section 33 of the 1944 Act empowered the Minister to make regulations defining 'the several categories of pupils requiring special educational treatment and making provision as to the special methods appropriate for the education of pupils of each category'. In addition, the Minister could rule on the requirements to be complied with as a condition of approval as a special school. This power illustrates a feature of modern legislation whereby Acts of Parliament express certain powers and duties in very general terms, and leave matters of detail to be dealt with by regulations which have the force of law. Such delegated legislation, although criticized on the ground that it is open to abuse, is nevertheless recognized as an essential necessity if parliamentary time is not to be taken up with the minutiæ of administration. Certainly, the Regulations which the Minister of Education laid before Parliament in 1945,[1] and the amending Regulations of 1953 and 1959,[2] conformed with the intention of the 1944 Act. In place of the five categories of handicapped children previously recognized,[3] there were now eleven. Moreover, the categories were defined in such a way as to avoid, as far as possible, the rigid separation of the handicapped from the normal.

In no way was this shown more clearly than in the definition of educationally sub-normal children. The new terminology not only replaced 'mentally defective' with its emotive connotations, but also abolished the necessity for certification. In addition, it allowed education authorities to provide special education for a much larger number of children than had previously been possible. In this, as in the abolition of certification, it followed the recommendations of the Wood Committee. No longer would children have to be considered feeble-minded before they could be sent to special schools or

[1] Statutory Rules and Orders No. 1076, The Handicapped Pupils and School Health Service Regulations 1945.
[2] Statutory Instrument No. 1156, The School Health Service and Handicapped Pupils Regulations 1953 and Statutory Instrument No. 365, The Handicapped Pupils and Special Schools Regulations 1959.
[3] Blind, deaf, epileptic and physically and mentally defective.

classes. Indeed, the term feeble-minded was not to be applied to children who were educable. Even though their lack of intellectual ability was such that they would previously have come under the Mental Deficiency Acts, the provisions of those Acts would be suspended while they were of school age. Therefore, within the definition of educational sub-normality came not only those children who, being of low intelligence, had in the past been considered suitable for special education, but also children who, for whatever reason, were markedly failing in their school work. The extent of the failure was not specified, for the definition was deliberately broad. In this respect it was in striking contrast to that in the 1921 Act which described mentally defective children as those who 'not being imbecile, and not being merely dull or backward, are defective, that is to say, . . . children [who] by reason of mental or physical defect are incapable of receiving proper benefit from the instruction in the ordinary public elementary schools, but are not incapable by reason of that defect of receiving benefit from instruction in . . . special classes or schools'.[1] Very different was the description of E.S.N. pupils as those who 'by reason of limited ability or other conditions resulting in educational retardation, require some specialized form of education wholly or partly in substitution for the education normally given in ordinary schools'.[2] Despite the fact that the degree of retardation is not mentioned, the Ministry did in fact suggest that any child whose school attainments were twenty per cent or more below the average attainment of children of the same age, might be considered to need special educational treatment.[3]

Of the other ten categories of handicapped children listed in the 1945 Regulations, three, the blind, the deaf and the epileptic, corresponded with existing categories, although the actual definitions differed. Certain changes were, however, made. Blind pupils were to be educated in residential schools. Therefore the few day schools which had previously made provision for them would have to close. Secondly, blind and deaf children were excluded from the mandate which allowed L.E.A.s to give special education in the ordinary school. For them, education in special schools would still be necessary. Finally, the existence of two new categories of handicapped children affected the existing schools for the blind and deaf. Following the recommendations of the Committees of Inquiry of 1934 and 1938, the partially sighted and partially deaf were recognized as

[1] 11 and 12 George V, c. 51, s. 55.
[2] The School Health Service and Handicapped Pupils Regulations 1953, regulation 14.
[3] Ministry of Education, *Pamphlet No. 5, Special Educational Treatment* (1946), p. 20.

separate categories of handicapped children. Consequently, schools for the blind which had previously provided for both blind and partially sighted children were asked to concentrate on one of the handicaps only. By 1960 only two schools remained which educated the blind and the partially sighted. Both had special dispensation. One, at Bridgend, is the only blind school in Wales; the other, at Liverpool, the only Catholic blind school in England and Wales.

Children who, prior to 1944, had been known as physically defective could, under the new regulations, fall into one of three categories, physically handicapped, delicate or diabetic. Delicate children were, of course, those who in the past had attended the open-air schools, but the realization of the need for special educational provision for diabetic children was recent. Until the discovery of insulin treatment in 1922 there was little prospect of survival for those who contracted diabetes. However, by 1939 there was a large number of such children, and the exigencies of evacuation drew them to the attention of the authorities. Because of the necessity for treatment and a special diet, it became difficult to billet diabetic children. Therefore the L.C.C., with the support of the Diabetic Association, opened a hostel for them. The children lived in the hostel but attended ordinary schools. By the end of the war there was a waiting list for admission to the hostel, and between then and 1953 five more hostels were established. They provide for diabetic children who come from divided or broken homes, or homes where the conditions are such that the strict regime necessary for diabetics cannot be maintained. The children in all the hostels attend local schools; the needs of the country have now been met; and in 1953 the separate category of diabetic pupils was included in the general category of delicate pupils.

Children in hospital schools had, in the pre-war years, been known as physically defective. Now they were physically handicapped. But the 1944 Act had a more profound effect than one of nomenclature. Under Section 56 L.E.A.s were permitted to educate children otherwise than at school. This made it possible for a group of children, too small to form a school, or even an individual child, to be taught in hospital. It also enabled L.E.A.s to appoint peripatetic teachers who would visit home-bound children.

The last two of the categories listed in the 1945 Regulations were children suffering from speech defects and maladjustment. Although both the categories were new, there was already some provision for the children concerned. However, not until 1945 did it become the duty of L.E.A.s to provide special educational treatment. Special arrangements for children who stammered were first made by

Manchester Education Committee in 1906, and by 1939 some ninety authorities had appointed speech therapists. But progress was inhibited by the fact that the therapists were organized in two separate bodies which were not always in agreement. In 1945 the associations agreed to amalgamate, and together they founded the organizing and examining College of Speech Therapists. Two years later the first special school was established. Moor House, Oxted is intended for children with speech defects too severe to be treated in speech clinics. It works in close co-operation with the plastic surgery unit of the Queen Victoria Hospital, East Grinstead. In 1958 a second school was opened at Worthing by the Invalid Children's Aid Association for young children who require speech therapy in a residential atmosphere. If at the age of nine they still require residential therapy, they move on to Moor House.

As with the diabetic, the difficulties experienced in billeting maladjusted children in 1939 showed the need for residential accommodation. Hostels were opened for them in the reception areas, and at the end of the war some were taken over as residential schools by L.E.A.s. Others continued to function as hostels, with the children attending local schools. These were satisfactory developments. Unfortunately, there were, and still are, insufficient schools and hostels to meet the needs of the maladjusted.

17

THE PERIOD OF CONSOLIDATION: II. THE PRESENT

ALL the problems of special education were not solved by the 1944 Act. In some respects problems were created by it. One of these was concerned with E.S.N. children. Under the new definition of educational sub-normality, between ten and fifteen per cent of the school population would require special educational treatment, and could in theory go to a special school. Obviously many of these would not need to be formally ascertained as E.S.N. Equally, only a very small proportion of them could, or would need to, attend a special school. The question however arose as to what children would comprise the small proportion. The Ministry, in 1946, had little doubt: 'Very few more than those who would have been certifiable under the old Act'.[1] This meant that the children in the special schools should, in the main, be those whose intelligence quotients were below 70 or, at least, below 75. Some authorities accepted the advice of the Ministry. Others used their powers under the definition of educational sub-normality to send to special schools children who, though not of very low intelligence, were extremely retarded in their school work. Some of these children, whose intelligence quotients were frequently as high as 85 or 90, had become retarded through ill health, prolonged absence from school, or sensory difficulties. Others, however, had marked behaviour difficulties, and could well have benefited from attendance at a child guidance clinic or a school for maladjusted children.

This policy of sending children of near average intelligence to E.S.N. schools has been widely criticized. While it cannot be denied that the small classes and the individual methods of the E.S.N.

[1] Ministry of Education, *Pamphlet No. 5, Special Educational Treatment* (1946), p. 21.

214

school are obviously beneficial to all children who have learning difficulties, it is hard to escape the conclusion that the policy has certain disadvantages. If E.S.N. schools are used as remedial centres for children who are failing at school for reasons other than low intelligence, there exists the danger that the education authorities concerned will feel that they have solved the problem of remedial education. Obviously this cannot be so, since the number of children requiring remedial education is far in excess of the number who can be admitted to special schools. Even if some children are assisted in the special schools, there still remains the need for special classes and individual teaching in the ordinary school, and, ideally, the appointment of peripatetic remedial teachers and the establishment of remedial centres. Moreover, it is presumed that if the remedial work in the E.S.N. school is successful the children concerned will return to the ordinary school. This constant transfer of children to the ordinary school may well have a disturbing effect on the more permanent inhabitants of the E.S.N. school, while the need to cater for the academic requirements necessary for transfer to the ordinary school might wean the special school away from its true rôle of providing a slow pace, a secure environment and an education based on the practical needs of children of low intellectual ability.

In the same way, the sending of emotionally disturbed children to E.S.N. schools may convince education authorities that they are doing all that is necessary for them. In fact they are being fair neither to the disturbed children nor to the other occupants of the schools. The former need treatment for their maladjustment which the E.S.N. school is unable to give. The latter, always easily led, may well come under the influence of the maladjusted who, with their superior intelligence, could become the leaders of the schools. But the most powerful argument against the admission of children of near normal intelligence to E.S.N. schools is that, while the present grave shortage of accommodation lasts, there remains the possibility that children of low intelligence, for whom the schools can be of greater use, are denied places.[1] This is the ground upon which the Ministry still takes its stand. The *Report of the Chief Medical Officer*, published in 1958, stated that 'in some schools the proportion of children with I.Q.s of 80 and above was considerably greater than might have been expected. It is not suggested that children with relatively high I.Q.s are unwisely placed when they are in special schools nor is this the place for a discussion of this question. But this selection for special school education of children with high I.Q.s causes one to consider

[1] For a good analysis of the factors involved in the selection of children for special schools, see Cleugh, *The Slow Learner* (1957), pp. 21–9.

what becomes of the children with low levels of intelligence—particularly those who are on the borderline of educability. Admission of these seriously retarded children to a special school provides their only opportunity of making progress, and of showing whether they are capable of receiving education at school.'[1] The most recent pronouncement, in July 1961, makes a similar point: 'The children most in need of the help which only special schools can provide are those with the greatest degree of handicap and, in the Minister's view, they should have first call on the existing places. It is undesirable that severely handicapped children should be allowed to remain in ordinary schools.'[2]

The question of which children should go to the E.S.N. special school is further complicated by the inadequacy of the provision for special educational treatment, the uneven nature of the process of ascertaining which children require special education, and the fact that in many areas the selection of children for special schools is carried out solely by medical officers. It was obvious that for some years after the passing of the 1944 Act there would be a shortage of accommodation for E.S.N. children. Even before the war there had been insufficient places, and the wartime decline of special schools, coupled with the new definition of educational sub-normality, had made the shortage more acute. Whereas there had been 16,000 children in schools for mentally defective children in 1926, there were only 11,000 in E.S.N. schools in 1946. The subsequent growth was commendably rapid. Ten years later there were 26,000, and by the end of 1960 the number had reached 34,500. But despite the increase in places available, the number of children on the waiting lists remained remarkably constant. With 15,500 children in E.S.N. schools in 1950 there were 12,500 awaiting admission. In 1960 the number waiting was the same, although there were twice as many places available. Moreover, a survey in 1956 showed that additional places were required for a further 27,000 children: more than double the number that L.E.A.s had shown on their annual returns. It is evident from these figures that some L.E.A.s are not identifying all the children who require special school education while there is still no reasonable hope that places can be found for them. The Minister is therefore planning to approve building programmes that will raise the number of special school places for E.S.N. children to 54,000.[3] It will be some years before this figure is reached, and one

[1] *Report for 1956 and 1957*, p. 141.
[2] Ministry of Education, *Circular 11/61, Special Educational Treatment for Educationally Sub-normal Pupils*, July 1961, p. 7.
[3] *Ibid.*, p. 9.

must endorse the comment that 'the shortage of special school places for the educationally sub-normal is the largest outstanding problem in the special school field'.[1]

It is by no means the only problem. The provision of special educational facilities in the ordinary school is still woefully inadequate. Where the special class exists, it is all too frequently regarded as a poor relation. Schools tend to concentrate on the examination successes of the brighter children, and while many dedicated teachers do excellent work in the special classes, others await the day of transfer to the A stream. Moreover, there is often a lack of realization of the true needs of the children in special classes. Teachers are unaware of the particular learning difficulties of individual children, and the shortage of educational psychologists makes the solution of the problem no easier.

The shortage of psychologists has other effects. Section 34 of the Education Act of 1944 retained the principle that medical officers should have a say in the selection of children for special schools. There was, however, one major change. Prior to 1944 the medical officer, by the very act of certification, decided that a child should go to a special school. But Section 34 makes it clear that the decision must now lie with the L.E.A., and that the opinion expressed and the recommendation made by the medical officer are in the nature of advice. It is the authority which must make the decision, and before doing so it should consider reports and information 'from teachers and other persons with respect to the ability and aptitude of the child'.[2] That such reports should be considered is highly desirable. If, as still sometimes happens, they are not, and the decision is made solely on the advice of the medical officer, then the latter is in fact making an educational judgement. Teachers in special schools are extremely critical of the present system, and while the Act remains unamended the best solution is that suggested by the Chief Medical Officer of the Ministry.[3] Recommendations concerning the admission of a child to an E.S.N. school should be made by a panel consisting of a school medical officer, the chief education officer or one of his deputies, an educational psychologist, and the head teacher of the present and/or proposed school. Some L.E.A.s have established such panels, but in other areas, reported the Chief Medical Officer, 'the advice of the medical officer appears to be accepted as sufficient and final and, where this is so, principal school medical officers are urged

---

[1] *Report of the Chief Medical Officer of the Ministry of Education for 1956 and 1957*, p. 134.
[2] 7 and 8 George VI, c. 31, s. 34.
[3] *Report for 1956 and 1957*, pp. 141 and 142.

to make representations to their authorities on the desirability of having arrangements for consultation such as have been described instead of leaving the medical officers with responsibility for an educational matter which is really outside their sphere'.[1]

With its emphasis on the community care of the mentally ill and mentally handicapped, the Mental Health Act 1959, although not directly concerned with E.S.N. children, introduced one important change in the procedure for dealing with them. Ever since the education of feeble-minded children became compulsory in 1914, it had been the duty of education authorities to notify the mental deficiency authorities of all children who would be likely to require care and supervision when they left the special schools at sixteen. This duty had been continued by Section 57 of the 1944 Act, but as the Mental Health Act abolished statutory supervision, so it relieved L.E.A.s of the duty of notifying leavers from special schools.[2] There will, however, still be children leaving special schools who might need the assistance previously given under the Mental Deficiency Acts. For these, local authorities and even the special schools themselves should provide some form of after-care. Birmingham has led the way in this respect with an After-Care Committee which has been in existence since 1901. Some authorities have provided special youth clubs, either as part of ordinary clubs or on the premises of E.S.N. schools. Others are following the example of the National Association for Mental Health by establishing hostels for children leaving residential schools who have no satisfactory home to which to return. Many have done nothing, and there is much room for the expansion of facilities to assist E.S.N. children with their problems of adjustment to working life.

There is room, too, for the expansion of facilities to assist children with adjustment problems of a different kind. The Committee on Maladjusted Children, appointed by the Minister of Education in 1950, published its *Report* in 1955. Among other things, it recommended that there should be a comprehensive child guidance service available for the area of every local education authority.[3] The service should include a school psychological service and child guidance clinics. It was expected that, as part of the former, educational psychologists would 'try to help within the setting of their school individual children who have learning or behaviour difficulties'.[4] Only when this was not possible would the children be referred to the clinic. The recommendation was accepted by the Minister, and in March 1959 it was suggested to L.E.A.s that they should

---

[1] *Report for 1956 and 1957*, p. 142.   [2] 7 and 8 Elizabeth II, c. 72, s. 11.
[3] *Report of the Committee*, p. 144.   [4] *Ibid.*, p. 145.

implement the recommendation.[1] Advance since then has been rapid. Other recommendations, however, still remain to be implemented. More day special schools and classes for maladjusted children are required, and there is still a great need for special schools for maladjusted children who are also educationally subnormal. Such schools will probably have to be established on a regional basis, and L.E.A.s have been urged to make use of their regional consultative machinery for this purpose.[2]

As far as physically handicapped children are concerned, many of the recent advances have been due to the work of voluntary bodies. The British Council for the Welfare of Spastics and the National Spastics Society, both established since the war, have been responsible for the foundation of a number of schools solely for children suffering from cerebral palsy. The first of these, St. Margaret's School, Croydon, opened in 1947, to be followed the following year by Carlson House, Birmingham. In 1949 a third school was established at Ivybridge, Devon. Since then others have been opened in various parts of the country, including some by L.E.A.s. All are small, and, because of the difficulties involved in educating cerebral palsied children, all have a very generous staff–pupil ratio. Consequently, the expenses of the schools have been high. This, allied to the big demand for places, has led some of the schools to confine admission to children within the normal range of intelligence, since it is felt that they are more likely to derive benefit from the education provided. Therefore, although there is now sufficient day school accommodation for physically handicapped children, there are still a number of severely disabled children for whom residential schooling is required but who are, as yet, at home. Many of these are cerebral palsied children of low intelligence. Some are being visited by home teachers, but a few remain without education of any kind.

A further post-war development in the field of physically handicapped children has been the establishment of a grammar school for boys. It was opened in September 1956 by the trustees of the Lord Mayor Treloar Training College at Alton. It has accommodation for seventy boys, and offers secondary technical in addition to secondary grammar education. There is a need for a similar school for girls, and it is to be hoped that the discussions at present in progress will result in one being established.

Between 1925 and 1945 the number of registered blind children

---

[1] Ministry of Education, *Circular 347, Special Educational Treatment for Maladjusted Children*, March 1959.
[2] Ministry of Education, *Circular 11/61, Special Educational Treatment for Educationally Sub-normal Pupils*, p. 10.

fell by almost half. There were, therefore, despite the disorganization caused by the war, sufficient special school places for the blind. In 1948, however, there was a marked and sudden increase in the registration of blind babies, which continued until 1954. The increase was due to retrolental fibroplasia in babies born prematurely. The discovery that the disease was caused by the administration of too much oxygen to premature babies, and the consequent reduction in the use of oxygen, resulted in the disease disappearing almost as dramatically as it had appeared. There remain, however, the unfortunate children who have been blinded. For a time their presence in schools for the blind will add substantially to the number of children in certain age groups.[1] The resulting shortage of accommodation should be of a temporary nature, and there is every reason to believe that there is adequate educational provision for the blind. One class of blind children presenting severe educational problems are those who have additional handicaps. In 1948 the Royal National Institute for the Blind, continuing a smaller scale, pre-war experiment, opened a special school for such children at Condover Hall, near Shrewsbury. It caters for blind children who are also physically handicapped, maladjusted, educationally sub-normal, epileptic or deaf. Although the academic achievements of many of the children are necessarily low, Condover Hall fills a long felt need, and, with Worcester and Chorleywood Colleges, ensures that there is suitable provision for blind children of all ranges of ability.

The post-war era has been one of advancement in the education of the deaf. In the years immediately following 1945 the number of children attending schools for the deaf increased substantially. Some of the increase was due to the belated implementation of the 1937 Act which lowered the compulsory school age from seven to five. Much of it was the result of the realization that the deaf should be educated from as young an age as possible, and of the entry to the schools of children aged two years and over. There was also an actual increase in the incidence of deafness. An epidemic of German measles in 1940 affected some expectant mothers and, consequently, the number of babies born deaf. The decade following 1945 therefore saw an expansion in schools for the deaf. Latterly, however, the trend has been reversed. The number of pupils classified as deaf has been diminishing. At the same time there has occurred an increase in the number of the partially deaf. The variations are not due to changes in the degree of hearing defects. On the contrary, they are the results of advances in electronic engineering which have made

[1] See Clarke, 'Retrolental Fibroplasia in the Sunshine Home Nursery School', *Teacher of the Blind*, Vol. 43, No. 4, April 1955, pp. 121–3.

available improved amplifying equipment in the form of group and individual hearing aids. Better aids and an earlier start to auditory training have therefore made it possible to upgrade to the category of partially deaf children who would previously have been rightly regarded as deaf.

There are, however, many children who may still be termed profoundly deaf. They are taught by the oral method. Some, when they leave school at sixteen, can hardly be said to have acquired speech. Moreover, the time and effort devoted to the acquisition of speech might well, in their case, have been better spent in improving their education, which all too often is also seriously lacking at sixteen. Although it is not suggested that there should be a large scale return to silent methods, there is certainly a need to consider whether, when a child is failing to succeed by oral methods, it would not be to his advantage to teach him by the manual system. Referring to similar suggestions, the Ministry of Education stated: 'These criticisms are a healthy sign; they emphasize that the education of the deaf is undergoing rapid change and development and that even after the demand for school places has been met . . . there will be no cause for complacency but on the contrary a greater need to concentrate on outstanding problems.'[1]

The comment is applicable not only to the education of the deaf but to all handicapped children. Progress there has been; progress from that day in 1760, when Thomas Braidwood first used his spatula-like instrument, to a day two hundred years later, when the Department of Education of the Deaf at Manchester advertised for a research fellow with qualifications in physics or electrical engineering. Progress there must yet be; progress in overcoming the problems that still exist in every aspect of the field of special education. As in the past, so in the future will voluntary effort and voluntary organizations play their part. As in the past, so in the future will they often lead the way. To be opened in 1962 is the first special school for maladjusted children with communication difficulties. It will be established by a voluntary body.

[1] Ministry of Education, *Pamphlet No. 30, Education of the Handicapped Pupil 1945–1955*, p. 12.

BIBLIOGRAPHY

ACTS OF PARLIAMENT

26 Henry VIII, c. 27 — Poor Law Act, 1535. [62n.]
43 Elizabeth I, c. 2 — Poor Law Act, 1601. [62n.]
4 & 5 William IV, c. 76 — Poor Law Amendment Act, 1834. [30]
8 & 9 Victoria, c. 100 — Lunatics Act, 1845. [135]
16 & 17 Victoria, c. 70 — Lunacy Regulations Act, 1853. [135]
25 & 26 Victoria, c. 43 — Poor Law Act, 1862. [97–8]
29 & 30 Victoria, c. 118 — Industrial Schools Act, 1886. [63]
30 & 31 Victoria, c. 6 — Metropolitan Poor Act, 1867. [57, 135]
30 & 31 Victoria, c. 102 — Representation of the People Act, 1867. [66]
33 & 34 Victoria, c. 75 — Elementary Education Act, 1870. [66–7, 76, 112, 116, 145]

34 Victoria, c. 26 — Universities Tests Act, 1871. [66]
34 & 35 Victoria, c. 31 — Trade Union Act, 1871. [66]
36 & 37 Victoria, c. 66 — Supreme Court of Judicature Act, 1873. [66]
38 & 39 Victoria, c. 55 — Public Health Act, 1875. [67]
39 & 40 Victoria, c. 79 — Elementary Education Act, 1876. [112, 116]
42 & 43 Victoria, c. 54 — Poor Law Act, 1879. [97]
43 & 44 Victoria, c. 23 — Elementary Education Act, 1880. [116]
49 & 50 Victoria, c. 25 — Idiots Act, 1886. [61, 135]
51 & 52 Victoria, c. 41 — Local Government Act, 1888. [106]
52 & 53 Victoria, c. 44 — Prevention of Cruelty to Children Act, 1889. [146–7]
53 Victoria, c. 5 — Lunacy (Consolidation) Act, 1890. [135]
53 & 54 Victoria, c. 43 — Education of Blind and Deaf-mute Children (Scotland) Act, 1890. [108]

54 & 55 Victoria, c. 65 — Lunacy Act, 1891. [135]
56 & 57 Victoria, c. 42 — Elementary Education (Blind and Deaf Children) Act, 1893. [110–12, 133–4, 168, 190n., 195, 201]
62 & 63 Victoria, c. 32 — Elementary Education (Defective and Epileptic Children) Act, 1899. [149n., 150, 157–8, 164–5, 168, 175, 181, 185, 188, 190n.]

2 Edward VII, c. 42 — Education Act, 1902. [112, 145, 170, 186]
3 Edward VII, c. 13 — Elementary Education (Defective and Epileptic Children) Amendment Act, 1903.

6 Edward VII, c. 57 — Education (Provision of Meals) Act, 1906. [169]
7 Edward VII, c. 43 — Education (Administrative Provisions) Act, 1907. [170]
1 & 2 George V, c. 13 — Parliament Act, 1911. [187]
3 & 4 George V, c. 28 — Mental Deficiency Act, 1913. [61, 187–8, 191, 193n., 211, 218]

Bibliography

4 & 5 George V, c. 45 — Elementary Education (Defective and Epileptic Children) Act, 1914. [188, 190]
8 & 9 George V, c. 39 — Education Act, 1918. [159, 165, 190n.]
10 & 11 George V, c. 49 — Blind Persons Act, 1920. [201]
11 & 12 George V, c. 51 — Education Act, 1921. [190n., 194, 209, 211]
17 & 18 George V, c. 33 — Mental Deficiency Act, 1927.
1 Edward VIII, c. 25 — Education (Deaf Children) Act, 1937. [202n., 220]
7 & 8 George VI, c. 31 — Education Act, 1944. [166, 208 ff.]
9 & 10 George VI, c. 81 — National Health Service Act, 1946.
11 & 12 George VI, c. 40 — Education (Miscellaneous Provisions) Act, 1948.
7 & 8 Elizabeth II, c. 72 — Mental Health Act, 1959. [61, 218]

STATUTORY REGULATIONS AND OFFICIAL CIRCULARS

Board of Education. *Circular 432, Defective and Epileptic Children* (Revised), 13th May 1904. [186n.]
Board of Education. Regulations for the Training of Teachers for Elementary Schools, 1908. [197n.]
Board of Education. *Circular 1388, Defective and Epileptic Children*, February 1927. [189n.]
Ministry of Education. Statutory Rules and Orders No. 1076, The Handicapped Pupils and School Health Service Regulations, 1945. [203n., 210]
Ministry of Education. *Circular 241, Handicapped Pupils and Medical Service Regulations*, 18th April 1945.
Ministry of Education. Statutory Instrument No. 1933, Handicapped Pupils and School Health Service Amending Regulations, 1949.
Ministry of Education. Statutory Instrument No. 1156, The School Health Service and Handicapped Pupils Regulations, 1953. [210n.–11n.]
Ministry of Education. *Circular 269, The School Health Service and Handicapped Pupils Regulations*, 25th August 1953.
Ministry of Education. *Circular 276, Provision of Special Schools*, 25th June 1954.
Ministry of Education. *Administrative Memorandum, Survey of Physically Handicapped Children*, 28th April 1955.
Ministry of Education. *Administrative Memorandum, The Lord Mayor Treloar College*, 23rd March 1956.
Ministry of Education. *Circular 347, Child Guidance*, 10th March 1959. [219n.]
Ministry of Education. *Circular 348, Special Educational Treatment for Maladjusted Children*, 10th March 1959.
Ministry of Education. Statutory Instrument No. 336, The Medical Examination (Sub-normal Children) Regulations, 1959.
Ministry of Education. Statutory Instrument No. 365, The Handicapped Pupils and Special Schools Regulations, 1959. [210n.]
Ministry of Education. *Circular 352, School Health Services, Medical Examinations and Handicapped Pupils Regulations*, 24th March 1959.
Ministry of Education. *Circular 11/61, Special Educational Treatment for Educationally Sub-normal Pupils*, 3rd July 1961. [216n., 219n.]

REPORTS OF ROYAL COMMISSIONS

Second Report of the Royal Commission on the Elementary Education Acts. H.M.S.O., 1887. [97, 107, 117n.]

Bibliography

Report of the Royal Commission on the Blind, the Deaf and Dumb and Others of the United Kingdom, 4 vols. H.M.S.O., 1889. [20n., 22n., 26n., 29n., 33n., 36n., 39n., 42n., 46n.-8n., 55-7, 58n., 60n., 62n., 69n.-74n., 77n.-80n., 82n., 84n., 86, 90n.-2n., 95-115, 117n., 118-20, 132, 134, 137n., 149, 196n.]

Report of the Royal Commission on Physical Training (Scotland), 2 vols. H.M.S.O., 1903. [168]

Report of the Royal Commission on the Care and Control of the Feeble-Minded, 8 vols. H.M.S.O., 1908. [181n., 183 ff.]

Report of the Royal Commission on the Poor Laws and Relief of Distress, Vol. I. H.M.S.O., 1909.

Report of the Royal Commission on the Law Relating to Mental Illness and Mental Deficiency. H.M.S.O., 1957.

REPORTS OF OFFICIAL COMMITTEES

Board of Education. *Report of the Inter-Departmental Committee on Medical Inspection and Feeding of Children attending Public Elementary Schools*, 2 vols. H.M.S.O., 1905. [128n., 158n., 169]

Board of Education. *Selected Reports, E. No. 5. Report on Schools attended by Very Poor Children in London*. H.M.S.O., 1911.

Board of Education and Board of Control. *Report of the Joint Departmental Committee on Mental Deficiency*, 3 vols. H.M.S.O., 1929. [56n., 188–92, 208–9]

Board of Education. *Report of the Committees of Inquiry into Problems Connected with Defective Vision in School Children*. H.M.S.O., 1931.

Board of Education. *Report of the Committee of Inquiry into Problems Relating to Partially Sighted Children*. H.M.S.O., 1934. [204–6, 208, 211]

Board of Education. *Report of the Committee of Inquiry into Problems Relating to Children with Defective Hearing*. H.M.S.O., 1938. [202–3, 208, 211]

Committee of Council on Education. *Reports of the Commissioners of Inquiry into the State of Education in Wales*. H.M.S.O., 1847. [43n.-4n.]

Education Department. *Report of the Departmental Committee on Defective and Epileptic Children*, 2 vols. H.M.S.O., 1898. [57n.-60n., 112n., 116n.-19n., 121n.-7n., 129n.-31n., 132-50, 153n.-4n., 175n., 180n., 192n.]

Local Government Board. *Report of the Departmental Committee appointed by the Local Government Board to Inquire into the Poor Law Schools*. H.M.S.O., 1896. [134n.]

Local Government Board. *Report of the Inter-Departmental Committee on Physical Deterioration*, 3 vols. H.M.S.O., 1904. [168-9, 171]

Local Government Board. *Report of the Departmental Committee on the Welfare of the Blind*. H.M.S.O., 1917. [201]

London County Council. *Report of the Conference on the Instruction of Crippled Children, July 1900*. London County Council, 1900.

London County Council. *Report of a Committee of Inspectors on Backwardness in Elementary Schools*. London County Council, 1937.

Ministry of Education. *Training and Supply of Teachers of Handicapped Pupils. Fourth Report of the National Advisory Council on the Training and Supply of Teachers*. H.M.S.O., 1954. [125n.]

Ministry of Education. *Report of the Committee on Maladjusted Children*. H.M.S.O., 1955. [193n., 218n.]

Ministry of Health and Board of Education. *A Study of the Deaf in England and Wales, 1930–1932, being a Report by Dr. A. Eichholz to the Minister of Health and the President of the Board of Education*. H.M.S.O., 1932. [197n., 202–3]

Ministry of Health. *Report of the Departmental Committee on the Voluntary Mental Health Services.* H.M.S.O., 1939.

Ministries of Health and Labour. *Report of the Working Party on the Employment of the Blind in Industry.* H.M.S.O., 1950.

Ministry of Health. *Report of the Working Party on Social Workers in the Local Authority Health and Welfare Services.* H.M.S.O., 1959.

Ministry of Labour. *Report of the Inter-Departmental Committee on the Rehabilitation and Resettlement of Disabled Persons.* H.M.S.O., 1943.

Ministry of Labour. *Standing Committee on the Rehabilitation and Resettlement of Disabled Persons. Services for the Disabled.* H.M.S.O., 1955.

Ministries of Labour and Health. *Report of the Committee of Inquiry on the Rehabilitation, Training and Resettlement of Disabled Persons.* H.M.S.O., 1956.

School Board for London. *Report of Conference on the Instruction of Blind Children, July 1876.* Reprinted by Spottiswoode and Company, 1886. [79n.]

Scottish Education Department. *Pupils who are Defective in Hearing. A Report of the Advisory Council on Education in Scotland.* H.M.S.O., 1950.

Scottish Education Department. *Pupils who are Defective in Vision. A Report of the Advisory Council on Education in Scotland.* H.M.S.O., 1950.

Scottish Education Department. *Pupils Handicapped by Speech Disorders. A Report of the Advisory Council on Education in Scotland.* H.M.S.O., 1951.

Scottish Education Department. *Pupils with Mental or Educational Disabilities. A Report of the Advisory Council on Education in Scotland.* H.M.S.O., 1951.

Scottish Education Department. *Pupils with Physical Disabilities. A Report of the Advisory Council on Education in Scotland.* H.M.S.O., 1951.

Scottish Education Department. *Pupils who are Maladjusted because of Social Handicaps. A Report of the Advisory Council on Education in Scotland.* H.M.S.O., 1952.

Scottish Education Department. *The Administration of Education for Handicapped Pupils. A Report of the Advisory Council on Education in Scotland.* H.M.S.O., 1952.

ANNUAL REPORTS

Association for the Oral Instruction of the Deaf and Dumb. *Annual Reports, 1874–1914.* [85n.–7n., 197n.]

Asylum for the Deaf and Dumb Children of the Poor, Old Kent Road, London. *Annual Reports, 1850–1874.*

Board of Education. *General Report on Schools for the Blind and Deaf for the Two Years ended 31st August 1900.* H.M.S.O.

Board of Education. *Annual Reports of the Chief Medical Officer, 1908–1938.* H.M.S.O. [36n., 128n., 150n., 157n., 160n., 162n., 164n.–7n., 171n.–4n., 176n., 181n.–2n., 184n., 186n., 188n., 192n.–3n., 196n.–7n., 199n., 201n.–2n., 204n.–205n.]

British and Foreign Blind Association. *1st–29th Reports, 1871–1913.* [71n.]

College of Teachers of the Deaf and Dumb. *Annual Reports, 1888–1899.* [196n.]

Education Department. *Reports of the Committee of Council on Education on Schools for the Blind and Deaf, 1896–1897, 1897–1898, and 1898–1899.* H.M.S.O. [112n.–13n.]

General Institution for the Blind, Edgbaston, Birmingham. *1st–62nd Annual Reports, 1848–1909.* [37n.–8n.]

General Institution for the Instruction of Deaf and Dumb Children Birmingham. *Account* [Report] *of the General Institution established in Birmingham for 1814.*

Bibliography

Invalid Children's Aid Association. *Sixtieth Annual Report, 1947.*

Liverpool School for the Deaf and Dumb. *Annual Report for 1852.* [28n.]

London Society for Teaching the Blind to Read. *Thirty-sixth Annual Report, 1874.* [34n., 47n.]

Ministry of Education. *Report of the Chief Medical Officer for the Years 1939–1945.* H.M.S.O. [193n., 208n.]

Ministry of Education. *Biennial Reports of the Chief Medical Officer, 1946–1959.* H.M.S.O. [216n.–18n.]

Ministry of Education. *Education 1900–1950. Report of the Ministry of Education for the year 1950.* H.M.S.O.

National Association for the Oral Instruction of the Deaf. *Annual Reports, 1915 and 1916.*

Royal Normal College and Academy of Music for the Blind. *1st–3rd Reports, 1873–1876.* [73n.–4n.]

St. Matthew's Church, Scotland Road, Liverpool. *Parish Magazine for January 1898.* [154n.]

School for the Blind, Liverpool. *Reports of the State of the School, 1846–1874.* [37n.–8n.]

Society for Training Teachers of the Deaf. *1st–35th Annual Reports, 1878–1912* and *Final Report, 1915.* [84n., 90n., 197n.]

Ulster Society for Promoting the Education of the Deaf and Dumb, and the Blind. *1st–9th Annual Reports, 1837–1845.* [39n.]

Victoria Women's Settlement, Liverpool. *1st–12th Annual Reports, 1898–1909.* [155n.]

Yorkshire School for the Blind, York. *Annual Reports, 1873–1882.* [32n.–3n., 38n.]

REPORTS OF CONFERENCES

Board of Education. *Special Reports on Educational Subjects*, Vol. 9, pp. 595–604: 'Report of the Congress on the Education of Feeble-minded Children, Augsburg, April 1901', by A. Eichholz. London, H.M.S.O., 1902.

Buckle, A. *Report on the International Congress for the Amelioration of the Condition of the Blind, Paris, 1878.* York, Yorkshire School for the Blind, 1879.

Buckle, A. *Report on Congress of Directors and Teachers of Blind Institutions, Frankfurt-on-the-Mayne, 1882.* York, Yorkshire School for the Blind, 1883.

Buckle, A. *Report on Congress of Instructors and Friends of the Blind, Cologne, August 1888.* York, Yorkshire School for the Blind, 1889.

Buxton, D. ed. *Speech for the Deaf, Essays, Proceedings, and Resolutions of the International Congress on the Education of the Deaf, Milan, September 1880.* London, W. H. Allen, 1880. [92n.]

College of Speech Therapists. *Report of the Conference on Speech Therapy, London, September 1948.* London, Tavistock Publications, 1949.

Horsfall, T. C. ed. *Proceedings of the Conference on Education under Healthy Conditions, Manchester 1885.* Manchester, John Heywood, 1885. [56n., 106n., 117n.]

Proceedings of the Seventh Convention of American Instructors of the Deaf and Dumb, Indianapolis, August 1870. Indianapolis, Indiana Institution, 1870.

Proceedings of the First Meeting of the American Association of the Blind, Boston, 1872. Boston, Mass., 1873.

Proceedings of the Conference of Head Masters of Institutions for the Education of the Deaf and Dumb, London, July 1877. London, no publisher given, 1877. [88n.]

Bibliography

Proceedings of the Conference of Headmasters of Institutions for the Education of the Deaf and Dumb, London, July 1881. London, W. H. Allen, 1882.

Proceedings of the Conference in the Mayor's Parlour on the Subject of State Aid for the Deaf and Dumb, Town Hall, Manchester, January 1885. Manchester, no publisher given, 1885. [93n.]

Proceedings of the Conference of Head Masters of Institutions for the Education of the Deaf and Dumb, London, June 1885. London, W. H. Allen, 1886. [29n., 41n.]

Proceedings of the Conference of Headmasters of Institutions for the Education of the Deaf and Dumb, London, July, 1885. London, W. H. Allen, 1886. [92n.–94n.]

Record of the Proceedings at the Interview of the Deputation Appointed to Wait on the Committee of Her Majesty's Privy Council for Education and Present a Memorial on the Subject of State Aid for the Deaf and Dumb, March 1885. Manchester, no publisher given, 1885. [93n.]

Report of the Fiftieth Meeting of the British Association for the Advancement of Science, Swansea 1880, pp. 216–19. 'Report of the Committee appointed to Consider and Report on the German and Other Systems of Teaching the Deaf to Speak'. London, John Murray, 1880. [92n.]

Report of the Proceedings of the Conference of the Governing Bodies of Institutions for the Education of the Deaf, London, March 1881. London, W. H. Allen, 1881.

Report of the Proceedings of the Conference of Headmasters of Institutions for the Education of the Deaf and Dumb, Doncaster, May, 1882. Doncaster, no publisher given, 1882. [93n.]

Report of the Conference of Managers, Teachers, and Friends of the Blind, York, July 1883. York, Yorkshire School for the Blind, 1889. [95n.]

Report of the Conference of the Blind and their Friends, Upper Norwood, July 1890. London, no publisher given, 1891.

Report of the Conference on the Education of the Blind, Birmingham, June 1894. Birmingham, no publisher given, 1894. [195n.]

Report of the Conference on Matters Relating to the Blind, Westminster, 1902. London, Farmer and Sons, 1902.

Report of the International Conference on the Blind, Edinburgh, 1905. Glasgow, W. Hodge, 1905.

Report of the Conference to mark the Centenary of the Home Teaching Service of the Blind, London 1957. London, Southern Regional Association for the Blind, 1957.

Transactions of the First and Second Conferences of Principals of Institutions for the Deaf and Dumb, London, July 1851 and Doncaster, July 1852. London, Varty and Owen, 1852. [88n.]

UNPUBLISHED PAPERS

Asylum for Indigent Blind, Liverpool. Minute Book, 1791–1803 and School for the Blind, Liverpool. Minute Books, 1804–1880. [17n.–19n., 31n., 38n.]

Bates, A. The Higher Education of the Deaf. Unpublished M.A. Thesis of Reading University, 1956.

Gorman, P. P. Certain Social and Psychological Difficulties Facing the Deaf Person in the English Community. Unpublished D.Phil. Thesis of Cambridge University, 1960.

Ministry of Education Archives. Various Education Class Files. [20n., 32n., 37n., 87n., 107n.–9n., 122n., 124n.–6n., 148n.–9n., 165, 172n.–6n., 202n.]

Bibliography

Public Record Office. Various Education Class Files. [120n.–1n., 126n., 132n.–134n., 142n., 152n., 157n.]

Watson, T. J. A History of Deaf Education in Scotland from 1760–1939. Unpublished Ph.D. Thesis of Edinburgh University, 1949. [40n.]

BOOKS AND PAMPHLETS

Alston, J. *Statements of the Education, Employments, and Internal Arrangements adopted at the Asylum for the Blind, Glasgow.* Glasgow, Asylum for the Blind, 1842. [46n.]

Amman, J. C. *A Dissertation on Speech.* Originally printed in Latin by John Wolters, Amsterdam, 1700. Translated by Baker, C. London, Low, Marston, Low and Searle, 1873. [6n.]

Anagnos, M. *Education of the Blind. Historical Sketch of its Origin, Rise and Progress.* Boston, Mass., Rand, Avery, 1882. [22n.]

Anonymous. *An Account of the School for the Indigent Blind in St. George's Fields, Surrey.* London, the Philanthropic Society, 1813. [22n.–3n., 31n., 41n.]

Anonymous. *History of the Education of the Deaf in the United States.* Reprinted from the *Encyclopaedia Americana.* Washington, Y. M. Stoddart, 1880.

Anonymous. *A Letter on the Education of the Blind.* Reprinted from the *Edinburgh Magazine and Review* for November 1774. London, Sampson Low, Marston, 1894.

Armitage, T. R. *The Education and Employment of the Blind.* London, published for British and Foreign Blind Association by R. Hardwicke, 1871. [72n.]

Arnold, T. *Education of Deaf-mutes: A Manual for Teachers*, 2 vols. London, The College of Teachers of the Deaf and Dumb, Vol. I 1888, Vol. II 1891. [12n., 21n., 27n.–9n., 35n., 40n., 83n.–4n., 89]

Arnold, T. *Arnold on the Education of the Deaf: A Manual for Teachers.* Revised and rewritten by Farrar, A. London, National College of Teachers of the Deaf, 2nd edn. 1954. [89]

Arrowsmith, J. P. *The Art of Instructing the Infant Deaf and Dumb.* London, Taylor and Hessey, 1819. [27, 28n.]

Barnhill, A. *A New Era in the Education of Blind Children.* Glasgow, Chas. Glass, 1875. [75n., 100n.]

Barr, M. W. *Mental Defectives: Their History, Treatment and Training.* London, Rebman, 1904.

Bartley, G. C. T. *The Schools for the People.* London, Bell and Daldy, 1871. [22n., 40n., 63n.–4n., 151n.]

Bede, The Venerable, *Ecclesiastical History of England also the Anglo-Saxon Chronicle.* Edited by Giles, J. A. London, H. G. Bohn, 1849. [4n.]

Bélanger, A. *Enseignement des Sourds-muets. Bibliographie générale de tous les Ouvrages parus en France ou en langue Française.* Paris, 1889.

Bender, R. E. *The Conquest of Deafness.* Cleveland, Ohio, The Press of Western Reserve University, 1960. [27n., 30n., 84n., 88n.]

Best, H. *The Deaf, Their Position in Society and the Provision for their Education in the United States.* New York, Thomas Y. Crowell, 1914.

Best, H. *Blindness and the Blind in the United States.* New York, Macmillan, 1934.

Binet, A. and Simon, T. *Mentally Defective Children.* Translated from the French by Drummond, W. B. London, E. J. Arnold, 1914. [53n., 279n.]

Birmingham Royal Institution for the Blind. *The Birmingham Royal Institution for the Blind.* Birmingham, Royal Institution for the Blind, not dated, 1948? [37n.]

Bibliography

Blair, R. H. *Education of the Blind.* Worcester, Deighton and Son, 1876. [70n.]

Board of Education. *The Education of Backward Children, Educational Pamphlet No. 112.* London, H.M.S.O., 1938.

Bonet, J. P. *Simplification of the Letters of the Alphabet and Method of Teaching Deaf-mutes to Speak.* Originally published Madrid, 1620. Translated from the Spanish by Dixon, H. N. London, no publisher given, 1890. [5n.]

Booth, C. *Life and Labour of the People in London.* Fifth Series: Poverty, Vol. 3. London, Macmillan, 1904.

Bosanquet, H. *Social Work in London—A History of the Charity Organisation Society.* London, John Murray, 1914. [61n.–2n.]

Buckle, A. *Report on the Blind Institutions of Denmark.* York, Yorkshire School for the Blind, 1878.

Bulwer, J. B. *Chirologia or The Natural Language of the Hand.* London, R. Whitaker, 1644.

Bulwer, J. B. *Philocophus, or The Deafe and Dumbe Man's Friend.* London, Humphrey Moseley, 1648. [5n.]

Buxton, D. *The German System of Teaching the Deaf.* A paper read to the British Association at Sheffield, 1879. London, W. H. Allen, 1879. [91n.]

Buxton, D. *Notes of Progress in the Education of the Deaf.* A paper read in the Education Department of the National Association for the Promotion of Social Science. London, W. H. Allen, 1882.

Campbell, C. F. F. *Two Outstanding American Blind Educators.* An address given to the World Conference on Work for the Blind. Cleveland, Ohio, 1931. No publisher given, not dated.

Campbell, F. J. *The Musical Education of the Blind.* A paper read at the Eighth Annual Conference of the Incorporated Society of Musicians, London, 1893. London, no publisher given, 1893. [34n.]

Charity Organisation Society. *Report of the Special Committee on the Training of the Blind.* London, Longmans Green, 1876. [33–4, 73n., 74–5]

Charity Organisation Society. *Report of the Sub-Committee on the Education and Care of Idiots, Imbeciles and Harmless Lunatics.* London, Charity Organisation Society, 1877. [61–2, 97]

Charity Organisation Society. *The Epileptic and Crippled Child and Adult. A Report on the Present Condition of these Classes of Afflicted Persons, with Suggestions for their Better Education and Employment.* London, Swan Sonnenschein, 1893. [64–5, 133, 151–2, 175n., 180n.]

Charity Organisation Society. *The Feeble-minded Child and Adult. A Report on an Investigation of the Physical and Mental Condition of 50,000 School Children, with Suggestions for the Better Education and Care of the Feeble-minded Children and Adults.* London, Swan Sonnenschein, 1893. [118–19, 133]

Charity Organisation Society. *Report on the Physical Condition of Fourteen Hundred School Children in Edinburgh.* London, Charity Organisation Society, 1906.

Clarke, A. M. and Clarke, A. D. B. *Mental Deficiency—the Changing Outlook.* London, Methuen, 1958.

Cleugh, M. F. *The Slow Learner.* London, Methuen, 1957. [215n.]

Commonwealth Office of Education. *Facilities for the Education of Handicapped Children in Australia.* Sydney, Commonwealth Office of Education, 1961.

Copleston, J. *How to Educate the Deaf and Dumb.* London, A. M. Pigott, 1866.

Craig, D. and Nettleton, J. S. *Yorkshire Institution for the Deaf, Doncaster. Centenary of the Founding of the Institution 1829–1929.* Doncaster, Yorkshire Institution, 1929.

Bibliography

Cresswell, D'Arcy. *Margaret McMillan, a Memoir*. London, Hutchison, 1948.

Dalby, W. B. *The Education of the Deaf and Dumb by means of Lip-reading and Articulation*. A paper read at the Social Science Congress, Leeds, 1871. London, J. and A. Churchill, 1872.

Dalgarno, G. *Didascalocophus or the Deaf and Dumb Mans [sic] Tutor*. First published at Oxford in 1680. Reprinted in Edinburgh by the Maitland Club, 1834. [5n.]

Davies, S. P. *The Mentally Retarded in Society*. New York, Columbia University Press, 1959.

De l'Epée, L'Abbé C. M. *La Véritable Maniere d'Instruire les Sourds et Muets*. Paris, Chez Nyon l'Aîné, 1784. [74n.]

Descoeudres, A. *The Education of Mentally Defective Children*. Translated from the 2nd French edition by Row, E. F. London, Harrap, 1928.

Diderot, D. 'Letter on the Blind for the Use of Those Who See' in *Early Philosophical Works*, pp. 88–104. Translated and edited by Jourdain, M. Chicago, Open Court Publishing Company, 1916.

Digby, Sir K. *The Private Memoirs of Sir Kenelme Digby etc. written by Himself*. London, Saunders and Otley, 1827. [5n.]

Fay, E. A. ed. *Histories of American Schools for the Deaf, 1817–1893*, 3 vols. Washington, Volta Bureau, 1893. [16n.]

Forster, S. S. *A Plea for the Higher Culture of the Blind*. A paper read at the Conference of Managers, Teachers, and Friends of the Blind, York, 1883. York, Yorkshire School for the Blind. 1883. [69n.]

Frampton, M. E. and Gall, E. D. ed. *Special Education for the Exceptional*, 3 vols. Boston, Mass., Porter Sargent, 1955. [205n.]

Frampton, M. E. and Kerney, E. *The Residential School: its History, Contributions and Future*. New York, New York Institute for the Blind, 1953.

Frampton, M. E. and Rowell, H. G. *Education of the Handicapped*. Vol. I History. London, Harrap, 1939. [12n, 14n., 63n.]

French, R. S. *From Homer to Helen Keller*. New York, American Foundation for the Blind, 1932.

Gall, J. *A Historical Sketch of the Origin and Progress of Literature for the Blind*. Edinburgh, J. Gall, 1834. [vii, 31n., 47n.]

Gall, J. *An Account of the Recent Discoveries which have been made for Facilitating the Education of the Blind*. Edinburgh, J. Gall, 1837. [46n.]

Gallaudet, E. M. *Life of Thomas Hopkins Gallaudet*. New York, Henry Holt, 1910.

Galton, F. *Hereditary Genius: an Inquiry into its Laws and Consequences*. London, Macmillan, 1869. [178]

Galton, F. *Natural Inheritance*. London, Macmillan, 1889. [178]

Galton, Sir Francis and others. *The Problem of the Feeble-Minded*. London, P. S. King, 1909.

Girdlestone, G. R. *The Care and Cure of Cripple Children*. Bristol, J. Wright and Sons, 1924. [159n.–60n., 162n.]

Glasgow Deaf and Dumb Institution. *A Brief Historical Sketch of the Origin and Progress of the Glasgow Deaf and Dumb Institution*. Glasgow, J. Smith, 1835.

Goddard, H. H. *The Kallikak Family*. New York, Macmillan, 1912. [179n.]

Green, F. *Vox Oculis Subjecta: A Dissertation on the Most Curious and Important Art of Imparting Speech, and the Knowledge of Language, to the Naturally Deaf, and (consequently) dumb; with a particular account of the Academy of Messrs. Braidwood of Edinburgh*. London, B. White, 1783. [13]

Hansard's Parliamentary Debates, 1st–4th Series, 1804–1908. [57n., 93n., 108n.–10n., 149n.–50n.]

Bibliography

Harris, W. and Turner, M. *Guide to Institutions and Charities for the Blind.* London, 1st edn. 1870, 2nd edn. 1884.

Hathaway, W. *Education and Health of the Partially Seeing Child.* New York, Columbia University Press, 1954. [204n.]

Haüy, V. *Essai sur l'Éducation des Aveugles.* Paris, Enfans-Aveugles et M. Clousier, 1786. [3, 21]

Haüy, V. *An Essay on the Education of the Blind.* Translated from the French by Blacklock, T. Edinburgh, Alexander Chapman, 1793. [21n.]

Hawker, R. *The History of the Asylum for the Deaf and Dumb.* London, Williams and Smith, 1805.

Hodgson, K. W. *The Deaf and Their Problems.* London, Watts, 1953. [5n., 20n., 27n.–8n., 30n., 38n., 40n., 42n., 78n., 84n., 88n.]

Holder, W. *Elements of Speech with an Appendix concerning Persons Deaf and Dumb.* London, J. Martyn, 1669. [5n.]

Hubert-Valleroux, M. E. *Des Sourds-muets et des Aveugles: Memoirs sur l'état actuel des Institutions a leur usage.* Paris, Victor Masson, 1852.

Hunt, Dame Agnes. *This is My Life.* London, Blackie, 1938. [160n.]

Illingworth, R. S. ed. *Recent Advances in Cerebral Palsy.* London, Churchill, 1958.

Illingworth, W. H. *History of the Education of the Blind.* London, Sampson Low, Marston, 1910. [70n.]

Invalid Children's Aid Association. *History of the Association 1888–1925.* London, Invalid Children's Aid Association, not dated, 1925?

Itard, J. M. G. *De l'Éducation d'un Sauvage.* Paris, Bourneville, 1894.

Itard, J. M. G. *The Wild Boy of Aveyron.* Translated from the French by Humphrey, G. and M. New York, The Century Company, 1932. [51n.–2n.]

Johns, B. G. *Blind People.* London, John Murray, 1867. [22n.–3n., 33n.]

Johnson, E. C. *Paris Exhibition, 1867. Report on Apparatus and Methods used in the Instruction of the Blind.* London, Eyre and Spottiswoode, 1868. [42n.]

Johnson, E. C. *London International Exhibition, 1871, Division II, Educational Works and Appliances. Report on the Methods of Teaching the Blind, and the Deaf and Dumb.* London, J. M. Johnson and Sons, 1871. [33n., 68n., 71n.]

Johnson, Samuel. *A Journey to the Western Islands of Scotland.* London, W. Strahan and T. Cadell, 1775. [12, 13n.]

Joint Committee of the College of Teachers of the Blind and the National Institute for the Blind. *The Education of the Blind, A Survey.* London, E. J. Arnold, 1936. [171n., 206n.]

Jones, K. *Lunacy, Law, and Conscience, 1774–1845.* London, Routledge and Kegan Paul, 1954. [56n.]

Jones, K. *Mental Health and Social Policy 1845–1959.* London, Routledge and Kegan Paul, 1960. [187n.]

Keir, S. *The Royal Albert Institution, Lancaster. Historical Synopsis.* Lancaster, Royal Albert Institution, 1929. [56n.]

Kekewich, Sir G. W. *The Education Department and After.* London, Constable, 1920. [141n.–2n.]

Kerr, J. *School Vision and the Myopic Scholar.* London, Allen and Unwin, 1925. [203n.–4n.]

Kimmins, G. T. (Dame Grace). *Heritage Craft Schools and Hospitals, Chailey, 1903–48, being an Account of the Pioneer Work for Crippled Children.* Privately published, 1948. [162n.]

Kirk, S. A. and Johnson, G. O. *Educating the Retarded Child.* New York, Houghton Mifflin, 1951.

Klemm, L. R. *European Schools.* New York, D. Appleton, 1891. [116n., 120]

Bibliography

Knie, J. G. *A Guide to the Proper Management and Education of Blind Children.* Translated from the German by Taylor, W. London, Simpkin, Marshall, 1861.

Lapage, C. P. *Feeblemindedness in Children of School Age with an Appendix on Sandlebridge by Mary Dendy.* Manchester, Manchester University Press, 2nd edn. 1920. [18ln.–3n.]

La Sizeranne, M. de. *The Blind as seen through Blind Eyes.* Translated from the French by Lewis, F. P. New York, Putnam, 1893.

Lawrence, C. E. *William Purdie Treloar.* London, John Murray, 1925. [162n.]

Leese, J. *Personalities and Power in English Education.* London, E. J. Arnold, 1950. [168n.]

Leff, S. and V. *The School Health Service.* London, H. K. Lewis, 1959. [157n., 168n.]

Lithiby, Sir J. *The Education Acts, 1870–1919, and Other Acts Relating to Education.* London, Charles Knight, 1920. [61n.]

Lowndes, G. A. N. *The Silent Social Revolution.* London, Oxford University Press, 1937. [168n., 170n.]

Mackenzie, W. L. *The Medical Inspection of School Children.* Edinburgh, Wm. Hodge, 1904.

Mansbridge, A. *Margaret McMillan, Prophet and Pioneer.* London, Dent, 1932. [128n.]

McMillan, M. *The Camp School: An Address Delivered to the National Liberal Club, Political and Economic Circle.* London, P. S. King, not dated, 1915? [174n.]

McMillan, M. and Sanderson, A. C. *London's Children: How to feed them and how not to feed them.* London, I.L.P., 1909.

Medhurst, C. E. *The Rev. [sic] Samuel Strong Forster: a Brief Account of his Life and Work on behalf of the Higher Education of the Blind.* Worcester, Deighton, 1891. [68n.–9n.]

Ministry of Education. *Special Educational Treatment, Pamphlet No. 5.* London, H.M.S.O., 1946. [211n., 214n.]

Ministry of Education. *Education of the Handicapped Pupil 1945–1955, Pamphlet No. 30.* London, H.M.S.O., 1956. [176n., 209n., 221n.]

Monk, P. *Though Land Be Out of Sight: the Early Years of Chorleywood College.* London, National Institute for the Blind, 1952. [199n.–200n.]

Montessori, M. *The Montessori Method.* Translated from the Italian by George, A. E. London, Heinemann, 1912. [178n.]

Mowat, C. L. *The Charity Organisation Society 1869–1913.* London, Methuen, 1916. [31n., 61n.]

National Association for the Education of the Deaf and Dumb Poor of Ireland. *Report of a Deputation from the National Association for the Education of the Deaf and Dumb Poor of Ireland who visited several Institutions for the Deaf and Dumb in Great Britain.* Dublin, J. Charles, 1856.

Nelson, W. and Lunt, J. *Royal Residential Schools for the Deaf Manchester. Centenary of the Founding of the Schools June 1823–June 1923. Historical Survey.* Manchester, Royal Residential Schools, 1923. [27n.–8n., 198n.]

Neufert, L. und Bendix, K. *Die Charlottenburger Waldschule.* Berlin, Urban und Schwarzenberg, 1905.

O'Connor, N. and Tizard, J. *The Social Problem of Mental Deficiency.* London, Pergamon Press, 1956. [179n.]

Pablasek, M., Moldenhawer, J. and Buckle, A. *The Education of the Blind.* Papers read at the International Congress for the Amelioration of the Condition of the Blind, Paris, 1878. York, Yorkshire School for the Blind, 1879.

Bibliography

Palin, J. H. *Bradford and Its Children: How they are fed.* London, I.L.P., 1908.

Pearson, K. *The Life, Letters and Labours of Francis Galton,* 4 vols. Cambridge, Cambridge University Press, 1914.

Pinsent, E. F. (Dame Ellen). *The Mental Health Services in Oxford City, Oxfordshire and Berkshire.* Oxford, Oxford University Press, 1937. [193n.]

Praagh, W. Van. *On the Establishment of Day Schools for the Deaf and Dumb.* London, Trübner, 1871.

Praagh, W. Van. *On the Oral Education of the Deaf and Dumb.* Reprinted from the Journal of Education. London, Association for the Oral Instruction of the Deaf and Dumb, 1878.

Praagh, W. Van. *On Training Colleges for Teachers of the Deaf and Dumb.* A paper read at the Conference of Headmasters of Institutions for the Education of the Deaf and Dumb at Doncaster, 1882. London, Association for the Oral Instruction of the Deaf and Dumb, 1882. [86n.]

Praagh, W. Van. *Lessons for the Instruction of Deaf and Dumb Children in Speaking, Lip-reading, Reading and Writing,* 2 vols. London, Trübner, 1884.

Richards, L. E. ed. *Letters and Journals of Samuel Gridley Howe,* 2 vols. Boston, L. C. Page, Vol. I 1906, Vol. II 1909.

Richards, L. E. *Samuel Gridley Howe.* New York, Appleton-Century, 1935. [54n., 72n.]

Ritchie, J. M. *Concerning the Blind.* Edinburgh, Oliver and Boyd, 1930. [22n., 26n., 35n., 39n., 48n., 70n., 75n., 95n., 171n.]

Roblin, J. *The Reading Fingers, Life of Louis Braille.* Translated from the French by Mandalian, R. G. New York, American Foundation for the Blind, 1952.

Roblin, J. *Louis Braille.* London, Royal National Institute for the Blind, not dated, 1960?

Roth, M. *The Physical Education of the Blind.* A paper read at the Conference of Managers, Teachers, and Friends of the Blind, York, 1883. York, Yorkshire School for the Blind, 1883.

Rowntree, B. Seebohm. *Poverty and Progress.* London, Longmans Green, 1901.

Royal National Institute for the Blind. *The History of Blind Welfare in England and Wales.* London, Royal National Institute for the Blind, 3rd edn. 1955.

Royal Normal College. *Historical Statement of the Higher Education of the Blind.* London, Watson and Hazell, 1873. [74n.]

Royal School for Deaf Children, Birmingham. *Royal School for Deaf Children Birmingham and Martley.* Birmingham, Royal School for Deaf Children, 1950.

Royal West of England Institution for the Deaf and Dumb, Exeter. *Historical Survey 1826–1926.* Exeter, Royal West of England Institution, 1926.

Runciman, J. *Schools and Scholars.* London, Chatto and Windus, 1887.

Sanborn, F. B. *Dr. S. G. Howe, the Philanthropist.* New York, Funk and Wagnalls, 1891.

School for the Blind, Liverpool. *An Address in Favour of the School for the Blind in Liverpool Instituted in the Year 1791.* Liverpool, School for the Blind, 1808. [39n.–40n.]

Schwartz, H. *Samuel Gridley Howe, Social Reformer, 1801–1876.* Cambridge, Mass., Harvard University Press, 1956. [54n.]

Scott, E. R. *The History of the Education of the Blind prior to 1830.* London, College of Teachers of the Blind, not dated, 1916?

Scott, W. R. *The Deaf and Dumb, their Education and Social Position.* London, Bell and Daldy, 1844. [28]

Séguin, E. *Traitement Moral, Hygiène et Éducation des Idiots et des Autres Enfants Arriérés.* Paris, J. B. Baillière, 1846. [54n.]

Bibliography

Séguin, E. *Idiocy: And its Treatment by the Physiological Method*. New York, Albany-Brandow Printing Company, 1866.

Shuttleworth, G. E. and Potts, W. A. *Mentally Defective Children; their Treatment and Training*. London, H. K. Lewis, 5th edn. 1922.

Society for Training Teachers of the Deaf and Diffusion of the German System. *Prospectus of the Society*. London, Society for Training Teachers of the Deaf, 1878. [91n.]

Spalding, T. A. and others. *The Work of the London School Board*. London, P. S. King, 2nd edn. 1900.

Spence, Rev. Mr. (*sic*). *An Account of the Life, Character and Poems of Mr. Blacklock, Student of Philosophy in the University of Edinburgh*. London, R. and J. Dodsley, 1754. [21n.]

Stainer, W. *The Powers of the School Board and the Poor Law Guardians in relation to the Care and Education of the Deaf and Dumb*. Margate, Keble's Gazette, 1888. [76n.]

Standing, E. M. *Maria Montessori*. London, Hollis and Carter, 1957.

Syle, H. W. *A Retrospect of the Education of the Deaf*. Philadelphia, W. R. Cullingworth, 1886.

Tarra, G. *The Pure Oral Method. Translations from the Writings, Speeches and Correspondence of Giulo Tarra*. Name of translator not given. London, W. H. Allen, 1883.

Taylor, W. W. and Taylor, I. W. *Special Education of Physically Handicapped Children in Western Europe*. New York, International Society for the Welfare of Cripples, 1960.

Thomas, M. G. *The First Seventy Years. Worcester College for the Blind 1866–1936*. London, National Institute for the Blind, not dated, 1937?

Thomas, M. G. *The Royal National Institute for the Blind, 1868–1956*. Brighton, Brighton Herald, 1957. [48n., 68n., 71n., 199n., 200n.]

Training College for Teachers of the Deaf and Dumb, Fitzroy Square, London. *Prospectus*, not dated.

Tredgold, A. F. *Mental Deficiency*. London, Ballière, Tindall and Cox, 2nd edn. 1914. [179n.]

Trevelyan, J. P. *The Life of Mrs. Humphry Ward*. London, Constable, 1923. [156n., 159n.]

Tropp, A. *The Growth of the Teaching Profession in England and Wales from 1800 to the Present Day*. London, Heinemann, 1957. [146n.]

Tuke, D. H. *Chapters in the History of the Insane in the British Isles*. London, Kegan Paul, 1882. [54n.–7n.]

Wait, W. B. *Education of the Blind: its Progress and Results*. New York, Bradstreet Press, 1880.

Wait, W. B. *Origin of the New York Institution for the Blind*. New York, Bradstreet Press, 1892.

Wallin, J. E. W. *The Education of Handicapped Children*. Boston, Houghton Mifflin, 1924.

Wallin, J. E. W. *Education of Mentally Handicapped Children*. New York, Harper, 1955.

Walther, E. *Geschichte des Taubstummen-Bildungswesens*. Bielefeld, Velhagen und Klasing, 1882.

Warner, F. *Report on the Physical and Mental Condition of 50,000 School Children*. London, Parkes Museum, 1892. [133n.]

Warner, R. *Report on the Scientific Study of the Mental and Physical Conditions of Childhood, with particular reference to Children of Defective Constitution and with Recommendations as to Education and Training.* London, Royal Sanitary Institute, 1895. [133n.]

Warner, F. *The Children: How to Study Them.* London, F. Hodgson, 1896.

Watson, F. *The Life of Sir Robert Jones.* London, Hodder and Stoughton, 1934. [159n.-60n., 162n.]

Watson, J. *Instruction of the Deaf and Dumb.* London, Darton and Harvey, 1809. [14n., 16n., 20n., 21]

Wilson, H. J. *Information with regard to Institutions, Societies, and Classes for the Blind in England and Wales.* London, Gardner's Trust for the Blind, 1887.

Winterbourn, R. *Educating Backward Children in New Zealand.* Christchurch, New Zealand, Whitcombe and Tombs for New Zealand Council of Educational Research, 1944.

ARTICLES

Adams, J. G. 'Visit to European Institutions for the Blind, in 1853-4.' *Nineteenth Annual Report of the Managers of the New York Institution for the Blind 1855*, pp. 35-44.

Andrews, A. 'Dr. Richard Elliott.' *Teacher of the Deaf*, Vol. 48, No. 286, August 1950, pp. 132-5.

Andrews, A. 'A Short History of the Education of the Deaf in Great Britain.' *The Education of Deaf Children, National Institute for the Deaf Booklet No. 486*, 1955, pp. 2-6.

Anonymous. 'Provision for Indigent Idiots and Imbeciles.' *The Journal of Mental Science*, Vol. 33, No. 144, January 1888, pp. 550-3.

Anonymous. 'How the Deaf-Mutes were cared for by L'Epée and Sicard.' *American Annals of the Deaf.* Vol. 73, No. 4, September 1928, pp. 366-77 and No. 5, November 1928, pp. 458-68.

Anonymous. 'Royal School for Deaf and Dumb Children, Margate.' *Teacher of the Deaf*, Vol. 44, No. 261, June 1946, pp. 74-5.

Anonymous. 'First Special School in Wales and Monmouthshire.' *Journal of Education*, Vol. 83, No. 979, February 1951, p. 80.

Anonymous. 'Mary Hare Grammar School.' *The Times Educational Supplement*, No. 1964, 19th December 1952, p. 1021. [201n.]

Askew, R. 'The Mary Hare Grammar School for the Deaf.' *The Education of Deaf Children, National Institute for the Deaf Booklet No. 486*, 1955, pp. 21-2. [201n.]

Baker, B. W. 'History of the Care of the Feeble-minded.' *Bulletin of the Massachusetts Department of Mental Diseases*, Vol. 14, Nos. 1 and 2, April 1930, pp. 19-29.

Beach, F. 'Facts Concerning Idiocy and Imbecility.' *The Health Exhibition Literature*, Vol. 11, pp. 534-45. London, International Health Exhibition, 1884. [54n., 117n.]

Beach, F. and Shuttleworth, G. E. 'Idiocy and Imbecility.' *A System of Medicine*, edited by Allbutt, Sir Clifford and Rolleston, H. D., Vol. 8, pp. 874-91.

Binet, A. et Simon, T. 'Méthods nouvelles pour le diagnostic du niveau intellectual des anormeaux.' *Archives de Psychologie*, Tome 11, 1905, pp. 163-90.

Blount, J. H. 'The Education of Deaf Children with Additional Handicaps.' *The Education of Deaf Children, National Institute for the Deaf Booklet No. 486*, 1955, pp. 24-6.

Brill, T. 'A Guide to the Literature on the Deaf.' *American Annals of the Deaf*, Vol. 81, No. 2, March 1936, pp. 100-12.

Bibliography

Burgwin, E. M. 'The Abnormal Child: The Physically and Mentally Defective.' *The Work of the London School Board*, by Spalding, T. A. and others, pp. 254–7. London, P. S. King, 1900.

Carter, W. R. 'State Aid to Blind Educational Institutions.' *Report of the Conference of the Blind and Their Friends, Upper Norwood, 1890*, pp. 30–47.

Clarke, E. 'Retrolental Fibroplasia in the Sunshine Home Nursery School.' *Teacher of the Blind*, Vol. 43, No. 4, April 1955, pp. 121–3. [220n.]

Cram, O. W. 'Elfrida Rathbone: Pioneer Worker for Sub-normal Children.' *Special Schools Journal*, Vol. 39, No. 3, October 1950, pp. 76–80.

De Motte, A. 'Schools for the Deaf in Europe.' *Volta Review* (U.S.A.), Vol. 34, No. 11, November 1932, pp. 568–73.

Denmark, F. L. 'The New Education Act and the Future of the Deaf Child.' *Teacher of the Deaf*, Vol. 42, No. 252, December 1944, pp. 151–5. [43n.]

Elstad, L. M. 'Historical Backgrounds of Types of Schools and Methods of Communication.' *American Annals of the Deaf*, Vol. 103, No. 2, March 1958, pp. 300–8.

Ewing, A. W. G. 'The Education of the Deaf: History of the Department of Education of the Deaf, University of Manchester, 1919–1955.' *British Journal of Educational Studies*, Vol. 4, No. 2, May 1956, pp. 103–28. [198n.]

Fay, E. A. 'The Braidwood Family.' *American Annals of the Deaf and Dumb*, Vol. 23, No. 1, January 1878, pp. 64–5. [12n.]

Fernald, W. E. 'History of the Treatment of the Feeble-Minded.' *Proceedings of the National Conference of Charities and Correction, 20th Annual Session, 1893*, pp. 203–21. Boston, Mass., 1893.

Gallaudet, E. M. 'Results of Articulation Teaching at Northampton.' *American Annals of the Deaf and Dumb*, Vol. 19, No. 3, July 1874, pp. 136–45.

Getliff, E. H. 'The College of Teachers of the Blind.' *Teacher of the Blind*, Vol. 43, No. 5, June 1955, pp. 190–201. [196n.]

Goldsmith, E. M. 'Schools for Crippled Children Abroad.' *Report of the United States Commissioner of Education*, Vol. I, pp. 503–11. Washington, 1909.

Greenaway, E. S. 'Higher Education for the Deaf: its Origins and Possible Developments.' *Teacher of the Deaf*, Vol. 47, No. 282, December 1949, pp. 188–92. [89n.]

Greene, M. C. 'The Abnormal Child: The Blind.' *The Work of the London School Board*, by Spalding, T. A. and others, pp. 248–51. London, P. S. King, 1900.

Harman, N. B. 'The Education of High Myopes.' *British Medical Journal*, 29th October 1910, pp. 1320–21.

Harris, J. W. 'Worcester College for the Blind.' *New Beacon*, Vol. 42, No. 494, April 1958, pp. 75–8.

Illingworth, W. H. 'Higher Education of the Blind.' *Report of the International Conference on the Blind, Edinburgh, 1905*, pp. 92–122. Glasgow, W. Hodge, 1905.

Langdon, J. N. 'The Royal Normal College.' *New Beacon*, Vol. 41, No. 485, July 1957, pp. 149–53. [200n.]

Lowenfeld, B. 'History and Development of Specialized Education for the Blind.' *The New Outlook for the Blind* (U.S.A.), Vol. 50, No. 10, December 1956, pp. 401–8.

McCarthy, W. V. 'The Beginning of Specialized Care of the Crippled.' *The Crippled Child* (U.S.A.), Vol. 15, August 1937, p. 63.

McMurtrie, D. C. 'Early History of the Care and Treatment of Cripples.' *Johns Hopkins Hospital Bulletin* (U.S.A.), Vol. 25, No. 276, 1914.

Bibliography

Nelson, W. 'The Abnormal Child: The Deaf.' *The Work of the London School Board*, by Spalding, T. A. and others, pp. 251–4. London, P. S. King, 1900.

Newman, Sir George. 'The Evolution and Policy of the School Medical Service.' *The Year Book of Education, 1933*, pp. 398–410. London, Evans Brothers, 1933. [168n.]

Peet, H. P. 'Memoir on the Origin and Early History of the Art of Instructing the Deaf and Dumb.' *American Annals of the Deaf and Dumb*, Vol. 3, No. 3, April 1851, pp. 129–60.

Pinsent, E. F. (Dame Ellen). 'On the Permanent Care of the Feeble-Minded.' *Lancet*, 21st February 1903, pp. 513–15. [183n.]

Potts, W. A. 'The Recognition and Training of Congenital Mental Defectives.' *British Medical Journal*, 9th May 1908, pp. 1097–99.

Powell, S. G. 'Mr. Ince Jones' School for Deaf Boys.' *Volta Review* (U.S.A.), Vol. 45, No. 4, April 1943.

Praagh, W. Van. 'Oral Instruction of the Deaf and Dumb.' *The Health Exhibition Literature*, Vol. 11, pp. 78–88. London, International Health Exhibition, 1884.

Pritchard, D. G. 'The Training of Teachers of Physically Handicapped and Educationally Sub-normal Children in England and Wales.' *The Slow Learning Child* (Australia), Vol. 6, No. 3, March 1960, pp. 145–51.

Rae, L. 'Historical Sketch of the Instruction of the Deaf and Dumb, before the time of de l'Epée.' *American Annals of the Deaf and Dumb*, Vol. I, No. 4, July 1848, pp. 197–208.

Roy, S. C. 'Education.' *History of the Development of Work for the Blind, A Symposium Sponsored by The Associated Blind, Inc.*, pp. 15–23. New York, The Associated Blind, Inc., 1954.

Sharpe, T. W. 'Provision for the Instruction of the Blind on Attaining 16 years of Age, and of those going Blind after that Age, having regard to the Act of 1893.' *Report of the Conference on Matters Relating to the Blind, Westminster, 1902*, pp. 29–44. London, Farmer and Sons, 1902.

Shuttleworth, G. E. 'In Memory of Edouard Séguin.' *The Journal of Mental Science*, Vol. 26, No. 119, October 1881.

Shuttleworth, G. E. 'The Health and Physical Development of Idiots.' *The Health Exhibition Literature*, Vol. 11, pp. 526–33. London, International Health Exhibition, 1884. [106n., 117n.]

Shuttleworth, G. E. 'The Education of Children of Abnormally Weak Mental Capacity.' *The Journal of Mental Science*, Vol. 34, No. 145, April 1888, pp. 80–4. [106n., 116n.–18n.]

Shuttleworth, G. E. 'On Some Slight Forms of Mental Defect in Children and their Treatment.' *British Medical Journal*, 3rd October 1903, pp. 828–9.

Shuttleworth, G. E. 'The Differentiation of Mentally Deficient Children.' *Transactions of the International Congress on School Hygiene, 1908*, p. 742. [138n.]

Shuttleworth, G. E. 'Exceptional School-Children.' *The Teacher's Encyclopaedia*, Vol. 5, 1912, pp. 214–38. London, Caxton Publishing Co., 1912. [60n.]

Smith, R. A. 'A History of London's Special Schools.' *Special Schools Journal*, Vol. 45, No. 4, November 1956, pp. 17–21.

Smith, R. A. 'Origin of Schools for Physically Defective Children.' *Special Schools Journal*, Vol. 46, No. 1, March 1957, pp. 25–7.

Spalding, J. 'Royal Residential Schools for the Deaf, Manchester-Trade Training Schools.' *The Education of Deaf Children, National Institute for the Deaf Booklet No. 486*, 1955, pp. 22–4.

Sullivan, W. C. 'Feeble-mindedness and the Measurement of the Intelligence by the Method of Binet and Simon.' *Lancet*, 23rd March 1912, p. 777.

Bibliography

Warner, F. 'A Method of Examining Children in Schools as to their Development and Brain Condition.' *British Medical Journal*, 22nd September 1888, pp. 659–60. [137n.]

Warner, F. 'Dull, Delicate, and Nervous Children.' *A System of Medicine*, edited by Allbutt, Sir Clifford and Rolleston, H. D., Vol. 8, pp. 964–84. London, Macmillan, 1910.

Whitton, H. 'Sir James E. Jones: Benefactor to the Deaf.' *Teacher of the Deaf*, Vol. 54, No. 321, June 1956, pp. 66–70. [197n.]

Whitton, H. 'An Early Infants' School for the Deaf.' *Teacher of the Deaf*, Vol. 57, No. 342, December 1959, pp. 223–9.

Wilkinson, W. M. 'The Present Public and Charitable Provision for Imbeciles, Compared with the Existing Legislation respecting them.' *The Journal of Mental Science*, Vol. 26, No. 113, April 1880, pp. 141–7.

INDEX

Index

Index

Farrar, Abraham, 88–9
Feeble-minded children: and lunatics, 61, 135; and the Committee on Defective and Epileptic Children, 121, 123, 132–47, 177; and the Royal Commission on the Blind and Deaf, 97, 105–7, 132; and the Royal Commission on the Care and Control of the Feeble-Minded, 183 ff.; and the Wood Committee, 189 ff.; and voluntary bodies, 180 ff.; association with adults, 61, 181–2; at Darenth, 60, 115; certification of, 121, 136, 185–7, 191, 210; confusion with idiots, 56, 135; first provision for, 54–61, 115 ff.; in idiot asylums, 54, 115; in Germany, 54, 68, 115–16, 121, 141–2; in ordinary schools, 115–19, 137, 190; in special schools and classes, 115, 118–31, 180 ff.; in voluntary schools, 145; in workhouses, 134; permanent care of, 181–3, 185; recommendations of Charity Organization Society, 61–2, 97; sense training of, 53, 122, 178, 181; views of geneticists, 178–80, 183
Fenton, Rev., 29
Fernald, Walter, 181
Ferrus, M., 54
Fisher, H. A. L., 159, 165
Fitzroy Square Training College and School for the Deaf, 77, 85–7, 90–1, 105, 113, 196–7
Forster, Rev. Samuel Strong, 68–70
Forster, W. E., 66, 76, 85
Foundling Hospital, 9
France: education of the blind, 3, 72; education of the deaf, 6, 7, 82; epileptics in, 175; partially sighted children in, 205
French Revolution, 3, 16, 25–6, 51
Frere, James Harley, 47
Froebel, Friedrich Wilhelm August, 116, 178
Fry, Edmund, 46
Fry, Elizabeth, 25

Gale, James, 70–1
Gall, James, vii, 30–1, 46–8
Gallaudet College of the Deaf, Washington, 201
Gallaudet, Thomas Hopkins, 15, 27
Galton, Sir Douglas, 192n.
Galton, Sir Francis, 178–9, 192
Gardner, Henry, 69n.
Gardner's Trust for the Blind, 69
Gavin, Miss H., 184n.
General Institution for the Blind, Birmingham, 37–8

General Institution for the Instruction of Deaf and Dumb Children, 15, 26, 30
George III, 13–14
George V, 187
Georgia Institution for the Deaf, 39 n.
Germany: education of feeble-minded children in, 54, 68, 115–16, 121, 141–142; education of physically handicapped children in, 62–3; education of the deaf in, 7, 8, 82–3, 86, 90; epileptics in, 68, 175; open-air schools in, 171; partially sighted children in, 205
Gilbert, Elizabeth, 41, 76n.
Girdlestone, G. R., 159
Girton College, 66
Gladstone, William Ewart, 66, 81n., 85, 93
Glasgow Asylum for the Blind, 46
Glasgow Institution for the Deaf and Dumb, 27n., 28, 42
Gloucester, Duchess of, 55
Goddard, H. H., 178–9
Goldsack, Irene, see Ewing, Lady Irene
Gordon Square Settlement, London, 156
Gorst, Sir John, 134
Gothenburg Industrial School for Cripples, 63
Grants for special education, 100, 103–104, 110–13, 133–4
Green, Francis, 13–14
Greene, Miss M. C., 79
Greenock Mid Parish School, 78
Grosvenor House, 73
Guggenbühl, Dr., 54
Guild of the Poor Brave Things, 161

Hackney School for the Deaf, 14–15, 20–1
Halifax Open-Air School, 171–3
Hamilton, Phoebe, 47n.
Hare, Mary, 200–1
Harman, N. Bishop, 203
Harris, F. D., 117, 138–9
Harrison, Damer, 184
Harrold, Elizabeth, 37
Harrold, William, 37
Harsdorffer, 2
Hartford School for the Deaf, U.S.A., 15
Harvard University, 72
Haüy, Valentin, 2, 18, 21, 32, 45, 74
Hay, Alexander, 45
Haynes, Catherine, 33
Healey, William, 193
Health at School, 167
Hearing aids, 198, 220–1

Index

International Library of Sociology

Edited by
John Rex
University of Warwick

Founded by
Karl Mannheim
as The International Library of Sociology
and Social Reconstruction

*This Catalogue also contains other Social Science
series published by Routledge*

Routledge & Kegan Paul   London and Boston

68-74 Carter Lane London EC4V 5EL
9 Park Street Boston Mass 02108

Contents

● *Books so marked are available in paperback*
All books are in Metric Demy 8vo format (216 × 138mm approx.)

GENERAL SOCIOLOGY

Belshaw, Cyril. The Conditions of Social Performance. *An Exploratory Theory. 144 pp.*

Brown, Robert. Explanation in Social Science. *208 pp.*

Cain, Maureen E. Society and the Policeman's Role. *About 300 pp.*

Gibson, Quentin. The Logic of Social Enquiry. *240 pp.*

Homans, George C. Sentiments and Activities: *Essays in Social Science. 336 pp.*

Isajiw, Wsevold W. Causation and Functionalism in Sociology. *165 pp.*

Johnson, Harry M. Sociology: *a Systematic Introduction. Foreword by Robert K. Merton. 710 pp.*

Mannheim, Karl. Essays on Sociology and Social Psychology. *Edited by Paul Keckskemeti. With Editorial Note by Adolph Lowe. 344 pp.*
Systematic Sociology: *An Introduction to the Study of Society. Edited by J. S. Erös and Professor W. A. C. Stewart. 220 pp.*

Martindale, Don. The Nature and Types of Sociological Theory. *292 pp.*

● **Maus, Heinz.** A Short History of Sociology. *234 pp.*

Mey, Harald. Field-Theory. *A Study of its Application in the Social Sciences. 352 pp.*

Myrdal, Gunnar. Value in Social Theory: *A Collection of Essays on Methodology. Edited by Paul Streeten. 332 pp.*

Ogburn, William F., and **Nimkoff, Meyer F.** A Handbook of Sociology. *Preface by Karl Mannheim. 656 pp. 46 figures. 35 tables.*

Parsons, Talcott, and **Smelser, Neil J.** Economy and Society: *A Study in the Integration of Economic and Social Theory. 362 pp.*

● **Rex, John.** Key Problems of Sociological Theory. *220 pp.*

Stark, Werner. The Fundamental Forms of Social Thought. *280 pp.*

FOREIGN CLASSICS OF SOCIOLOGY

● **Durkheim, Emile.** Suicide. *A Study in Sociology. Edited and with an Introduction by George Simpson. 404 pp.*
Professional Ethics and Civic Morals. *Translated by Cornelia Brookfield. 288 pp.*

● **Gerth, H. H.,** and **Mills, C. Wright.** From Max Weber: *Essays in Sociology. 502 pp.*

Tönnies, Ferdinand. Community and Association. *(Gemeinschaft und Gesellschaft.) Translated and Supplemented by Charles P. Loomis. Foreword by Pitirim A. Sorokin. 334 pp.*

SOCIAL STRUCTURE

Andreski, Stanislav. Military Organization and Society. *Foreword by Professor A. R. Radcliffe-Brown. 226 pp. 1 folder.*

● **Cole, G. D. H.** Studies in Class Structure. *220 p.*

Coontz, Sydney H. Population Theories and the Economic Interpretation. *202 pp.*

Coser, Lewis. The Functions of Social Conflict. *204 pp.*

Dickie-Clark, H. F. Marginal Situation: *A Sociological Study of a Coloured Group. 240 pp. 11 tables.*

Glass, D. V. (Ed.). Social Mobility in Britain. *Contributions by J. Berent, T. Bottomore, R. C. Chambers, J. Floud, D. V. Glass, J. R. Hall, H. T. Himmelweit, R. K. Kelsall, F. M. Martin, C. A. Moser, R. Mukherjee, and W. Ziegel. 420 pp.*

Glaser, Barney, and **Strauss, Anselm L.** Status Passage. *A Formal Theory. 208 pp.*

Jones, Garth N. Planned Organizational Change: *An Exploratory Study Using an Empirical Approach. 268 pp.*

Kelsall, R. K. Higher Civil Servants in Britain: *From 1870 to the Present Day. 268 pp. 31 tables.*

König, René. The Community. *232 pp. Illustrated.*

● **Lawton, Denis.** Social Class, Language and Education. *192 pp.*

McLeish, John. The Theory of Social Change: *Four Views Considered. 128 pp.*

Marsh, David C. The Changing Social Structure in England and Wales, 1871-1961. *272 pp.*

Mouzelis, Nicos. Organization and Bureaucracy. *An Analysis of Modern Theories. 240 pp.*

Mulkay, M. J. Functionalism, Exchange and Theoretical Strategy. *272 pp.*

Ossowski, Stanislaw. Class Structure in the Social Consciousness. *210 pp.*

SOCIOLOGY AND POLITICS

Crick, Bernard. The American Science of Politics: *Its Origins and Conditions. 284 pp.*

Hertz, Frederick. Nationality in History and Politics: *A Psychology and Sociology of National Sentiment and Nationalism. 432 pp.*

Kornhauser, William. The Politics of Mass Society. *272 pp. 20 tables.*

Laidler, Harry W. History of Socialism. *Social-Economic Movements: An Historical and Comparative Survey of Socialism, Communism, Co-operation, Utopianism; and other Systems of Reform and Reconstruction. 992 pp.*

Mannheim, Karl. Freedom, Power and Democratic Planning. *Edited by Hans Gerth and Ernest K. Bramstedt. 424 pp.*

Mansur, Fatma. Process of Independence. *Foreword by A. H. Hanson. 208 pp.*

Martin, David A. Pacificism: *an Historical and Sociological Study. 262 pp.*

Myrdal, Gunnar. The Political Element in the Development of Economic Theory. *Translated from the German by Paul Streeten. 282 pp.*

Verney, Douglas V. The Analysis of Political Systems. *264 pp.*

Wootton, Graham. Workers, Unions and the State. *188 pp.*

4

FOREIGN AFFAIRS: THEIR SOCIAL, POLITICAL AND ECONOMIC FOUNDATIONS

Bonné, Alfred. State and Economics in the Middle East: *A Society in Transition. 482 pp.*
    Studies in Economic Development: *with special reference to Conditions in the Under-developed Areas of Western Asia and India. 322 pp. 84 tables.*

Mayer, J. P. Political Thought in France from the Revolution to the Fifth Republic. *164 pp.*

CRIMINOLOGY

Ancel, Marc. Social Defence: *A Modern Approach to Criminal Problems. Foreword by Leon Radzinowicz. 240 pp.*

Cloward, Richard A., and **Ohlin, Lloyd E.** Delinquency and Opportunity: *A Theory of Delinquent Gangs. 248 pp.*

Downes, David M. The Delinquent Solution. *A Study in Subcultural Theory. 296 pp.*

Dunlop, A. B., and **McCabe, S.** Young Men in Detention Centres. *192 pp.*

Friedlander, Kate. The Psycho-Analytical Approach to Juvenile Delinquency: *Theory, Case Studies, Treatment. 320 pp.*

Glueck, Sheldon, and **Eleanor.** Family Environment and Delinquency. *With the statistical assistance of Rose W. Kneznek. 340 pp.*

Lopez-Rey, Manuel. Crime. *An Analytical Appraisal. 288 pp.*

Mannheim, Hermann. Comparative Criminology: *a Text Book. Two volumes. 442 pp. and 380 pp.*

Morris, Terence. The Criminal Area: *A Study in Social Ecology. Foreword by Hermann Mannheim. 232 pp. 25 tables. 4 maps.*

Trasler, Gordon. The Explanation of Criminality. *144 pp.*

SOCIAL PSYCHOLOGY

Bagley, Christopher. The Social Psychology of the Child with Epilepsy. *320 pp.*

Barbu, Zevedei. Problems of Historical Psychology. *248 pp.*

Blackburn, Julian. Psychology and the Social Pattern. *184 pp.*

● **Fleming, C. M.** Adolescence: *Its Social Psychology: With an Introduction to recent findings from the fields of Anthropology, Physiology, Medicine, Psychometrics and Sociometry. 288 pp.*

●   The Social Psychology of Education: *An Introduction and Guide to Its Study. 136 pp.*

Homans, George C. The Human Group. *Foreword by Bernard DeVoto. Introduction by Robert K. Merton. 526 pp.*
    Social Behaviour: *its Elementary Forms. 416 pp.*

Klein, Josephine. The Study of Groups. *226 pp. 31 figures. 5 tables.*
Linton, Ralph. The Cultural Background of Personality. *132 pp.*
Mayo, Elton. The Social Problems of an Industrial Civilization. *With an appendix on the Political Problem. 180 pp.*
Ottaway, A. K. C. Learning Through Group Experience. *176 pp.*
Ridder, J. C. de. The Personality of the Urban African in South Africa. *A Thematic Apperception Test Study. 196 pp. 12 plates.*
● **Rose, Arnold M.** (Ed.). Human Behaviour and Social Processes: *an Interactionist Approach. Contributions by Arnold M. Rose, Ralph H. Turner, Anselm Strauss, Everett C. Hughes, E. Franklin Frazier, Howard S. Becker, et al. 696 pp.*
Smelser, Neil J. Theory of Collective Behaviour. *448 pp.*
Stephenson, Geoffrey M. The Development of Conscience. *128 pp.*
Young, Kimball. Handbook of Social Psychology. *658 pp. 16 figures. 10 tables.*

SOCIOLOGY OF THE FAMILY

Banks, J. A. Prosperity and Parenthood: *A Study of Family Planning among The Victorian Middle Classes. 262 pp.*
Bell, Colin R. Middle Class Families: *Social and Geographical Mobility. 224 pp.*
Burton, Lindy. Vulnerable Children. *272 pp.*
Gavron, Hannah. The Captive Wife: *Conflicts of Household Mothers. 190 pp.*
George, Victor, and **Wilding, Paul.** Motherless Families. *220 pp.*
Klein, Josephine. Samples from English Cultures.
    1. Three Preliminary Studies and Aspects of Adult Life in England. *447 pp.*
    2. Child-Rearing Practices and Index. *247 pp.*
Klein, Viola. Britain's Married Women Workers. *180 pp.*
    The Feminine Character. *History of an Ideology. 244 pp.*
McWhinnie, Alexina M. Adopted Children. *How They Grow Up. 304 pp.*
Myrdal, Alva, and **Klein, Viola.** Women's Two Roles: *Home and Work. 238 pp. 27 tables.*
Parsons, Talcott, and **Bales, Robert F.** Family: *Socialization and Interaction Process. In collaboration with James Olds, Morris Zelditch and Philip E. Slater. 456 pp. 50 figures and tables.*

SOCIAL SERVICES

Bastide, Roger. The Sociology of Mental Disorder. *Translated from the French by Jean McNeil. 264 pp.*
Carlebach, Julius. Caring For Children in Trouble. *266 pp.*
Forder, R. A. (Ed.). Penelope Hall's Social Services of Modern England. *352 pp.*
George, Victor. Foster Care. *Theory and Practice. 234 pp.*
    Social Security: *Beveridge and After. 258 pp.*

● **Goetschius, George W.** Working with Community Groups. *256 pp.*

Goetschius, George W., and **Tash, Joan.** Working with Unattached Youth. *416 pp.*

Hall, M. P., and **Howes, I. V.** The Church in Social Work. *A Study of Moral Welfare Work undertaken by the Church of England. 320 pp.*

Heywood, Jean S. Children in Care: *the Development of the Service for the Deprived Child. 264 pp.*

Hoenig, J., and **Hamilton, Marian W.** The De-Segration of the Mentally Ill. *284 pp.*

Jones, Kathleen. Lunacy, Law and Conscience, *1744-1845: the Social History of the Care of the Insane. 268 pp.*

Mental Health and Social Policy, 1845-1959. *264 pp.*

King, Roy D., Raynes, Norma V., and **Tizard, Jack.** Patterns of Residential Care. *356 pp.*

Leigh, John. Young People and Leisure. *256 pp.*

Morris, Pauline. Put Away: *A Sociological Study of Institutions for the Mentally Retarded. 364 pp.*

Nokes, P. L. The Professional Task in Welfare Practice. *152 pp.*

Timms, Noel. Psychiatric Social Work in Great Britain (1939-1962). *280 pp.*

● Social Casework: *Principles and Practice. 256 pp.*

Trasler, Gordon. In Place of Parents: *A Study in Foster Care. 272 pp.*

Young, A. F., and **Ashton, E. T.** British Social Work in the Nineteenth Century. *288 pp.*

Young, A. F. Social Services in British Industry. *272 pp.*

SOCIOLOGY OF EDUCATION

Banks, Olive. Parity and Prestige in English Secondary Education: a Study in Educational Sociology. *272 pp.*

Bentwich, Joseph. Education in Israel. *224 pp. 8 pp. plates.*

● **Blyth, W. A. L.** English Primary Education. *A Sociological Description.*

1. Schools. *232 pp.*

2. Background. *168 pp.*

Collier, K. G. The Social Purposes of Education: *Personal and Social Values in Education. 268 pp.*

Dale, R. R., and **Griffith, S.** Down Stream: *Failure in the Grammar School. 108 pp.*

Dore, R. P. Education in Tokugawa Japan. *356 pp. 9 pp. plates*

Evans, K. M. Sociometry and Education. *158 pp.*

Foster, P. J. Education and Social Change in Ghana. *336 pp. 3 maps.*

Fraser, W. R. Education and Society in Modern France. *150 pp.*

Grace, Gerald R. Role Conflict and the Teacher. *About 200 pp.*

Hans, Nicholas. New Trends in Education in the Eighteenth Century. *278 pp. 19 tables.*

● Comparative Education: *A Study of Educational Factors and Traditions. 360 pp.*

Hargreaves, David. Interpersonal Relations and Education. *432 pp.*
● Social Relations in a Secondary School. *240 pp.*
Holmes, Brian. Problems in Education. *A Comparative Approach. 336 pp.*
King, Ronald. Values and Involvement in a Grammar School. *164 pp.*
● **Mannheim, Karl,** and **Stewart, W. A. C.** An Introduction to the Sociology of Education. *206 pp.*
Morris, Raymond N. The Sixth Form and College Entrance. *231 pp.*
● **Musgrove, F.** Youth and the Social Order. *176 pp.*
● **Ottaway, A. K. C.** Education and Society: *An Introduction to the Sociology of Education. With an Introduction by W. O. Lester Smith. 212 pp.*
Peers, Robert. Adult Education: *A Comparative Study. 398 pp.*
Pritchard, D. G. Education and the Handicapped: *1760 to 1960. 258 pp.*
Richardson, Helen. Adolescent Girls in Approved Schools. *308 pp.*
Simon, Brian, and **Joan** (Eds.). Educational Psychology in the U.S.S.R. *Introduction by Brian and Joan Simon. Translation by Joan Simon. Papers by D. N. Bogoiavlenski and N. A. Menchinskaia, D. B. Elkonin, E. A. Fleshner, Z. I. Kalmykova, G. S. Kostiuk, V. A. Krutetski, A. N. Leontiev, A. R. Luria, E. A. Milerian, R. G. Natadze, B. M. Teplov, L. S. Vygotski, L. V. Zankov. 296 pp.*
Stratta, Erica. The Education of Borstal Boys. *A Study of their Educational Experiences prior to, and during Borstal Training. 256 pp.*

SOCIOLOGY OF CULTURE

Eppel, E. M., and **M.** Adolescents and Morality: *A Study of some Moral Values and Dilemmas of Working Adolescents in the Context of a changing Climate of Opinion. Foreword by W. J. H. Sprott. 268 pp. 39 tables.*
● **Fromm, Erich.** The Fear of Freedom. *286 pp.*
The Sane Society. *400 pp.*
● **Mannheim, Karl.** Diagnosis of Our Time: *Wartime Essays of a Sociologist. 208 pp.*
Essays on the Sociology of Culture. *Edited by Ernst Mannheim in co-operation with Paul Kecskemeti. Editorial Note by Adolph Lowe. 280 pp.*
Weber, Alfred. Farewell to European History: *or The Conquest of Nihilism. Translated from the German by R. F. C. Hull. 224 pp.*

SOCIOLOGY OF RELIGION

Argyle, Michael. Religious Behaviour. *224 pp. 8 figures. 41 tables.*
Nelson, G. K. Spiritualism and Society. *313 pp.*

Stark, Werner. The Sociology of Religion. *A Study of Christendom.*
Volume I. *Established Religion. 248 pp.*
Volume II. *Sectarian Religion. 368 pp.*
Volume III. *The Universal Church. 464 pp.*
Volume IV. *Types of Religious Man. 352 pp.*
Volume V. *Types of Religious Culture. 464 pp.*
Watt, W. Montgomery. Islam and the Integration of Society. *320 pp.*

SOCIOLOGY OF ART AND LITERATURE

Beljame, Alexandre. Men of Letters and the English Public in the Eighteenth
Century: *1660-1744, Dryden, Addison, Pope. Edited with an Introduction
and Notes by Bonamy Dobrée. Translated by E. O. Lorimer. 532 pp.*
Jarvie, Ian C. Towards a Sociology of the Cinema. *A Comparative Essay
on the Structure and Functioning of a Major Entertainment Industry.
405 pp.*
Rust, Frances S. Dance in Society. *An Analysis of the Relationships between
the Social Dance and Society in England from the Middle Ages to the
Present Day. 256 pp. 8 pp. of plates.*
Schücking, L. L. The Sociology of Literary Taste. *112 pp.*
Silbermann, Alphons. The Sociology of Music. *Translated from the German
by Corbet Stewart. 222 pp.*

SOCIOLOGY OF KNOWLEDGE

Mannheim, Karl. Essays on the Sociology of Knowledge. *Edited by Paul
Kecskemeti. Editorial note by Adolph Lowe. 353 pp.*
Stark, Werner. The Sociology of Knowledge: *An Essay in Aid of a Deeper
Understanding of the History of Ideas. 384 pp.*

URBAN SOCIOLOGY

Ashworth, William. The Genesis of Modern British Town Planning: *A Study
in Economic and Social History of the Nineteenth and Twentieth Centuries.
288 pp.*
Cullingworth, J. B. Housing Needs and Planning Policy: *A Restatement of
the Problems of Housing Need and 'Overspill' in England and Wales.
232 pp. 44 tables. 8 maps.*
Dickinson, Robert E. City and Region: *A Geographical Interpretation.
608 pp. 125 figures.*
The West European City: *A Geographical Interpretation. 600 pp. 129 maps.
29 plates.*
● The City Region in Western Europe. *320 pp. Maps.*

Humphreys, Alexander J. New Dubliners: *Urbanization and the Irish Family.* *Foreword by George C. Homans. 304 pp.*

Jackson, Brian. Working Class Community: *Some General Notions raised by a Series of Studies in Northern England. 192 pp.*

Jennings, Hilda. Societies in the Making: *a Study of Development and Redevelopment within a County Borough. Foreword by D. A. Clark. 286 pp.*

Kerr, Madeline. The People of Ship Street. *240 pp.*

● **Mann, P. H.** An Approach to Urban Sociology. *240 pp.*

Morris, R. N., and **Mogey, J.** The Sociology of Housing. *Studies at Berinsfield. 232 pp. 4 pp. plates.*

Rosser, C., and **Harris, C.** The Family and Social Change. *A Study of Family and Kinship in a South Wales Town. 352 pp. 8 maps.*

RURAL SOCIOLOGY

Chambers, R. J. H. Settlement Schemes in Africa: *A Selective Study. 268 pp.*

Haswell, M. R. The Economics of Development in Village India. *120 pp.*

Littlejohn, James. Westrigg: *the Sociology of a Cheviot Parish. 172 pp. 5 figures.*

Williams, W. M. The Country Craftsman: *A Study of Some Rural Crafts and the Rural Industries Organization in England. 248 pp. 9 figures. (Dartington Hall Studies in Rural Sociology.)*

The Sociology of an English Village: *Gosforth. 272 pp. 12 figures. 13 tables.*

SOCIOLOGY OF INDUSTRY AND DISTRIBUTION

Anderson, Nels. Work and Leisure. *280 pp.*

● **Blau, Peter M.,** and **Scott, W. Richard.** Formal Organizations: *a Comparative approach. Introduction and Additional Bibliography by J. H. Smith. 326 pp.*

Eldridge, J. E. T. Industrial Disputes. *Essays in the Sociology of Industrial Relations. 288 pp.*

Hetzler, Stanley. Technological Growth and Social Change. *Achieving Modernization. 269 pp.*

Hollowell, Peter G. The Lorry Driver. *272 pp.*

Jefferys, Margot, *with the assistance of Winifred Moss.* Mobility in the Labour Market: *Employment Changes in Battersea and Dagenham. Preface by Barbara Wootton. 186 pp. 51 tables.*

Millerson, Geoffrey. The Qualifying Associations: *a Study in Professionalization. 320 pp.*

Smelser, Neil J. Social Change in the Industrial Revolution: *An Application of Theory to the Lancashire Cotton Industry, 1770-1840. 468 pp. 12 figures. 14 tables.*

Williams, Gertrude. Recruitment to Skilled Trades. *240 pp.*

Young, A. F. Industrial Injuries Insurance: *an Examination of British Policy.* *192 pp.*

ANTHROPOLOGY

Ammar, Hamed. Growing up in an Egyptian Village: *Silwa, Province of Aswan. 336 pp.*

Brandel-Syrier, Mia. Reeftown Elite. *A Study of Social Mobility in a Modern African Community on the Reef. 376 pp.*

Crook, David, and **Isabel.** Revolution in a Chinese Village: *Ten Mile Inn. 230 pp. 8 plates. 1 map.*

The First Years of Yangyi Commune. *302 pp. 12 plates.*

Dickie-Clark, H. F. The Marginal Situation. *A Sociological Study of a Coloured Group. 236 pp.*

Dube, S. C. Indian Village. *Foreword by Morris Edward Opler. 276 pp. 4 plates.*

India's Changing Villages: *Human Factors in Community Development. 260 pp. 8 plates. 1 map.*

Firth, Raymond. Malay Fishermen. *Their Peasant Economy. 420 pp. 17 pp. plates.*

Gulliver, P. H. Social Control in an African Society: a Study of the Arusha, Agricultural Masai of Northern Tanganyika. *320 pp. 8 plates. 10 figures.*

Ishwaran, K. Shivapur. *A South Indian Village. 216 pp.*

Tradition and Economy in Village India: *An Interactionist Approach. Foreword by Conrad Arensburg. 176 pp.*

Jarvie, Ian C. The Revolution in Anthropology. *268 pp.*

Jarvie, Ian C., and **Agassi, Joseph.** Hong Kong. *A Society in Transition. 396 pp. Illustrated with plates and maps.*

Little, Kenneth L. Mende of Sierra Leone. *308 pp. and folder.*

Negroes in Britain. *With a New Introduction and Contemporary Study by Leonard Bloom. 320 pp.*

Lowie, Robert H. Social Organization. *494 pp.*

Mayer, Adrian C. Caste and Kinship in Central India: *A Village and its Region. 328 pp. 16 plates. 15 figures. 16 tables.*

Smith, Raymond T. The Negro Family in British Guiana: *Family Structure and Social Status in the Villages. With a Foreword by Meyer Fortes. 314 pp. 8 plates. 1 figure. 4 maps.*

DOCUMENTARY

Meek, Dorothea L. (Ed.). Soviet Youth: *Some Achievements and Problems. Excerpts from the Soviet Press, translated by the editor. 280 pp.*

Schlesinger, Rudolf (Ed.). Changing Attitudes in Soviet Russia.

2. *The Nationalities Problem and Soviet Administration. Selected Readings on the Development of Soviet Nationalities Policies. Introduced by the editor. Translated by W. W. Gottlieb. 324 pp.*

SOCIOLOGY AND PHILOSOPHY

Barnsley, John H. The Social Reality of Ethics. *A Comparative Analysis of Moral Codes. 448 pp.*

Douglas, Jack D. (Ed.). Understanding Everyday Life. *Toward the Reconstruction of Sociological Knowledge. Contributions by Alan F. Blum. Aaron W. Cicourel, Norman K. Denzin, Jack D. Douglas, John Heeren, Peter McHugh, Peter K. Manning, Melvin Power, Matthew Speier, Roy Turner, D. Lawrence Wieder, Thomas P. Wilson and Don H. Zimmerman. 358 pp.*

Jarvie, Ian C. Concepts and Society. *216 pp.*

Roche, Maurice. Phenomenology, Language and the Social Sciences. *About 400 pp.*

Sklair, Leslie. The Sociology of Progress. *320 pp.*

International Library of Social Policy

General Editor Kathleen Janes

Jones, Kathleen. Mental Health Services. *A history, 1744-1971. About 500 pp.*

Thomas, J. E. The English Prison Officer since 1850: *A Study in Conflict. 258 pp.*

Primary Socialization, Language and Education

General Editor Basil Bernstein

Bernstein, Basil. Class, Codes and Control. *2 volumes.*
1. *Theoretical Studies Towards a Sociology of Language. 254 pp.*
2. *Applied Studies Towards a Sociology of Language. About 400 pp.*

Brandis, Walter, and **Henderson, Dorothy.** Social Class, Language and Communication. *288 pp.*

Cook, Jenny. Socialization and Social Control. *About 300 pp.*

Gahagan, D. M., and **G. A.** Talk Reform. *Exploration in Language for Infant School Children. 160 pp.*

Robinson, W. P., and **Rackstraw, Susan, D. A.** A Question of Answers. *2 volumes. 192 pp. and 180 pp.*

Turner, Geoffrey, J., and **Mohan, Bernard, A.** A Linguistic Description and Computer Programme for Children's Speech. *208 pp.*

Reports of the Institute of Community Studies and the Institute of Social Studies in Medical Care

Cartwright, Ann. Human Relations and Hospital Care. *272 pp.*
Parents and Family Planning Services. *306 pp.*
Patients and their Doctors. *A Study of General Practice. 304 pp.*
Dunnell, Karen, and **Cartwright, Ann.** Medicine Takers, Prescribers and Hoarders. *About 140 pp.*
● **Jackson, Brian.** Streaming: *an Education System in Miniature. 168 pp.*
Jackson, Brian, and **Marsden, Dennis.** Education and the Working Class: *Some General Themes raised by a Study of 88 Working-class Children in a Northern Industrial City. 268 pp. 2 folders.*
Marris, Peter. Widows and their Families. *Foreword by Dr. John Bowlby. 184 pp. 18 tables. Statistical Summary.*
Family and Social Change in an African City. *A Study of Rehousing in Lagos. 196 pp. 1 map. 4 plates. 53 tables.*
The Experience of Higher Education. *232 pp. 27 tables.*
Marris, Peter, and **Rein, Martin.** Dilemmas of Social Reform. *Poverty and Community Action in the United States. 256 pp.*
Marris, Peter, and **Somerset, Anthony.** African Businessmen. *A Study of Entrepreneurship and Development in Kenya. 256 pp.*
Runciman, W. G. Relative Deprivation and Social Justice. *A Study of Attitudes to Social Inequality in Twentieth Century England. 352 pp.*
Townsend, Peter. The Family Life of Old People: *An Inquiry in East London. Foreword by J. H. Sheldon. 300 pp. 3 figures. 63 tables.*
Willmott, Peter. Adolescent Boys in East London. *230 pp.*
The Evolution of a Community: *a study of Dagenham after forty years. 168 pp. 2 maps.*
Willmott, Peter, and **Young, Michael.** Family and Class in a London Suburb. *202 pp. 47 tables.*
Young, Michael. Innovation and Research in Education. *192 pp.*
● **Young, Michael,** and **McGeeney, Patrick.** Learning Begins at Home. *A Study of a Junior School and its Parents. 128 pp.*
Young, Michael, and **Willmott, Peter.** Family and Kinship in East London. *Foreword by Richard M. Titmuss. 252 pp. 39 tables.*

Medicine, Illness and Society
General Editor　W. M. Williams

Robinson, David. The Process of Becoming Ill.
Stacey, Margaret. *et al.* Hospitals, Children and Their Families. *The Report of a Pilot Study. 202 pp.*

Routledge Social Science Journals

The British Journal of Sociology. *Edited by Terence P. Morris. Vol. 1, No. 1, March 1950 and Quarterly. Roy. 8vo. Back numbers available. An international journal with articles on all aspects of sociology.*

Economy and Society. *Vol. 1, No. 1. February 1972 and Quarterly. Metric Roy. 8vo. A journal for all social scientists covering sociology, philosophy, anthropology, economics and history.*

Printed in Great Britain by Lewis Reprints Limited
Brown Knight & Truscott Group, London and Tonbridge   21972